# MEDIEVAL AND MONASTIC DERRY

*To the memory of
Dermot Francis*

# Medieval and monastic Derry: sixth century to 1600

BRIAN LACEY

FOUR COURTS PRESS

Typeset in 10.5 pt on 12.5 pt EhrhardtMTPro *by*
Carrigboy Typesetting Services for
FOUR COURTS PRESS LTD
7 Malpas Street, Dublin 8, Ireland
www.fourcourtspress.ie
*and in North America for*
FOUR COURTS PRESS
c/o ISBS, 920 NE 58th Avenue, Suite 300, Portland, OR 97213.

© Brian Lacey and Four Courts Press 2013

A catalogue record for this title is available
from the British Library.

ISBN 978–1–84682–383–1

All rights reserved.
Without limiting the rights under copyright
reserved alone, no part of this publication may be
reproduced, stored in or introduced into a retrieval system,
or transmitted, in any form or by any means (electronic, mechanical,
photocopying, recording or otherwise), without the prior
written permission of both the copyright owner and
publisher of this book.

SPECIAL ACKNOWLEDGMENT

Sponsorship of some of the research published here was provided by the Heritage
Lottery Fund, Holywell Trust City Walls Heritage Project, Derry.

Printed in England
by CPI Antony Rowe Ltd, Chippenham, Wilts.

# Contents

| | | |
|---|---|---|
| ABBREVIATIONS | | vi |
| INTRODUCTION AND ACKNOWLEDGMENTS | | vii |
| 1 | The 'island' of Derry | 1 |
| 2 | The legend of the foundation of the monastery | 14 |
| 3 | The historical evidence: Daire Calgaich and the Cenél Conaill | 25 |
| 4 | Derry and the Cenél nEógain | 40 |
| 5 | The Mac Lochlainns and Doire Coluim Chille | 53 |
| 6 | The medieval settlement: its layout and structures | 77 |
| 7 | Derry in the late twelfth and early thirteenth centuries | 93 |
| 8 | Archbishop Colton's visit to Derry in 1397 | 111 |
| 9 | The Uí Domhnaill and the end of medieval Derry | 127 |
| 10 | Memorializing and reinterpreting Columban Derry | 138 |
| 11 | Summary and conclusions | 147 |
| BIBLIOGRAPHY | | 151 |
| INDEX | | 157 |

# Abbreviations

| | |
|---|---|
| ab. | abbot |
| AConn. | *Annála Connacht: The Annals of Connacht, AD1224–1544*, ed. A.M. Freeman (Dublin, 1996) |
| AFM | *Annals of the kingdom of Ireland by the Four Masters*, ed. J. O'Donovan (7 vols, 2nd ed., Dublin, 1851–6; repr. Dublin, 1998) |
| ARos. | *The Annals of Roscrea*, ed. D. Gleeson and S. Mac Airt, *Proceedings of the Royal Irish Academy*, 59C (1958), 138–80. Also Bart Jaski and Daniel Mc Carthy, *The Annals of Roscrea: a diplomatic edition* (Roscrea, 2012); 'A facsimile edition of the Annals of Roscrea' by Bart Jaski and Daniel Mc Carthy: www.scss.tcd.ie/misc/kronos/editions/ |
| ATig. | *Annals of Tigernach*, ed. W. Stokes, *Revue Celtique*, 16–17 (1895–7) |
| AU | *Annals of Ulster (to AD1131)*, ed. S. Mac Airt and G. Mac Niocaill (Dublin, 1983). Also W.M. Hennessy and B. MacCarthy (eds), *Annála Uladh: The Annals of Ulster 431–1131, 1155–1541* (4 vols, Dublin, 1887–1901, repr. 1999) |
| bp | bishop |
| *CPR* | *Calendar of papal registers* |
| *CPRI* | *Calendar of patent rolls, Ireland* |
| *CS* | *Chronicum Scotorum*, ed. W.M. Hennessy (London, 1866) |
| *CSPI* | *Calendar of state papers, Ireland* |
| d. | died |
| *fl.* | *floruit*, alive at the time |
| Inquisition(s) | *Inquisitionum in officio rotulorum cancellariae Hiberniae repertorium*, II: *Ultonia*, appendix iv, Derrie (Dublin, 1829) |
| k. | king |
| MIA | *Miscellaneous Irish Annals, AD1114–1437*, ed. Séamus Ó hInnse (Dublin, 1947; repr. 2001, 2004) |
| n.d. | no date (given) |
| RCAHMS | Royal Commission on the Ancient and Historical Monuments of Scotland |
| *RIA Dictionary* | *Dictionary of the Irish language, based mainly on old and middle Irish materials*, compact ed. (Dublin, 1998) |
| *s.a.* | *sub anno*, 'under' or 'at the year' |

# Introduction and acknowledgments

Derry is one of the oldest more or less continuously documented places in Ireland. The story covered in this book extends over a little more than one thousand years. During that time, apart from anything else, language itself – especially the names of people, places and things – evolved and changed. It is extremely difficult to establish one standard version to cover those names as they changed over time, but in the text below an attempt to do so has been made (usually silently with regard to extracts from medieval sources), except when using quotations from modern authors.

In the middle of the seventeenth century, John Colgan seems to have been the first person in print to cast doubt on the traditional understanding of the origins of Derry. His uncertainty related to the year that the church there came into being rather than the identity of its founder. However, despite a formidable ancient and modern tradition that Derry's ancient 'monastery' was established by Columba or Colum Cille,[1] historical evidence does not support that claim. Nor can either of the two well-known dates – 535 in the Annals of the Four Masters or 545/6 in the Annals of Ulster – be accepted. Arguments against this 'official' account can be made on three grounds: (i) there is no contemporary historical evidence that Columba was the founder; (ii) there is almost certainly contemporary evidence pointing to someone else as the founder; and (iii) it is possible to explain plausibly why, and to some extent even when, the well-known 'legend' was developed.

While Colum Cille's role in the foundation continues to be affirmed in most modern publications, doubts have been raised about the traditional version on many occasions. For example, Richard Sharpe queried the date of the foundation and suggested that some of the evidence, itself of course open to question, points to a date as late as the 580s or subsequently, and almost definitely after 569 (1995, 255–6). William Reeves raised the problem of the age of the alleged donor of the site, the king Áed mac Ainmerech (1857, 160–1). In the seminal *Ordnance Survey memoir … parish of Templemore* there is a discussion in the section 'drawn up by Mr George Petrie, aided by Mr John O'Donovan' about the chronological problems inherent in the traditional account of the foundation of Derry (Colby 1837, 6 and 18). Already in 1647, in the *Trias Thaumaturga*, John Colgan had drawn attention to some of the

---

1 Colum Cille is an Irish-language phrase meaning 'Columba (or 'dove') of the church'. Almost certainly it does not date from his own lifetime but is a hagiographical development of the Latin Christian name Columba, post-dating his death.

confusion, mentioning the subject on several occasions. In a note to his version of Manus Ó Domhnaill's sixteenth-century Life of Saint Colum Cille, Colgan correctly casts doubt on the date of 535 as given by the Four Masters (Ó Riain 1997, 450, n. 46). Again, at the section called *De fundatione Monasterij Dorensis* in the fifth appendix to the Lives of the saint, he repeats his doubts: *Unde licet annus fundat[ioni]s illius Monasterij mihi manet incertus* or 'whence the year of the foundation of that monastery remains uncertain to me'. He goes on to say, however, that it is certain that it was founded some years before Columba and his associates went to Britain, around 562 (Ó Riain 1997, 502–3). But, as we will see below, it is not so certain at all!

When I started to study the history of Derry in the mid-1970s, I was inevitably drawn to the beautiful Long Tower church, at that time believed to have been constructed on the very location of Colum Cille's first and best-loved foundation. During many visits, I was able to examine the various works of art and the antiquities in the church and its precincts that collectively, and according to what I later discovered was a deliberate narrative scheme, outlined the story of Colum Cille and of his foundation of the monastery of Derry. With great interest, I read the commemorative plaques inserted into the floor of the church and surrounding churchyard. These drew attention, with apparent archaeological precision, to the exact locations of structures and events associated with the sixth-century saint. However, over subsequent years I gradually came to realize that the sixth-century monastic church had almost certainly been located at a different site – St Augustine's chapel-of-ease (Lacy 1988, 390–3) – and that it was extremely unlikely, anyway, that it had been founded by Colum Cille (ibid., 37, Lacey 1997a, 29–30 and below).

The cult of and traditions about St Columba, and the dossier of writings about him, started to develop immediately after his death at the end of the sixth century. Almost a thousand years later, in the early sixteenth century, Manus Ó Domhnaill composed his *Betha Colaim Chille*, which was, in effect, a summary of much, if not all, of what had been written and told in story about the saint before that time. Several different kinds of influence have been claimed for that work, but it was especially influential in shaping the 'traditional' picture of the ancient monastery of Derry as this was understood, and indeed 'exploited', particularly at the end of the nineteenth century. Ó Domhnaill's 'Life' of the saint was exceptionally influential on Fr William Doherty, who, at the beginning of the twentieth century, was the principal 'builder' of the new Long Tower. That church, which was designed to be – in effect – a 'text to be read', became the principal physical expression of the legend of Colum Cille's foundation of Derry. However, such actual historical evidence as exists does not support that traditional story. The origin of the ancient monastery of Derry has been told largely as legend rather than as 'history'. But the real history of the origins of Derry and its development over

*Introduction and acknowledgments* ix

the following thousand years can be reconstructed, at least in part. That is what is attempted in this book.

Written evidence for the history of Derry can be pushed as far back as the middle of the sixth century. For many centuries afterwards, however, the records are meagre, very partial and often ambiguous or unclear. As is usual with this early period, there are many things for which we can find little or no evidence. Speculation is necessary to fill in the gaps, but that speculation must be based on the evidence that does survive, freed from any obligation to maintain a given tradition. Although it may occasionally get in the way of the narrative, it is also necessary to show how we know what we know, or why we think something to be so. It is clear that such documentation as we have records only a fraction of what actually happened – and not always the most important events. We also know that all medieval texts were propaganda of one kind or another. Ancient chroniclers always perceived the need 'to reshape the past to meet [their] present aspirations' (Ó Corráin 2001, 250). Legends evolved or were deliberately concocted to explain the present, not the past. A process similar to how modern historians work – taking the small scraps of actual information that survive and speculating as to how they can be assembled into a narrative whole – is in fact the method that was used in ancient times by those who constructed the legends. Except, we have more information and a clearer sense of judgment and perspective. The key to unravelling the medieval history of Derry lies in understanding the changing political geography of the area in which it is located. Much of what follows here will be concerned with that matter.

This book is addressed to two readerships: medieval specialists who will already know something about the subject, and who may be irritated by the secondary explanations necessary for its more general readers – the non-specialists who wish to know something about the ancient origins of such a fascinating and beautiful place. I hope it will be of some interest and benefit to both.

The Derry/Londonderry bid document campaigning for designation as UK City of Culture 2013 stated that 'four innovative components' would be central to the city's programme in the event of its success. One of those was to create 'a new story [for the city] which will be underpinned by joyous celebration and purposeful inquiry'. A new story for this ancient and historic city is something we all look forward to. This book aims at formulating a new telling of that section of its story for the thousand years or so prior to the seventeenth century: the story of Derry before Londonderry. While based on detailed 'purposeful inquiry' over many years of research, hopefully it will also be read as a 'joyous celebration' of that thousand years.

I am indebted to a number of people who have helped to bring this project to fruition. My interest in the medieval history and archaeology of Derry was stimulated almost forty years ago by a colleague then at Magee University College, Frank D'Arcy, and the members of a study group he had set up in the early 1970s, Project Lough Foyle. I am very grateful to the anonymous referees who recommended this book's publication and who provided an extremely detailed proofing of an earlier draft. I am especially thankful to Nollaig Ó Muraíle who made many suggestions and corrections, and to Pádraig Ó Riain who commented on my ideas about Da Cualén. I am grateful to John Bryson of Derry – whose own work on the physical layout of medieval Derry has been very valuable for me – who read and commented on an early draft of this text. Richard Sharpe helped me with some Latin translation from the *Liber Hymnorum*. I am indebted to the Holywell Trust (Derry), which, in this important year for the city, provided financial assistance from the City Walls Heritage Project to enable part of the research for this book. I am also very grateful for the support of the Heritage and Museum Service of Derry City Council. Finally, as on so many other occasions, I am indebted to all the staff at Four Courts Press – most especially Michael Potterton – for publishing this book and for making its preparation for the printer a very pleasurable experience. Any errors and misinterpretations that remain are my own.

CHAPTER 1

# The 'island' of Derry

To start at the end; early in the summer of 1600 during the Nine Years War, Sir Henry Docwra led an English military expedition into Gaelic Ulster, sailing around the north coast into Lough Foyle. After various mishaps, on 16 May the expedition landed at Culmore, a tiny peninsula on the west shore at the north end of the narrows where the River Foyle enters the lough. After six days reconnoitring at Culmore and its vicinity, most of the troops set off again to take possession of Derry, or 'the Derry' as they called it. For over a thousand years, Derry had been one of the chief places in the political and religious life of the north-west of Ireland, but its character was about to change radically. Fourteen years later, Docwra gave an account of that day's events:

> On the 22nd of May wee put the Army in order to marche, & … wee went to the Derry 4 myles of[f] vpon the River side a place in manner of an Iland Comprehending within it 40 [recte 200] acres [of] Ground, wherein were the Ruines of a old Abbay, of a Bishopp's house, of two Churches, & at one of the ends of it of an old Castle, the River called loughfoyle encompassing it all on one side, & a bogg most commonlie wett, & not easilie passable except in two or three places dividing it from the maine land.
>
> This peece of Ground we possest our selves of without Resistance, & iudging it a fitt place to make our maine plantation in, being somewhat hie, & therefore dry, & healthie to dwell vpon, att that end where the old Castle stood, being Close to the water side, I pressentlie resolved to raise a fforte to keep our stoore of Munition and victuells in, & in the other a little aboue, where the walls of an old Cathedrall church were yet standing, to [erect] another [fort] for our future safetie & retreate vnto upon all occasions …
>
> A Quarrie of stone & slatt wee found hard at hand. Cockle shells to make Lyme, we discouered infinite plentie of, in a little Iland in the mouth of the Harbour as we came in, and with those helpes, togeather with the Provisions wee brought, & the stones and rubbidge of the old [medieval] Buildings wee found, we sett our selues wholie … to fortefying & framing & setting vpp of howses such as we might be able to liue in.
>
> (Kelly 2003, 43–5)

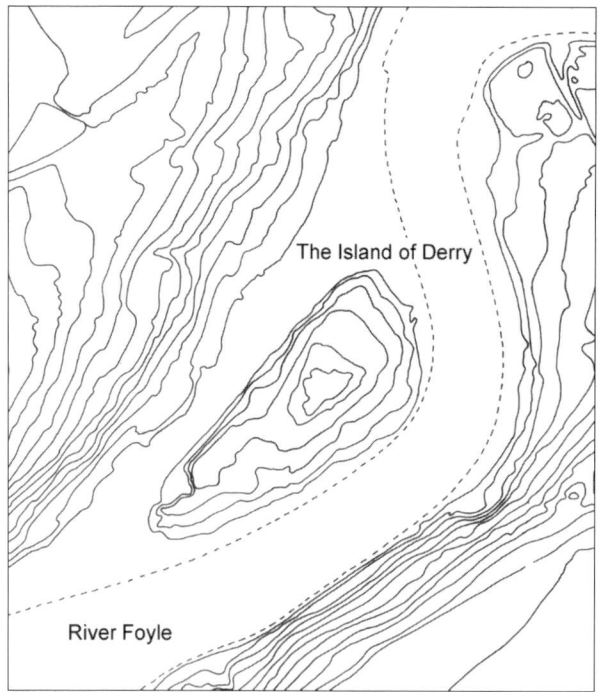

1 The 'Island' of Derry, showing the modern river course and contours at twenty-foot intervals (map by Dermot Francis).

What Docwra found at Derry was the ruined remains of a medieval and monastic settlement that had been growing in one form or another since at least the middle of the sixth century. The place also had a reasonably continuously recorded history, which was as old if not older than that of most other settled places on the island of Ireland.

Docwra's description is the earliest detailed account we have from which we can begin to build a picture of what medieval Derry actually looked like. What he found that day must have been similar (although, of course, a lot less tidy) to what visitors see today when they arrive at some of the other ancient Irish monastic sites that have survived undeveloped to the present, particularly those at lake- or riverside locations such as Devenish in Co. Fermanagh or Clonmacnoise in Co. Offaly. In May 1600, the remains at Derry consisted of a cluster of ruined medieval stone buildings – including the iconic round tower – standing in the midst of an agricultural landscape on a hillside rising above the River Foyle. As well as the main buildings, there must have been the bedraggled remnants ('the stones and rubbidge') of other lesser structures and monuments: houses of the former inhabitants; wells – including 'holy wells'; high crosses and cross-slabs; and cemeteries dating back a thousand years that contained the graves of monks, 'saints' and kings, as well as mere ordinary mortals.

# The 'island' of Derry

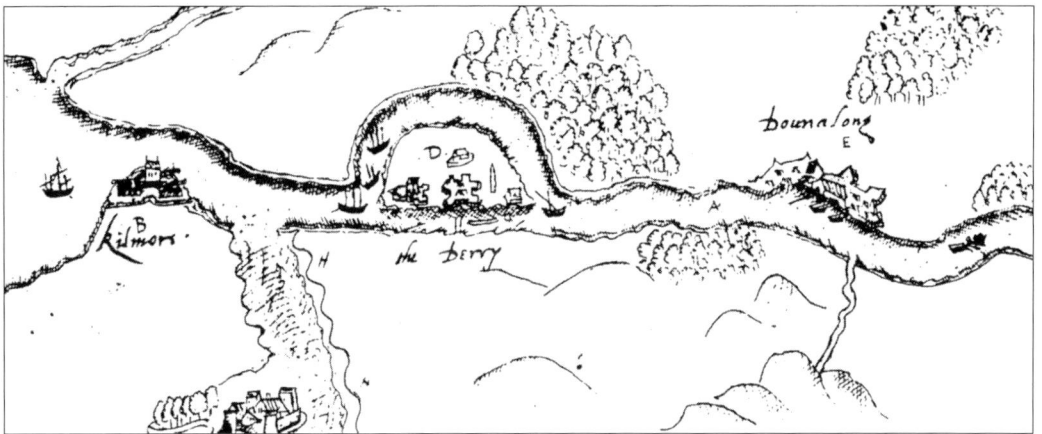

2 Detail from a contemporary sketch-map illustrating Sir Henry Docwra's expedition of 1600, showing sites along the River Foyle: 'Kilmore' (Culmore), Derry and Dunalong. The O'Doherty castle at Elagh (see also fig. 14) is shown at bottom left (National Library of Ireland, MS 2656, no. 16).

Docwra's account can be cross-checked with a sketch map made on the same expedition. This – the earliest known map of Derry, dated in London 27 December 1600 – is itself usefully annotated and labelled.[1] The structures mentioned by Docwra can all be recognized, as can the general topography and layout of Derry at the time. Most obvious is the settlement's location on an isolated hill ('in manner of an Iland'), defined on one side by a strip of marshy land (fig. 1). That bog cut the hill off on its western side from the adjacent 'mainland', which was then still part of the recently shired Co. Donegal. On its other sides, the hill was delimited by a wide bend of the Foyle. The river had been the artery that brought Docwra there and that would allow him, later, to penetrate further into western Ulster on his campaign against the rebellious Gaelic Irish (fig. 2). It was the river also that had been the *raison d'être* for the settlement's existence in the first place. Archaeological finds from along their shores and banks prove that the network formed by Lough Foyle and the River Foyle and its tributaries had served as important water highways leading into the interior of the north-west of Ireland from the beginning of Mesolithic times – about 8000BC – onwards.

The earliest name by which Derry is known is Daire Calgaich, meaning something like 'the oak wood' or 'oak grove' of Calgach. There are a number of stories dating to later in the medieval period that indicate some special or taboo

---

[1] National Archives, London: PRO SP 63/207, pt vi, no. 84 (I). Reproduced in Thomas 2005, Map 5; see also fig. 29, below. Ferguson (2005, 1–2) says that the map was enclosed with despatches dated 19 December, so, evidently, it had been prepared earlier than that.

qualities that attached to the trees of Derry. We know that oak trees held a special position in the belief systems of the ancient European peoples who are usually known to us – possibly inaccurately – as the Celts. It is likely that at least some of the stories about the Derry trees (which will be examined in later chapters) derive from such pre-Christian beliefs; but it would be difficult to prove that.

The name Daire Calgaich – or its equivalents – is referred to, apparently, for the first time at the year 619 in different versions of the medieval Irish annals.[2] Although the manuscripts and texts in which these 'embedded' annals have come down to us are much later, it is very likely that the original entry from which those later forms were copied (and re-copied) was written originally in the early seventh century into the lost document known now as the 'Iona chronicle', or its exemplar.[3] The Iona chronicle was the evolving historical record kept at the influential monastery on the Scottish island of Iona, which had been founded about 563 by the Donegal monk Columba. The Iona chronicle no longer survives, but it can be partially reconstructed from the substantial quotations from it that do survive, preserved as verbal 'fossils' in the 'matrices' of later texts. Although no longer in existence – strictly-speaking – the Iona chronicle is still the principal historical source for the 'history' of Ireland and Scotland up to about the year AD740. We do not know for certain when its compilation began or if it was started as far back as Columba's time, but there can be little doubt that the earliest allusion to Daire Calgaich in it was inserted contemporaneously or, at worst, near contemporaneously with the event it describes. The detail of that event will be returned to below; here the emphasis is on the issue of the oldest name for Derry.

The earliest surviving written form of Derry's name occurs in a copy of the Latin text *Vita Columbae* – Life of (St) Columba – composed about AD690–700, also on Iona, by Adomnán, its ninth abbot and Columba's relative. While that text also survives in a number of manuscripts from the later Middle Ages now housed in the British Library, the oldest copy is preserved at Schaffhausen in Switzerland.[4] Known by its catalogue label as *Generalia* I, it can be dated to the early eighth century and almost certainly to before 713 when the death of its presumed copyist, Dorbéne, is recorded. The manuscript was probably taken to a monastery with Irish connections on the Continent

---

2 As is to be expected, there is much confusion in the earliest medieval sources for dates. I am using here the table of synchronisms prepared by Daniel Mc Carthy, as published on the internet at: 'Chronological Synchronisation of the Irish Annals' (www.cs.tcd.ie/misc/kronos/chronology/synchronisms/annals-chron.htm, accessed 14 November 2011). Occasionally, there are discrepancies between Mc Carthy's dates and those that have been accepted more widely in the past.   3 Although the part of the entry that contains the name 'Daire Calgaich' is probably a secondary addition to the original shorter entry (see ch. 3).   4 Full accounts of these manuscripts and their histories can be found in various secondary sources, for example: Anderson and Anderson 1961, 3–18; Sharpe 1995, 235–8.

# The 'island' of Derry

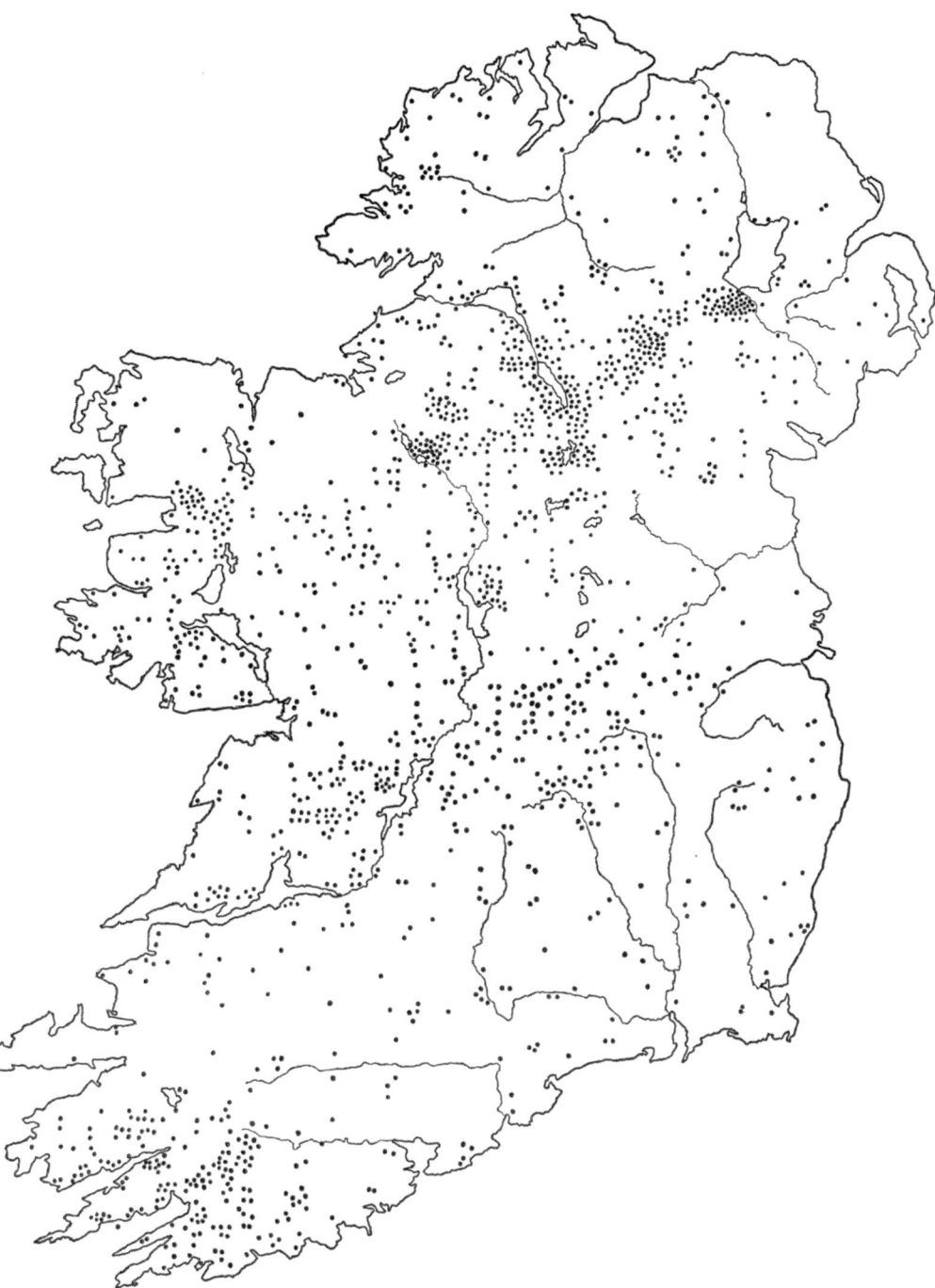

**3** Distribution of townland names that contain the word 'derry' (McCracken 1971, Map 2).

shortly after being finished. It was kept for much of the Middle Ages at the island monastery of Reichenau on Lake Constance, but in the upheavals following the French Revolution it ended up in the public library – the Stadtbibliotek – of the small Swiss town where it remains to the present day.

Derry is mentioned three times in the text: once in an Irish language form of its name as *Daire Calcig*, and twice in Latin as *Roboretum Calgachi*, a literal translation where *Roboretum* – also meaning something like 'oak wood' – is the direct equivalent of the Irish word Daire.[5] The subject matter of those references will be returned to below. In addition, a list of names of people associated with Columba that accompanies the later manuscripts of Adomnán's text includes a nephew of the saint, Bran, who is said to have been buried in Derry. We do not know its date for certain, but Richard Sharpe thinks that '[o]n linguistic grounds ... this list dates from Adomnán's time or very soon after' (1995, 354), that is about 700. At any rate, for what it is worth, the name of Derry is given in the lists in an Irish form as *Dairu Calchaich* (Anderson and Anderson 1961, 546).

The anglicized form Derry and its variants is a common name in Ireland; very frequently occurring as part of a composite place-name. The townland index records more than one thousand instances of 'derry' throughout the country, and there would be many more if minor place-names were included. This high number clearly reflects the ubiquity of oak trees in ancient times (fig. 3). It has also contributed some confusion to the modern interpretation of the ancient sources. As we will see, some references that have previously been understood as indicating Derry should actually have been attributed to other similarly named locations.

Some of those 'derry' places – such as the sites at and near the ruined early church of Derrynaflan in Co. Tipperary (where a magnificent set of early medieval, decorated metal liturgical objects was found – Ryan 1983) – are 'islands' of higher dry land rising out of the surrounding 'seas' of peat bog. To some extent at least, Derry must have been just such an 'island'; that is how it was described by Docwra when he captured it in 1600 – 'in manner of an Iland'.

The original settlement of Derry was located on a pear-shaped hill, 200 acres in extent and up to 120 feet in height.[6] Although more or less completely built over now, in earlier times – by comparison with the surrounding countryside – it must have been good agricultural land; in 1600, the English found it 'for the most part sown with corn' (*CSPI*, 1600–1, 93).

The River Foyle is still tidal and fast-flowing as it passes the eastern side of the hill. It is about forty feet in depth at high water and about one thousand

---

5 Anderson and Anderson 1961: in Irish 428 (90a); in Latin 206 (11b) and 248 (26a).
6 Lacy 1988; Lacey 2006, 128–30. See also map of medieval Derry by John Bryson (forthcoming) and Ó Baoill (forthcoming).

# The 'island' of Derry

4 Holywell Hill, formerly Knockenny > Cnoc Énnai. The 'holy well' of the name is actually a rain-filled, stone-lined cist sunk into a probably prehistoric cairn. The border between Northern Ireland and the Republic of Ireland (also Cos Donegal and Derry) passes through the cairn, which is below (in the photograph to the right of) the RTÉ television mast on the summit of the hill. The hill has been a boundary marker since, at least, the sixth century.

feet wide. There was no bridge across the river prior to the late eighteenth century; thus in ancient times it could only be crossed – with some difficulty – by ferry. The river was a dangerous and formidable physical barrier and in medieval times it was additionally a substantial political boundary. It was also, simultaneously, a considerably important water highway which facilitated access to much of western Ulster through its tributaries and its outlet to the ocean.

Since 1922, Derry has been a border city, located on the frontier between Northern Ireland and the southern Irish state. In some ways, however, for much of the time that we have had records about it, Derry was a border place – even an important 'boundary marker' as will be argued below. The hill of Derry is itself the easternmost limit of a small range of isolated hills and low mountains, the western edge of which is defined by Greenan Mountain in Co. Donegal. The latter – five miles north-west of Derry – rises eight hundred feet above Lough Swilly and on its top stands the imposing ancient (but now greatly 'restored') structure known as the Grianán of Aileach (fig. 15). Lying roughly halfway between the two is Holywell Hill (850 feet), which was known to the Elizabethan surveyors as Knockenny (Bryson 2001, 197) (fig. 4). Knockenny was probably a reflex of the Irish Cnoc Énnai(?), a name that almost certainly confirms that it was once the northern boundary of the little Cenél nÉnnai kingdom, just as it now marks the boundary between the two modern states. As we will see below, Cenél nÉnnai was a tiny kingdom that effectively ceased to exist as a separate entity (until it re-emerged about five hundred years later) around the end of the third quarter of the sixth century.

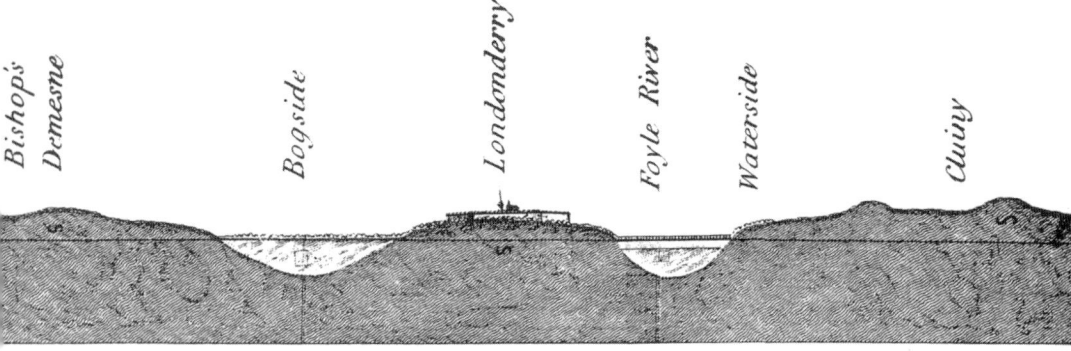

5 Detail of an imagined cross-section through the landscape at Derry to illustrate its 'original' island nature. From George Vaughan Sampson's chart of County Londonderry, 1813.

The western side of the hill of Derry is defined by a relatively steep-sided (at least in some places) valley, which in prehistoric times had been a second channel of the River Foyle (fig. 5). At the time of the so-called maximum marine transgression (perhaps $c$.3000BC), when sea-level rose to its highest relative to land-level, Derry would have been a true island – somewhat similar now to the nearby Inch Island in Lough Swilly. However, by the time the first ecclesiastical settlement ('monastery')[7] was established there in the late sixth century, the river level had dropped as a consequence of the final post-glacial adjustments to relative land- and sea-levels. The former river channel was memorialized as a strip of marshy wetland – 'the Bogside', by which name the area became famous in the late 1960s (Lacy 1990, 1–5). That boggy strip could only be crossed easily in medieval times by two or three artificially constructed causeways.[8]

To the north of the hill of Derry, there was another boggy valley (also a former channel of the River Foyle), which crossed the isthmus at the base of the Inishowen Peninsula. That valley is sometimes referred to as the Pennyburn Depression (fig. 6). The valley has been drained and largely built-on in modern times,[9] but the strip of bogland could also only be crossed by a limited number of causeways in pre-modern times. From at least the middle of the sixth to the end of the eighth century, that boggy valley had also acted as a political border: first as the northern frontier of the Cenél nÉnnai kingdom, and later – after the latter had been conquered – as the northern frontier of the

[7] There is an extensive literature discussing the nature of early Irish church settlements, particularly the degree to which the word 'monastery' is appropriate. Its use here implies no particular organizational character. The earliest relevant terminology for Derry is Adomnán's *eclesiam* of $c$.700, and *civitatum* in an entry in AU 882. For a full analysis of the issue, see Etchingham 1999.   [8] AFM 1600 explicitly refers to an *urdhrochat* – bridge (O'Donovan 1857, vi, 2206–7).   [9] Although localized place-names such as Moss Road/Park still memorialize its ancient condition.

The 'island' of Derry

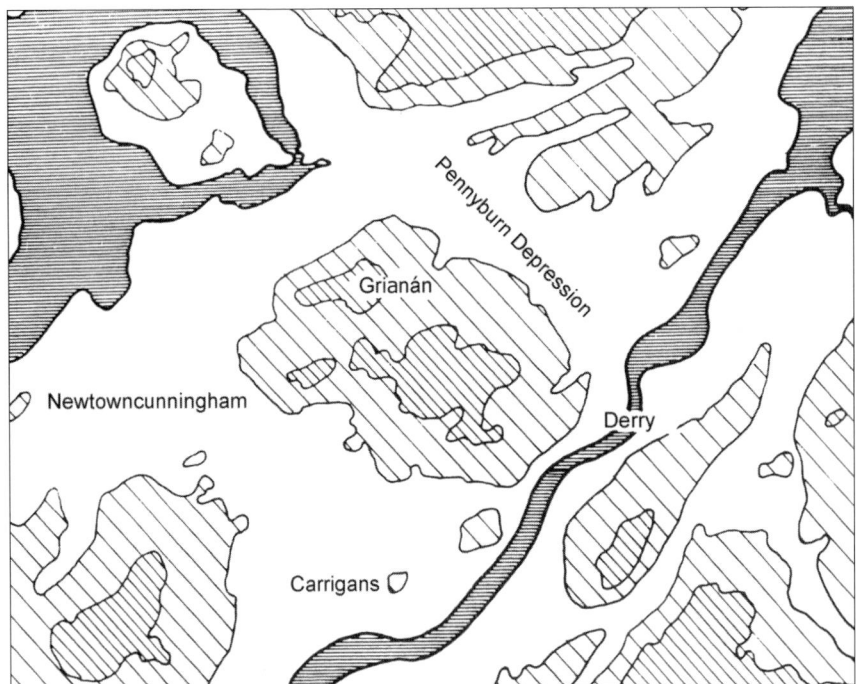

6 The area of high ground between Derry and the Grianán of Aileach, isolated to the north and south by low-lying boggy valleys. Holywell Hill (fig. 4) is at the centre of the highest land. The low land (former river channel) to the north (the Pennyburn Depression) separates the area from the Inishowen Peninsula further to the north (map by Dermot Francis).

Cenél Conaill, Columba's people. To the north of that natural frontier was the separate territory of the Cenél Conaill's neighbours and traditional enemies, the Cenél nEógain of Inishowen.

The second part of the earliest form of the name by which Derry is known is the Irish language masculine personal name Calgach, which itself seems to mean something like 'pointed' or 'piercing'.[10] We cannot be sure who the Calgach in question was. Some nineteenth-century writers – almost certainly mistakenly – attempted to identify him with the southern Scottish warrior Galgacus or Calgacus who fiercely opposed the Roman military leader Agricola in the first century AD.[11] That Calgacus, whom Alfred Smyth characterized as 'the first named inhabitant of Scotland' (2003, 14), is not known to have had any associations with Ireland and there is absolutely no evidence to support his identification with the person connected with Derry.

10 *RIA Dictionary* 132, col. 325 'colg'. Reeves suggested that the word became 'a proper name in the sense of "fierce warrior"' (1857, 160). 11 See, for instance, O'Doherty 1902, 1–12. For Calgacus' career, see Duncan 2000, 20; Smyth 2003, 14, 37, 46, 49, 52, 56.

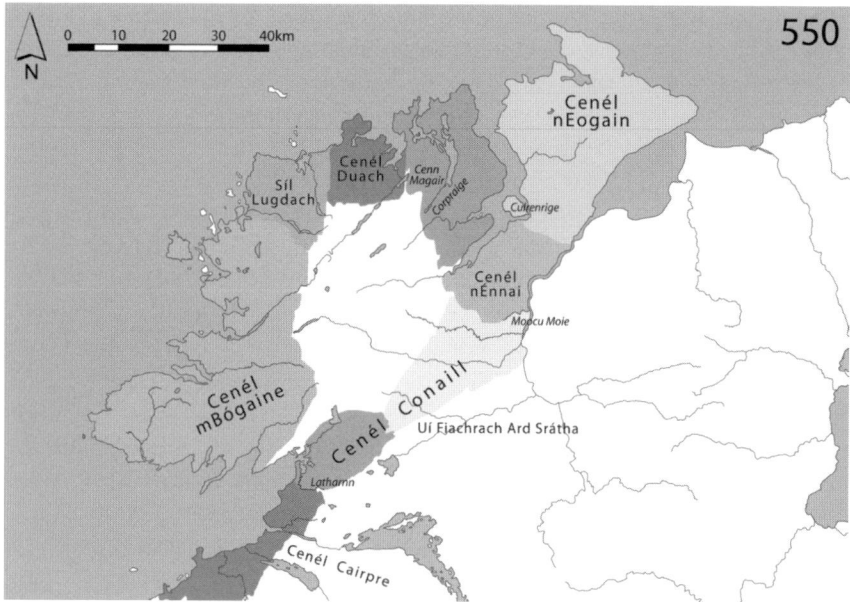

7 Generalized map of the kingdoms of Donegal, c.AD550. The Cenél nÉnnai kingdom, including the 'island' of Derry (not marked), is shown extending from the Swillyburn northwards to the southern edge of the Pennyburn Depression (map by Robert Shaw).

There is some circumstantial evidence that may allow us to tentatively identify the latter. The Iona chroniclers (whose record was later transmitted through the Annals of Ulster) recorded the death in 595 of a man called Tipraite mac Calgaich. The surviving record includes no identifying information about who he or his father were. But the fact that his death was recorded on Iona seems to indicate that he was a significant public figure and that there must have been some particular curiosity about him there. It is at least possible that the reason he was of interest to the Columban monks was because his father was the Calgach whose name was incorporated in the contemporary name for Derry (Lacey 2006, 128–9). Almost certainly by 595 there was a church at Derry – Daire Calgaich – which was linked to the growing number of Columban establishments under the leadership of Iona.

Up to shortly before that time Derry had probably been a secular fortification belonging to the Cenél nÉnnai kingdom (fig. 7). The Cenél nÉnnai are frequently referred to in modern texts as, at best, a shadowy, short-lived dynastic kingdom. Indeed, although they appear in the origin legends for the earliest kingdoms of Donegal (Lacey 2006, 41–6), their real existence has been questioned (Byrne 2001, xvi). But there are good reasons for believing that they did exist at the very period when Ireland, particularly the north-west of Ireland, was emerging from prehistory, that is when records begin to become available that allow some light to be shed on contemporary political geography (Lacey 2006, 120–31). No direct evidence survives for the Cenél nÉnnai at that time, but a certain amount of circumstantial evidence for them can be gleaned, particularly from the records relating to the sixth-century ecclesiastical figure Brugach mac Dega. Brugach's church was at a place called Ráith Maige Oenaig or Enaig, which has been variously identified as Raymoghy or Rateen, both in east Co. Donegal, twelve to ten miles respectively south-west of Derry.[12] Ráith Maige Oenaig was probably a southern boundary marker for the Cenél nÉnnai kingdom, just as the range of hills stretching from Derry through Holywell Hill (formerly Knockenny < Cnoc Énnai?) to Greenan Mountain formed their northern boundary. The relatively insignificant stream just north of present-day Lifford, known now as the Swillyburn, was probably the actual southern border of their kingdom (Lacey 2006, 121–3). Their territory lay between those boundaries to the north and south, and between the River Foyle and Lough Swilly to the east and west. Immediately south of their kingdom was the territory of Columba's own people, the Cenél Conaill (ibid., 131–43).

In the Book of Fenagh there is (an admittedly late) medieval poem in which words are addressed to Énna, the alleged eponymous 'founder' of the Cenél nÉnnai, by Conall, the alleged eponymous 'founder' of the Cenél Conaill.

| Ergsi co Doiri na ndam; | Go thou to Doire of the troops; |
| Faidfetsa anoir co Cruachan. | I will stretch eastwards to Cruachan.[13] |
| | |
| Gabas Enna a nDoiri dil, | Enna settled in faithful Doire, |
| Dun Chalgaich mic Aithemuin; | The fort of Calgach, Aitheman's son. |
| | (Hennessy and Kelly 1875, 402–3) |

Although the poem dates to at least five or six hundred years after the events it purports to describe, in it Derry is identified unambiguously as a Cenél nÉnnai *dún* or fortification. As Derry was at no time in the fully historic period a Cenél nÉnnai fortification, it is hard to see why anyone would have invented such a claim if there had not been some truth in it originally. The most logical explanation is that Derry was indeed a Cenél nÉnnai *dún* prior to its being captured by the Cenél Conaill. The Calgach son of Aitheman mentioned in the poem may have been a Cenél nÉnnai king who 'lived' in Derry and gave his name to it. In addition, although there can be no certainty about it, the only historical evidence that we have might suggest that Tipraite mac Calgaich who died in 595 may have been the latter's son.

---

12 For arguments in favour of Rateen, see Lacey 2006, 124–6.   13 Croaghan Hill – south-west of Lifford, Co. Donegal – the Cenél Conaill caput (Lacey 2006, 134–40).

TABLE 1. Suggested pedigree of Tipraite mac Calgaich (d. 595).

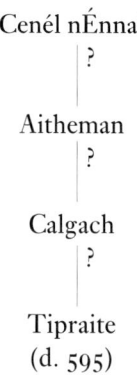

It is probably of some significance that in the admittedly later hagiography the cleric Brugach mac Dega is claimed as having been baptized by St Patrick. Whether that was true or not, he certainly seems to have been remembered as belonging to the earliest cohort of Christians in Ireland. In the Middle Irish Homily or Life of Colum Cille – composed in Derry about 1150 – to which we will return below, Colum Cille while still a child was brought at Christmastime to visit Brugach at Ráith Maige Oinaig/Enaig.

> [Colum Cille] and his fosterer went at Christmas-time to Brugach mac Dega, the bishop of Rátha Muige Enaig in Tír Énda. His fosterer, the cleric, was given charge of performing priestly duties in that place on the festival day. He, however, was seized with self-consciousness and was unable to chant his allotted psalm, which was *Misericordias*. Thereupon the son of grace, Colum Cille, recited the psalm on behalf of his fosterer, though previously he had read only his alphabet, and the names of God and Colum Cille were magnified by that great miracle.
>
> (Herbert 1988, 253)

The meaning of the story is not clear, but in hagiographical terms it seems to suggest that Brugach – in reality his 'clerical successors' who by then may have been located at the church of Raphoe (Lacey 2006, 250 and 317) – owed some debt to Colum Cille; realistically to his twelfth-century 'heirs', the senior clergy in Derry. In fact, as we will see below, in the mid-twelfth century the revived or re-emerged Cenél nÉnnai kingdom came under attack from various sources including the Uí Dochartaigh, a Síl Lugdach people who had a special devotion to the cult of Colum Cille.

Whatever their origins in the strictly prehistoric period, Cenél nÉnnai did not survive as an independent polity for long into the historic era. Although we have no contemporary documentation to demonstrate it, it seems very probable – again from the circumstantial evidence – that under their powerful king Áed mac Ainmerech, Columba's own people, the Cenél Conaill, conquered the Cenél nÉnnai territory including the hill or 'island' of Derry sometime around 578 (Lacey 2006, 114, 130). The Cenél Conaill conquest of the area right up to the former northern boundary of the Cenél nÉnnai kingdom seems to be confirmed by the Battle of Druim Meic Ercae in 578 in which the Cenél Conaill king Áed mac Ainmerech is recorded as having defeated the Cenél nEógain of Inishowen. Druim Meic Ercae has sometimes been identified with sites in Co. Tyrone (for example, MacShamhráin 2000, 82 n. 17), but it seems illogical that two Donegal kingdoms would have been fighting each other at such locations. A more likely possibility is that this was an attack by the Cenél Conaill on the Cenél nEógain, near the borders of the latter's territory at the southern end of the Inishowen Peninsula. The high ridge, running between the Scalp and Eshkaheen Mountains across the southern end of the peninsula, was the effective border of Cenél nEógain territory. Today, there are several places in the southern foothills of those mountains that have 'Drum' names, although none of them now, apparently, reflects the form Druim Meic Ercae. If such was the location of the battle in 578, then the place-name was probably derived from Muirchertach Mac Ercae, the influential but shadowy early member of the Cenél nEógain whose death was remembered as occurring in the 530s.[14]

Just south of those foothills was the strip of bogland – mentioned above – that ran between Lough Foyle and Lough Swilly, isolating Inis Eógain to the north and that survived down to the seventeenth century and beyond – the so-called Pennyburn Depression. Further south again is the range of low hills running between Greenan Mountain at the west and the hill of Derry at the east. The hill of Derry faced north across that former bog, towards Inis Eógain. This is, classically, border country. The church of Derry was probably established there specifically to mark and 'fix' the northern extent of the Cenél Conaill's expansion, just south of the Cenél nEógain border.

The defeat of the latter by the Cenél Conaill in 578 was probably accompanied by the extinction of the 'independence' of the Cenél nÉnnai and by the acquisition of their site at Derry. Derry had probably been some sort of border fortification belonging to that kingdom, which was then transferred by the Cenél Conaill to the church for the location of a 'boundary monastery'. That matter will be dealt with more fully in ch. 3.

14 For the historicity of Muirchertach Mac Ercae, see Byrne and Mac Shamhráin 2005, 178–81.

CHAPTER 2

# The legend of the foundation of the monastery

As with most other early Irish churches, no contemporary records exist of how the foundation of the Christian settlement at Derry came about. In fact, it is unlikely that such records ever existed. In the absence of contemporary written narratives and for various later propaganda purposes, legendary versions of the story evolved and grew more elaborate over time. Those stories are now well known. Basically, they state that Colum Cille founded the church there as a very young man – his first and, thus, most loved foundation – the site having been granted to him by his relative Áed mac Ainmerech who is often credited with being king of Ireland at the time. The date of AD545 (sometimes amended to 546) is usually assigned to that 'event'; that is, many years before Columba left Ireland for Scotland.

Who was this Columba who is credited with the 'foundation' of Derry? Much of what we think we know about him (and, generally, of this period of

TABLE 2. Genealogy of Columba and some of his relatives.

*Niall Noígiallach*
|
*Conall Gulban*
|
Fergus
|
┌──────────────┴──────────────┐
Eithne = Fedelmid          Brendan
|                              |
┌────┬──────┬──────┬──────┐
Cuimne  Sinech  Iogen  Mincoleth  Columba      Baithéne
                                  (d. 593)     (d. 596)
                                               (2nd ab. of
Bran            sons of Énán                   Iona)
(buried         (after whom
in Derry)       Kilmacrenan is
                named)

(source: Anderson and Anderson 1961, 546–9)

8 Map showing the distribution of the early population groups that claimed their descent from an individual known as Conall, or from a character with an equivalent cognate name (map by Robert Shaw).

the Irish past) turns out on examination to be legend instead of verifiable history, tales developed for both religious and secular propaganda purposes much later than the period of his actual life. Nevertheless, there can be little doubt that he was a real historical character and that, when we strip away the later accretions to his story, we can still recover some of the real facts about his actual historical life. We have very few pieces of real information, but the fact that we can say anything at all with reasonable authority is testament to his importance and influence (Lacey 2013).

Columba was probably born in the year 520 (or thereabouts) into the highly influential dynasty, the Cenél Conaill, who would give their name in the form Tír Chonaill to what is now the greater part of Co. Donegal. They claimed descent from an individual called Conall who was said to have been one of the sons of the legendary Niall Noígiallach, 'Niall of the Nine Hostages'. Whether Conall or Niall ever actually existed is debatable and probably impossible to establish with certainty. If the two had lived, they would have done so before the beginnings of historical documentation and therefore the alleged facts of their lives are not amenable to scientific scrutiny. Niall is claimed as giving rise to the people called the Uí Néill who *did* rule over much of the northern half of

Ireland for most of the second half of the first millennium – roughly AD 500–1000. Apart from the historicity of Niall himself, it is unlikely that the Conall of the Cenél Conaill had any real genealogical connection with him.[1] In fact, many peoples across the northern part of Ireland, particularly but not exclusively in Ulster, claimed descent from a character called Conall or from an 'ancestor' with a cognate name (fig. 8).

Notwithstanding doubts about the legend of their origins, the Cenél Conaill were evidently a powerful and expansionist dynasty from at least the sixth century who would retain significant power in the north-west of Ireland until the end of the eighth century. During that period, as well as dominating Donegal, individual Cenél Conaill kings also attained the position of king of Tara, believed to be the most influential office – at least in the northern half – of Ireland. Although a number of very early Cenél Conaill kings were described in contemporary or near contemporary sources as 'kings of Ireland', those claims were at best inflated propaganda self-assertions. The claims did give rise, however, to the later exaggerated legends that Columba himself could have been a candidate for the kingship of Ireland until he voluntarily gave up that inheritance in order to enter the service of the church.

Columba was probably born in the Gartan area of Donegal, in the territory of what almost certainly were his mother's people, the Corpraige of Fanad. According to a very early list of his relatives, his father was called Fedelmid and his mother Aethne or Eithne.[2] He had three sisters and a brother that we know about, and one of his first cousins, Baithéne, would later succeed him as abbot of Iona. One of his sisters had a son Bran who was believed to have been buried in Derry. Another sister was the mother of the sons of a man called Énán. Allegedly, those 'sons of Énán' – meic nÉnán – gave their name to the church of Cill mac nÉnán (Kilmacrenan, Co. Donegal), which was located at a place originally called Daire Eithne 'the oak wood of Eithne'.

We actually know little about Columba's early life and Christian education, but it may be significant that close to the *caput* of his father's people, the Cenél Conaill, at Croaghan Hill (just south of Lifford, Co. Donegal), there is an ancient church site with the indicative name of Domnach Mór Maige nItha, Donaghmore. Churches that incorporate the element *domnach* in their names are believed to have been among the earliest Christian churches in Ireland and are therefore often said to have been founded by St Patrick, as is the case here. Another indication of the already Christian environment in which the young Columba may have grown up is that in (admittedly late) hagiography he is

---

1 The meaning of the name Niall is uncertain, but seems to be 'connected with *nél* "a cloud"' (Ó Corráin and Maguire, 1981, 145). Conall seems to mean 'strong as a wolf' (ibid., 56).
2 Anderson and Anderson 1961, 546–9; Sharpe 1995, 354. The list also contains information on other members of his family that has not been included here. As Eithne was also the name of a widely honoured territorial goddess, we have to be cautious about accepting it as Columba's mother's real name.

associated, as we saw above, with the clerical figure Brugach mac Dega, himself said to be associated with St Patrick. Thus, in legend, and more persuasively in geography, Columba is linked to some of the earliest Christians and Christian places in the north-west of Ireland.

Little is known factually about Columba until 562 when he is recorded as leaving Ireland (as legend and folklore claim, from sites still pointed out in Derry) and subsequently founding the monastery on Iona. Iona developed into an institution of astonishing influence in Ireland, Scotland and the north of England. Many other churches were founded from it, including in the 580s Dairmag (Durrow, Co. Offaly). Dairmag is another 'oak' place-name, a factor that may have contributed later to the stories about Columba's involvement with Derry. Columba himself died in the 590s – probably in 593 although 597 was the generally accepted date until quite recently.

Legends claim that before he left for Scotland Columba had founded the monastery of Derry. Unfortunately for those particularly attached to that story, most of the narrative details cannot be substantiated when examined in the light of the admittedly meagre contemporary historical sources. The deconstruction of those legends and an analysis of the facts that can be gleaned from the historical evidence will be returned to in ch. 3, but first the medieval written versions of the legends in the chronological order in which they have been preserved will be outlined here.

While there may have been earlier oral versions (and even written versions that have not survived), the earliest surviving written account purporting to be a record of the foundation of Derry by Colum Cille occurs in the text known as the Irish *Liber Hymnorum*. The *Liber Hymnorum* – surviving in two closely related manuscripts[3] of about the early twelfth century (Bhreathnach and Cunningham 2007, 106) – contains an anthology 'apparently compiled in the tenth century', but probably after the year 989 (Herbert 1989, 67–8). The anthology includes three hymns or poems in Latin said to have been composed by Colum Cille: *Noli Pater Indulgere, Altus Prosator*[4] and *In te Christe*, and refers to a fourth, *Adiutor Laborantium*, which, until recently, was thought to have been lost (Clancy and Márkus 1995, 69–70). There is no certainty that any of these poems was composed by the saint, and many scholars would reject that possibility totally.[5] In the *Liber Hymnorum*, the three poems included are

---

3 Bernard and Atkinson, who edited the text in 1898, labelled the manuscripts (i) T, i.e. E.4.2 (now TCD 1441) in the library of Trinity College Dublin; and (ii) F, a manuscript that, in the early seventeenth century, belonged to the Franciscan convent of Donegal. This is now in the Franciscan collection in the library of University College Dublin (UCD-OFM A2).   4 The 'preface' in the *Liber Hymnorum* to the *Altus Prosator* says it was composed on Iona, but the equivalent 'preface' in the early fifteenth-century *Leabhar Breac* claims that it was composed '*in Cellula Nigra .i. isin dúib-recles i nDoire Choluim Cille* – the Dubreclés in Derry' (Bernard and Atkinson 1898, i, 62).   5 For instance, it has been argued that *Adiutor laborantium* was actually composed by Adomnán (Márkus 2010).

introduced separately by almost certainly fictional 'prefaces' – themselves apparently composed before the late tenth century – which claim to give details about the *locus*, the place of; the *tempus*, the time of; and the *causa*, the cause or reason for their composition.

The 'preface' to the poem *Noli Pater Indulgere* is of particular significance here, as it contains what appears to be the oldest surviving version of the alleged story of the foundation of the monastery of Derry. That preface – written in a mixture of Latin and Irish – although relatively brief, presents the 'bones' of the story that would be 'fleshed out' in the later versions.[6]

The following is the (slightly amended) Bernard and Atkinson translation of the Trinity College version, with my editorial intrusions inserted in square brackets.

> *Noli Pater*. Colum Cille *fecit hinc hymnum eodem modo ut* '*In te Christe*' [Colum Cille made this hymn in the same manner as (he composed) '*In te Christe*]. *Locus*, the door of the hermitage [*dorus dísert*] of Daire Calcaig; *tempus idem*, [the time of] Áed mac Ainmerech [king of Cenél Conaill who died *c*.596]; *causa*, Colum Cille *aliquando venit ad colloquium regis* [once came to a meeting with the king] to Derry, and there was offered to him the place with its appurtenance [*in port co n-airliud*]. At that time Colum Cille refused the place, *quia prohibuit* [because it had been forbidden by] Mo Bíí in his case *accipere mundum* [to accept the gift (?)][7] till he should hear of his [Mo Bíí's] death. But thereafter, when Colum Cille came to the door ['gate'?] of the place [*co dorus an bale*], there met him three persons of the folk [*muintir* 'monastic community'] of Mo Bíí, having with them Mo Bíí's girdle [*cris*, 'belt'], *et dixerunt, mortuus est Mobi*; [and said, Mo Bíí was dead]: *et dixit* Colum Cille [and Colum Cille said]
>
>> Mo Bíí's girdle
>> Was never closed around 'lua' (?)
>> Not only was it never opened to (allow) satiety,
>> It was never shut around a lie.

---

**6** The 'preface' to the enigmatic 'Hymn of St Cummain the Tall', also in the *Liber Hymnorum*, claims that it 'was composed in Daire Calcaig'. Although the preface mentions the Cenél Conaill king Áed mac Ainmerech, his son Domnall and Colum Cille, it is not clear what the connection of St Cummain – otherwise associated with Munster, Clonfert and Kilcummin in Co. Mayo – is with Derry. The editors considered that the hymn dated to 'before the ninth century at least' (Bernard and Atkinson 1898, i, 18; ii, 10, 108–9).   **7** The word *mundum* does not seem to make sense here. Richard Sharpe has suggested (pers. comm.) that the original may have been *munus* 'gift', first corrupted to *mundus* and then (by supposed grammatical correction, though in fact nonsense) to *mundum*.

*The legend of the foundation of the monastery* 19

> Colum Cille went back to the king, *et dixit regi* [and said to the king], 'the offering thou gavest me early this morning, give it me *nunc* [now]'. 'It shall be given', said the king. Then the place is burnt with all that was in it. 'That is wasteful', said the king, 'for if it had not been burnt, there would be no want of garment or food therein till Doom'. 'But (people) shall be there from henceforth', said [Colum Cille], '(and to) the person who shall be staying therein, there shall be no night of fasting'. Now the fire from its size threatened to burn the whole oak-wood, and to protect it this hymn was composed. Or it was the Day of Judgment that he [Colum Cille] had in mind, or the fire of John's Feast [*féile Eoin*],[8] and it is sung against every fire and every thunder from that time to this; and whosoever recites it at lying down and at rising up, it protects him against lightning flash, and it protects the nine persons of his household whom he chooses.
>
> (Bernard and Atkinson 1898, vol. I, 87; vol. II, 28)

The following variation of a section of the last paragraph occurs in the Franciscan manuscript.

> Or it is to preserve the oakwood [*daire* = Derry] when a thunder-bolt set fire to the place, after it had been given by Áed mac Ainmerech, and the fire sought to consume it, so it was on that account this hymn was composed.
>
> (ibid.)

The next major instalment in the development of this legend that has survived is the mid-twelfth-century work known as the Middle Irish Homily or Life of Colum Cille. Although it has been argued that this text originated in Armagh (Bannerman 1993, 41), Máire Herbert has demonstrated fairly conclusively that it was in fact composed in Derry, probably in association with the transfer to there from the monastery of Kells (Co. Meath) of the headquarters of the Columban confederation of churches – the *familia Columbae* – (Herbert 1985, 132; 1988, 199); that matter will be returned to below. The Middle Irish Life is cast in the form of a homily for preaching on the saint's feastday, 9 June. As Máire Herbert argued, it was probably composed between the year 1150, when Derry took over the leadership of the Columban churches, and 1182, when one of the treasures of Derry that it mentions – the *Soiscél Martain* (which will be returned to below) – was lost (ibid., 193). In fact, the Life was probably composed before 1169, the year of the Anglo-Norman 'invasion' of Ireland. The text makes no allusion to that momentous event,

---

8 This seems to suggest that the making of bonfires on St John's Eve (night of 23/24 June) was a custom practised in Derry from the late tenth century at least.

despite the fact that some of the leading Columban churches in Leinster quickly came within the sphere of influence of the 'invaders' (ibid.). The following is the Middle Irish Life's account of the foundation of Derry.

> Then Colum Cille went to Derry, the royal fortress [*rigdún*] of Áed mac Ainmirech. The latter was king of Ireland at that time. The king offered the fortress [*dún*] to Colum Cille, who refused on account of Mo Bíí's [of the monastery of Glasnevin in Dublin] precept [*timmna*. In the previous section of the text, there is the sentence: 'Furthermore, he told Colum Cille that he should not accept land until he himself, Mo Bíí, should permit him']. However, when he [Colum Cille] was coming out of the fortress, he met two of Mo Bíí's household [*muintir*], who had Mo Bíí's belt [*criss*] for him, and the permission to accept land, as Mo Bíí had died. *Ut dixit* Colum Cille [as Colum Cille said]:
> 
> > Mo Bíí's belt
> > was not like rushes round water;
> > it was neither opened on account of satiety
> > nor fastened round falsehood.
> 
> Afterwards, Colum Cille settled in Áed's fortress and founded a church [*eclais*] there, in which were performed numerous miracles.
> 
> (Herbert 1988, 255–6)

The Middle Irish Life survives in seven medieval manuscripts as well as in many other copies of a later date (Herbert 1988, 211–12). Both the *Leabhar Chlainne Suibhne* and the National Library of Scotland versions (each dating to the fifteenth or early sixteenth century) have two additional details relating to Derry. The first of these is as follows:

> Then having received it from the king, Colum Cille burnt the place [*bailí*] with all in it. 'That is an unprofitable act', said the king, 'for if it were not burnt, there would never be a scarcity of clothing or food (there)'. 'It will be thus from henceforth', replied he [Colum Cille], 'and the person who will dwell there will not spend any night fasting'. On account of its size, the fire was on the point of burning all the oak-wood, until Colum Cille composed a hymn for its protection, *Noli Pater Indulger*[*e*].
> 
> (Herbert 1988, 230 n. 2; 256 n. 1)

The second additional anecdote that occurs in these two versions is as follows:

> Colum Cille left Da Cualén, a cleric of his community, as his successor [*ina comarbus*] in Derry. The latter was a cleric from his own native territory, and Colum Cille granted that the office of prior [*secnabuigecht*] of the same monastery [*baili*] and the headship of its senior monks [*cendus a sruithe*] should be the prerogative of Cenél Conaill.
>
> (Herbert 1988, 231 n. 2; 257 n. 2)

The main text of the Middle Irish Life was composed at a time when the Mac Lochlainn family, who belonged to the Cenél nEógain, were rulers in Derry. Presumably the Cenél Conaill appendix (second addition) must derive from a period when the latter had regained some power there, as they seem to have done from about 1180 onwards (see below). We will return also (in ch. 7) to a discussion about who the Da Cualén was who is mentioned in the appendix. Manus Ó Domhnaill's *Betha Colaim Chille* 'Life of Colum Cille' composed in 1532 has a broadly similar statement about the Cenél Conaill, but he does not name the cleric in question (O'Kelleher and Schoepperle 1918, 78–9; Lacey 1998a, 51).

The most developed version of the legend is contained in that Ó Domhnaill Life. The idea for that work may have arisen as some sort of millennial memorial marking the one-thousandth anniversary of the birth of the saint (Lacey 1998a, 7), which would have occurred in 1520.[9] Ó Domhnaill's work was, in effect, a summary of much, if not all, of what had been written and told in story about the saint before that time. In accordance with what were the prevailing legends at the time, Ó Domhnaill gave great prominence to Derry as the first and most beloved of the saint's churches. He located the foundation very early in the saint's life, immediately following his alleged period as a student at St Mo Bíí's monastery at Glasnevin. According to the legend, a plague broke out and the students were dispersed back to their home territories for their protection. Colum Cille headed north to Derry in the land of his own people, the Cenél Conaill.

> That settlement of Derry was the home of Áed mac Ainmerech at the time. Áed offered the place to Colum Cille but he refused it as he did not have Mo Bíí's permission to accept it. However, as Colum Cille was leaving the fortification he met two of Mo Bíí's community who had brought Mo Bíí's belt for him, after the latter's death. For Mo Bíí had sent them to Colum Cille with permission to accept the land, along with the belt. And as Colum Cille took the belt from them he said: 'A good man had this belt because it was never opened for gluttony nor ever closed on a lie'. Then he made this verse:

---

9 The year of Colum Cille's birth, 520, is the only *anno domini* date used by Ó Domhnaill in the *Betha*, with the exception of 1532, the year in which the text was completed.

> Mo Bíí's inflexible belt,
> It was not like the rushes in a lake.
> It was never loosened for greediness,
> Nor tightened around the false or the fake.

Colum Cille then took the place from Áed and, when the latter had left it, he burned it and everything that was in it, erasing from it the works of worldly men so that he might consecrate it to God and to himself. 'That's folly', said Áed, 'for had the place not been burned, no one in it would ever lack food or clothes; now I fear that there'll always be want there'. But then Colum Cille said: 'Everyone there will always get from God what he needs'. So great was the fire and the blaze that it nearly destroyed the grove of oak trees there, so that Colum Cille made this hymn to protect it:

> *Noli Pater Indulgere ...* [10]
>
> Father, keep under
> The tempest and thunder,
> Lest we should be shattered
> By Thy lightning's shafts scattered.
> Thy terrors while hearing,
> We listen still fearing,
> The resonant song
> Of the bright angel throng,
> As they wander and praise Thee,
> Shouts of honour still raise Thee.
> To the King ruling right,
> Jesus, lover and light.
>
> As with wine and clear mead,
> Filled with God's grace indeed,
> Precursor John Baptist's word,
> Told of the coming Lord,
> Whom, blessed for evermore,
> All men should bow before.
> Zacharias, Elizabeth,
> To this Saint begot.
> May the fire of Thy love live in my heart yet,
> As jewel of gold in a silver vase set!
>
>                                                           Amen.

---

10 A recent scholarly edition and translation of the poem can be found in Clancy and Márkus 1995, 84–5. I have preferred, however, to use here an older rhyming version by the 'Nun of Kenmare', Sr Mary Frances Cusack (n.d., 790).

And this hymn is said against all fires and all thunders since then. And if a person recites it when they lie down and when they get up, it will protect any nine persons whom they choose from fire and thunder and lightning. Having received, moreover, the very noble and very honourable order of priesthood, and having been chosen against his will as the abbot of the black monks ['*na ab manuch ndub*'] in that settlement of Derry, and having blessed it and made his dwelling there, he took it in hand to feed a hundred poor people every day for the sake of God (Lacey 1998a, 45–6).

Ó Domhnaill's *Betha* has several other stories about Derry, which will be examined below.

A chronicler – almost certainly working in Derry in the twelfth century, and on very insubstantial grounds – went so far as to give the date of 545 (AU, sometimes amended to 546) as the year in which the foundation of the monastery there occurred. That date was chosen, apparently, as it was the year immediately following that in which the death of St Mo Bíí of Glasnevin is said to have occurred – in accordance with the legend that says that the latter had to give his permission for the foundation to take place (Anderson and Anderson 1961, 71). In the later forms of the legend, Colum Cille's church is usually identified with the institution called the Dubreclés or the 'Black Abbey'. A church of that name certainly did exist in Derry in medieval times, because, when it was burnt in a major fire in 1166, the annalist adds that this was something that 'had not been heard of from ancient times' (AU). However, the 1166 entry is the first time that the term Dubreclés is used in the annals. Notwithstanding the legend, therefore, we cannot say how old the Dubreclés was at that time. We will return to that matter in ch. 5.

Despite a formidable ancient and modern tradition, contemporary historical evidence does not support either a 545/6 date for the establishment of the monastery or the identification of Columba as its founder (Lacey 1998b, 35–47; Lacey 2006, 128–31; and see below, ch. 3). That story was almost certainly a later rationalisation and simplification of a complex reality that arose from Derry having been captured in the late sixth century from the tiny Cenél nÉnnai kingdom by the saint's people, the powerful Cenél Conaill. The legendary version can be challenged on various grounds. For instance, no historical source supports the idea that Columba was a student at the monastery of Glasnevin or that he was taught by Mo Bíí, its founder. Indeed, for what they are worth, other – admittedly equally late – traditions suggest that Colum Cille and Mo Bíí were both contemporary students of St Finnian of Clonard.

Precisely what the historical explanation for the connection with the saint of Glasnevin is remains unclear, but the hypocoristic (or endearing) form Mo Bíí [Mobhaoi] is an *alias* for Baithéne (Ó Riain 1985a, 123). That is the name of

Columba's first cousin and successor as abbot of Iona, who was listed by John Colgan in the seventeenth century as a Derry 'saint' (Ó Riain 1997, 506).[11] Baithéne's feastday (9 June) coincides with that of Columba and a story recorded in an early seventeenth-century manuscript claims that Baithéne 'was four years in the abbacy of Derry ... after Colum Cille' (Meyer 1893, 229). It seems possible that some genuine tradition about Baithéne (Mobhaoi) became confused with a story about Mo Bíí of Glasnevin. This could have come about because of the similarity of the hypocoristic forms of the names and at a time when genuine memories of Baithéne had receded. It has been suggested recently that the story about Mo Bíí's belt seems to indicate the existence of a valued relic of that name in Derry in the second half of the twelfth century – at the time of the writing of the Middle Irish Life – on which oaths were sworn.[12] Whatever its meaning, that legend is as old, at least, as the *Liber Hymnorum* preface to the *Noli Pater Indulgere*, that is, as far back as the late tenth century or possibly even earlier.

Áed mac Ainmerech, the king who is said to have given Derry to Colum Cille, was probably only about thirteen years of age in 545 and certainly was not king, even of his own dynasty the Cenél Conaill, before the 560s when his predecessor and father Ainmere is said (with some probability) to have attained the higher office of king of Tara. More persuasively, there is separate evidence that the monastery of Derry was founded some time later and by someone other than Columba. That matter will be fully explored in the next chapter.

---

**11** Baithéne was commemorated at, among other places, the church of Tech Baithéne (Taughboyne), modern St Johnstown, about seven miles south-west of Derry. By the last quarter of the sixth century, that area would have been part of Cenél Conaill territory, although almost certainly it was not so around the time of Baithéne's birth, probably in the 530s. **12** Ó Floinn 1997, 154. Ó Floinn inferred the connection with oath-taking from the reference to a lie in Ó Domhnaill's *Betha*. Related references to lies and falsehoods also occur in the earlier *Liber Hymnorum* and Middle Irish Life.

CHAPTER 3

# The historical evidence: Daire Calgaich and the Cenél Conaill

Modern accounts of the foundations of ancient Irish churches often seem to suggest that these were isolated religious or philanthropic events relatively unconnected with the secular world surrounding them. The very opposite was usually the case. The reasons behind many of those foundations can often be understood only in the context of the local geo-politics of the time. The foundation of Derry is very much a case in point.

In the legendary sources, Derry is said to have been the site of a fortress belonging to Áed mac Ainmerech before it became a monastery or a church settlement of some sort. There is, of course, no historical support for this claim; no archaeological evidence has come to light either. But, it would have been a very appropriate location for a fortification. In fact, it has been argued

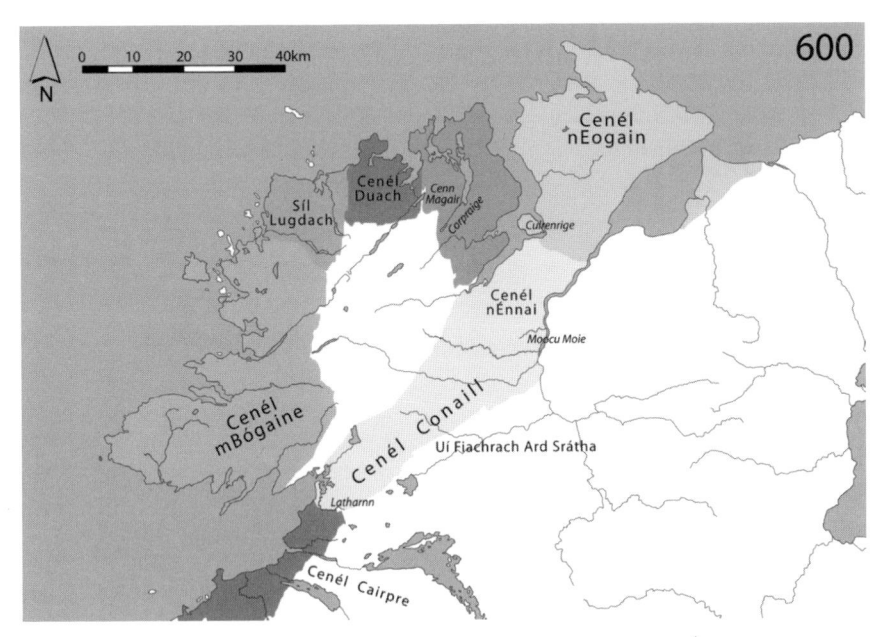

9 Generalized map of the kingdoms of Donegal, c.AD600. The Cenél nÉnnai kingdom has been conquered by their stronger, southern neighbours, the Cenél Conaill. Derry, not marked but located on the southern edge of the Pennyburn Depression, is by then one of the northern boundary markers of the enlarged Cenél Conaill kingdom (map by Robert Shaw).

above that it is likely to have been a frontier fortification of some kind belonging to the Cenél nÉnnai kingdom before that was conquered about 578 by the Cenél Conaill (fig. 9). If that is the case, then Áed mac Ainmerech is likely to have taken control of it before, in turn, handing it over to the church.

One of the so-called Donegal poems in the Book of Fenagh, *Estid re Conall Calma* 'List ye to the mighty Conall', says that the fortress in question was occupied previously by three Cenél Conaill kings, although it names only two of them – Báetán mac Ninnida and Áed mac Ainmerech, before it 'fell to Colum of the Cells' (Hennessy and Kelly 1875, 405). The Book of Fenagh dates to 1516 (Kenney 1929, 401), but the dates of the individual poems in it are more difficult to establish. Katharine Simms showed that, whatever the date of the language in which the poems have come down to us, the subject matter of the Donegal poems is 'relevant to the period from the eleventh to the early thirteenth centuries' (2008, 37). The following are the 'Derry' verses in *Estid re Conall Calma*:

| | |
|---|---|
| Doiri Longpurt Baedan binn | Derry was the seat of pleasant Baedan,[1] |
| Ua Ainmirech mic Chonuill, | Grandson of Ainmire, Conall's son, |
| Remi ri bliadain gan fell, | Before, and for a year without fault, |
| Ar ngabail rige nErend. | After assuming the kingship of Ireland. |
| | |
| Ba Longpurt he d'Aed na mbend, | It was the seat of Aedh-na-mBenn[2] – |
| Doiri Chailgich na ngeben, | Was Doire-Chalgaigh of the fetters – |
| Gur thuit ri Colam na cell, | Till it fell to Colum of the Cells, |
| Ar crabud ar crosifigell. | Thro' devotion, thro *cros-figells*[3]. |
| | |
| Tri righ a Conall na cath, | Three kings, from Conall of the battles, |
| Tainic re Colam craibdech; | Came before Colum the devout. |
| Ised tucsadar a ngeill, | The place to which they their pledges brought, |
| Co Doiri nuasal naigbeil. | Was formidable, noble Derry. |
| | (Hennessy and Kelly 1875, 404–5) |

Once again, there is no contemporary (that is, sixth-century) historical support for the claims outlined in the poem.

Patently, none of the legendary accounts outlined in the last chapter is contemporary with the events it claims to describe. But what of the sources

---

1 Baedan's pedigree as given here is incorrect, even in terms of the probably incorrect traditional understanding that makes him descend from Ninnid son of Fergus son of Conall Gulban. However, it is extremely unlikely that Baedan (Báetán) – who belonged to the Cenél Duach – had any real connection with the Cenél Conaill, at least on his father's side (Lacey 2006, 97–8, 198–9).  2 Áed mac Ainmerech, the Cenél Conaill king who is said to have given Derry to Colum Cille.  3 'Cross-vigils', a devotional practice in which an individual

that might, more realistically, be considered to preserve factual evidence from the sixth century? At the year 535 the Annals of the Four Masters say: *Eaclais Doire Calgaigh do fhothughadh la Colom Cille, iar nedhbairt an bhaile do dia derbfhine fén .i. Cenel cConaill Gulban mic Néll* 'The church of Doire-Calgaigh was founded by Colum Cille, the place having been granted to him by his own tribe [dynasty], i.e. the race of Conall Gulban, son of Niall'. There is no independent support for this entry, most especially for the date. John Colgan has a fairly lengthy section in the *Trias Thaumaturga* of 1647 in which he describes how the Four Masters – who had completed their famous work only eleven years earlier – had arrived at that date (Ó Riain 1997, 502). He tells us that the compilers of those 'annals' give the incorrect date of 592 as the year in which Colum Cille died, at the age of 'seventy-seven'. This in turn gave the year 516 for his birth. As the Four Masters and Colgan himself assumed, for reasons that are not clear, that the saint had founded the monastery in his twentieth year, the former concluded, therefore, that Derry had been founded in 535. However, Colgan himself, accepting the date of 520 for Colum Cille's birth, argues that the foundation of the monastery had to be *circa annum Christi quinqentisimum quadragesimum*, that is 'about 540' (ibid.).

The Annals of Ulster, which is regarded as one of our best surviving witnesses to the contents of the original Iona chronicle, gives the date of the foundation of Derry as 545. The well-known entry reads: *Daire Coluim Cille fundata est* 'Derry of Colum Cille was founded'. Perhaps significantly, the entry does not state, nor for that matter does it necessarily imply, the name of the founder. The date itself is not compatible with the legendary accounts. Apart from any other consideration, such evidence as we have would suggest that, while Colum Cille may have been about twenty-five years of age at the time, Áed mac Ainmerech, the king who is alleged to have given him the site, would have been only about thirteen. When Áed's death is recorded in the Annals of Tigernach for 598[4] there is a reference to the fact that he was 66 years of age at that time, suggesting that his birth occurred about 532. Independently of the question of his age, it is extremely unlikely that he would have been in a position to grant Derry to the church (if, indeed, it was he who gave it) prior at least to the death of his father Ainmere mac Sétnai in 568.

The name given to Derry in the 545 entry is also problematic. It is the only occasion until 1121 when Derry is referred to in the Annals of Ulster by the cultic form of the name, Daire Coluim Cille. At all other times, until the panegyric entry recording the death of Domnall Ua Lochlainn in 1121 (which will be discussed below), Derry is always referred to by the earliest form in which we know it, Daire Calgaich, or, from the late tenth century onwards, by

---

prays with arms extended, imitating the shape of a Latin cross.   4 ATig. = AU 598, *s.a.* 597 = Mc Carthy 596.

the simple form Daire. Even in the Annals of the Four Masters (composed as a single literary work in the early seventeenth century) the name Doire (modern form of Daire) Coluim Chille is avoided before the twelfth century except on two occasions, 950 and 1025, both of which will be discussed further below.

It is clear that the annalistic entries and the legendary accounts purporting to describe the foundation of the monastery of Derry contradict each other, to some extent at least. However, it is now widely accepted anyway – on linguistic grounds – that the 545 entry in the Annals of Ulster cannot be a contemporary record of that foundation. There are various suggestions as to when the entry might have been inserted in the record; among these is the period in the late twelfth and early thirteenth centuries when the exemplar of the Annals of Ulster was being kept and updated in Derry (Mac Niocaill 1975, 24), as we will see below, in ch. 7.

There is thus no historical basis for believing that the entries in the annals claiming that the foundation occurred in either 535 or 545 are a contemporary or even a near contemporary record of that event. The Andersons, who gave us the principal scholarly edition of Adomnán's *Vita Columbae*, provided an explanation as to why the anonymous scribe (almost certainly based in Derry) who retrospectively inserted the 545 entry in the annals chose that particular year:

> That date is based upon a legend that connected the foundation with the death of [St Mo Bíí of Glasnevin], whose death was entered under the previous year. The date is little to be trusted.
>
> (Anderson and Anderson 1961, 71)

As has been pointed out in the last chapter, it seems likely that Mo Bíí of Glasnevin had become confused – either accidentally or deliberately – with the hypocoristic form of the name Baithéne, the name of Columba's cousin and successor as abbot of Iona. Whatever its origins, the legend of the connection with the Glasnevin saint was 'authenticated' by the existence in Derry from at least the tenth century onwards of a relic known as Mo Bíí's Belt.

Adomnán mentions Derry three times in the *Vita Columbae* of *c*.690–700. In none of these instances is there any implication that Columba had founded a monastery or church there. The first episode involves 'two monks of Saint Columba ... [who] recently rowed from Britain and today have come from the oakwood of Calgach [*roboreto Calgachi* > Derry]' (Anderson and Anderson 1961, 206–9). It is likely, although not strictly necessary, that Derry is mentioned in this reference as the place where the monks landed following their journey from Britain. The incident is said to have occurred shortly after Columba's death; that is, presumably some time in the 590s.[5]

---

5 Dates from 592 to 597 are variously recorded for the saint's death. The synchronisms prepared by Mc Carthy suggest 593.

The second reference to Derry in Adomnán's *Vita* is the story of a prediction by Columba that the apparently Columban cleric, Baítán nepos niath Taloirc, would be buried in a place where 'a woman will drive sheep across his grave' (Anderson and Anderson 1961, 248–51). The cleric, having been blessed by the saint on Iona and after 'circuitous voyaging through the windy seas', returned to Ireland and spent some time as the head of the church at a place called *Lathreg Inden*. *Lathreg Inden* has not been positively identified but there is some consensus that it was in northern Donegal in the vicinity of Derry,[6] as the story continues with Baítán apparently moving to live in Derry.

> … After some seasons in the oakwood of Calgach [Derry] he died and was buried there. And about the same time, it happened that because of an attack by enemies the neighbouring lay-people, with their women and children, took refuge in the church [*eclesiam*] of that place. And so it came about that one day a woman was observed driving her sheep through the burial-place [*sepulchrum*] of that man, who recently had been buried there …

Adomnán goes on to say that a priest who saw what had happened in Derry exclaimed that the prophecy made by Columba 'many years ago' had been fulfilled. The priest, perhaps significantly called Mailodranus [Máelodrán] mocu-[Cu]rin although otherwise unidentified, later related the story to Adomnán. The monk's tribal affiliation, mocu-Curin, possibly links him with the Cuirenrige or Culenrige, who are said to have been located in the vicinity of Inishowen, possibly on Inch Island in Lough Swilly.[7] Notwithstanding his origins, however, the story proves that there was definitely a church and a graveyard in Derry within the lifetime of Máelodrán (whatever his dates), and before Adomnán wrote the Life at the end of the seventh century. It also implies that Columba, before he died in the 590s, had some knowledge of Derry and possibly, but again not certainly, of a church and a graveyard there. Aidan MacDonald has queried whether the word 'church' (*eclesia*) used in such contexts in the *Vita* refers to a building or a Christian community (MacDonald 1984, 280). However, the sense of the paragraph quoted above would seem to suggest that a physical structure is being referred to. At any rate, it is clear from the text that a Christian settlement of some sort existed in Derry at the time.

The cumulative evidence of the story also seems to confirm the Columban nature of that settlement, at least by the mid-seventh century: Columba's alleged knowledge of the place and possibly of a church there; the fact that it was the final resting place of the apparently Columban cleric Baítán; the

---

6 See suggestion of Birdstown, near Burnfoot, Co. Donegal, in Bryson 2001, 8, 109.
7 Lacey 2006, 105. Other suggestions such as Inishtrahull (which seems unlikely) and the Malin Peninsula (much more likely) have also been made.

connections between Adomnán and Máelodrán – a priest who clearly had spent some time in Derry; and possibly even the priest's own Christian name, which may reflect a connection with the monk Odrán whose life was commemorated, at least in later times, on Iona in various ways. In fact, for what it is worth, John Colgan listed 'Odrán a monk of Derry, buried in Iona', as one of the 'Saints of Derry', whose feastday was celebrated on 27 October. He also listed Baítán, the subject of the story, as a Derry 'saint' with a feastday on 29 November (Ó Riain 1997, 506).

The third reference to Derry in Adomnán's *Vita Columbae* is in the story about 'Librán of the reed-plot' (Anderson and Anderson 1961, 428–31). Adomnán establishes the reference to Derry in this fairly lengthy story during Columba's own lifetime but, apparently, not too long before the saint's death. Whether it is significant or not, there is no mention of a church or a monastery in this story. Librán arrives in Derry and wishes to set out for Britain, his ultimate destination being Iona. He finds 'a ship under sail, setting out from the harbour [*a portu*]' of Derry. Despite his entreaties, the sailors would not let him on board because, we are told: 'they were not monks of Saint Columba'. The implication seems to be that it would have been quite usual for sailors in the harbour of Derry to have been Columban monks. A miracle occurred subsequently and the convinced sailors then took Librán on board, 'and after their arrival in British land, Librán left the ship, and … made his way to Saint Columba, who was living in the island of Io[na]'.

Thus, both in the first and the third of these stories, Derry 'harbour' is indicated during (or, at least, shortly after) Columba's own lifetime as a port of embarkation and destination on the journey between Ireland and Britain, and indirectly to and from Iona. From the second mention we can conclude that there was a church and a Christian burial place in Derry before Adomnán wrote the *Vita*, and possibly before Columba's death.

There is one further, apparently early, reference to Derry in the list of Columba's relatives attached to the later medieval versions of Adomnán's *Vita*. Despite the fact that the list is not attached to the earlier Schaffhausen version, Sharpe believes, as we have seen, that the 'list dates from Adomnán's time or very soon after' (Sharpe 1995, 354). The list includes a reference to 'Bran who is buried in *Daire Calcig*'. There have been some differences in the reading of this text leading to the identification of Bran as a sister of Columba (Sharpe ibid.), or as a nephew of the saint (for example, Anderson and Anderson 1961, 547). Bran was almost certainly male, a son of Cuimne, one of Columba's three named sisters. The Latin text of the list has the masculine form *Bran qui sepultus est* and all of the more than forty Brans listed in the index to the *Corpus Genealogiarum Hiberniae* (O'Brien 1962) are male. However, for our purposes here the matter is of little importance. What does seem clear is that a close relative and almost certainly an overlapping 'contemporary' of Columba was buried in Derry. While it is not stated explicitly, given the source of the reference, I think we can also assume that the burial was in a Christian context. Bran was almost certainly buried in a church cemetery; in fact, again for what it is worth, he is listed by Colgan as one of the 'saints' of Derry, with a feastday on 18 May (Ó Riain 1997, 506).

What seems to be the earliest contemporary reference to Derry in the annals is found at the year 619. In that year, allowing for the usual corrections between the differing sets of annals, the death of Fiachra mac Ciaráin meic Ainmerech meic Sétnai is recorded in the Annals of Ulster, the Annals of the Four Masters, the Annals of Tigernach, *Chronicum Scotorum* and the Annals of Roscrea. All of these references, of course, derive from the one original source. The Annals of Ulster and the Annals of the Four Masters merely record Fiachra's name and the year of his death; there is no additional explanation as to who he was or why he was of interest to the chroniclers. The other three references, but with some slight variations, tell us that Fiachra was the *alius* [or '*alii*'] *fundatoris* [or *fundatorius*] *Daire Calcaigh*,[8] a phrase that seems to mean 'the other founder of Derry'. There is no reason to doubt that at least part of this entry in the later annals derives from a contemporary early seventh-century record made in the Iona chronicle, but it is also clear that the original notice has undergone a process of editing in some way. This may have occurred through the later addition in some of the annals (all with a Clonmacnoise connection) of the explanatory gloss about who Fiachra was or – a less likely possibility – the removal of that information (if it was in the original record) for propaganda reasons at some point in the development of the sets of annals with an Ulster provenance.

Who was Fiachra and what was his role in the foundation of the monastery of Derry? Reeves mentioned the entry from the Annals of Tigernach but did not discuss it further, other than to use it as confirmation of the donation of the site to the church by the Cenél Conaill (Reeves 1857, 277). It might be taken, therefore, that he understood Fiachra to be a lay patron of the monastery, perhaps the Cenél Conaill king. Máire Herbert refers to Fiachra in a manner similar to that of Reeves (Herbert 1988, 279). David Dumville (1999, 102) also suggests that Fiachra's role may have been as the donor of the site. Richard Sharpe seems to identify Fiachra explicitly as a Cenél Conaill king (1995, 398) but there is no evidence to substantiate such a suggestion. Conall Cú probably succeeded his father Áed mac Ainmerech (who died *c*.596) as king of the Cenél Conaill. Máel Coba, who died as king of Tara in 613, must have succeeded his brother Conall Cú (who died in 602) as king of the Cenél Conaill at least (Lacey 2006, 328). Likewise, Máel Coba must have been immediately followed as Cenél Conaill king by his brother Domnall mac Áedo,

8 See below, p. 33.

although Domnall did not succeed to the kingship of Tara until 628 (ibid.). There is no evidence of a gap in the line of Cenél Conaill kings around this time that might have been filled by Fiachra.

Unless we dismiss the reference as a total fabrication, we are surely obliged to accept that Fiachra played some important role in the establishment of the church in Derry, either as a layman or as a cleric. Yet, other than the various annalistic entries mentioned above, he is completely ignored in all the early literature about Derry. He appears in none of the legendary accounts of its foundation. He is not listed in the fairly full Cenél Conaill secular genealogies for the period, which would be unusual if he had been a king. Nor is he listed in the genealogies of the saints: for example in the *Genealogiae Regum et Sanctorum Hiberniae* compiled by the Four Masters in 1630, where a large amount of space was devoted to many relatively obscure Cenél Conaill saints (Walsh 1918).

Fortunately, Fiachra's pedigree as given in the annals allows us to identify him as: (i) a member of the Cenél Conaill, (ii) a nephew of the king, Áed mac Ainmerech, and (iii) a second cousin, once removed, of Columba. However, for whatever reason, his identity is not elucidated in the surviving annals from Ulster (AU; AFM). We could be forgiven for being particularly suspicious that the most important of Donegal chroniclers, the Four Masters, did not take a special interest in this early member of the Cenél Conaill. Surely they recognized his genealogical connections when they copied the entry about him into their own version of the annals in the early seventeenth century.

To obtain more information as to who Fiachra was, we have to turn to the annals compiled in the midlands and the south, all connected originally with Clonmacnoise (ATig.; CS; ARos.). The compilers of these – or their exemplar(s) – were almost certainly too far removed from the ecclesiastical politics of Derry, on the one hand, to wish to fabricate an identity for Fiachra, but, equally, to be concerned about hiding his true identity if this proved to be an embarrassment, as we might suspect it would have been for some northern devotees of Columba.

The precise relationships between the various surviving sets of annals are still not clear, but the reference to Fiachra in the Annals of Roscrea seems to be particularly instructive. The modern editors of that text claimed that it represents

> ... fragments of annals which, unlike the major ... collections, have not come under the hand of a medieval editor to any great extent ... a detailed analysis of them ... will serve to increase our knowledge of how our annals were set down (say) in the seventh century and eighth century as distinct from the edited product which we find in post-eleventh century mss ...
>
> (Gleeson and Mac Airt 1958)

Dumville has suggested that references to Fiachra are derivative of the tenth century 'Chronicle of Clonmacnoise' (1999, 101), however Mc Carthy (pers. comm.) has suggested that the identification phrase appears to be a gloss inserted 'after Cuanu's redaction of the Clomancnoise annals in *c*.1022'.[9]

There is a slight grammatical problem with some of the entries about Fiachra that might help in their analysis. The entry in the Annals of Tigernach is characteristically a mixture of Latin and Irish: *Bass Fiachrach, maic Ciarain, maic Ainmirech, maic Setna, id est, alii fundatoris Dairi Chalgaigh*[10] 'The death of F ..., that is, of the other founder of Derry'. Both the *Chronicum Scotorum* and the Annals of Roscrea commence the entry with the Latin word *Mors*, and identify Fiachra as the *alius fundatoris*. The Annals of Roscrea, transcribed according to its editors between 1636 and 1642, uses the more modern form of the name in Irish for Derry, Doire Calgaigh; otherwise the reference there is similar to that in the *Chronicum Scotorum*. To be grammatically correct, however, the Latin phrase should have been written as *Mors F ... alii fundatoris*, where the genitive *alii* following *mors* 'death of' would agree with the genitive *fundatoris*. If *alius* (or *alii*) was part of the original entry, it could be understood to have had either of two meanings: 'other' in the sense of 'as distinct from', or 'other' in the sense of 'one of two'. However, it may be that the word *alius* (as reproduced in ATig., CS and ARos.) is a later interpolation, and that the earlier post-*c*.1022 glossed entry would have read simply *Mors F ... , id est fundatoris Daire Calgaigh* 'The death of F ... that is, of the founder of Derry'. Perhaps the word 'other' (in the incorrect form *alius*) was inserted later in the common exemplar of these three sets of annals to deal with an obvious embarrassment at a time when the legendary account of the foundation of Derry had already become established. Further, on the grounds that it is the simplest explanation, I would argue that Fiachra was not a lay benefactor who granted the site to the church but, instead, the real clerical founder of Derry.

Peculiarly Brendan (or Bonaventure) O'Connor, who transcribed the only surviving manuscript of the Annals of Roscrea, worked at Louvain along with John Colgan. Despite this link, Colgan, whose *Trias Thaumaturga* definitely post-dates the Annals of Roscrea, makes no reference to Fiachra in his fairly comprehensive list of events and people associated with Derry – which, admittedly, he says is drawn mainly from the Annals of the Four Masters as well as 'other cited authorities' (Ó Riain 1997, 503–6). Nor does he include

---

9 The original Iona record may have contained no more than what appears in AU/AFM. For Cuanu, see Mc Carthy 2008, especially ch. 7.   10 This is how the entry has been reproduced in the Whitley Stokes printed edition. However, the latter adds in a footnote that the manuscript actually reads *alius funditorius daire chalgaidh*, as can be seen on MS Rawlinson B.488, fo. 9v, first column, roughly two thirds from the top. For the publication, Whitley Stokes altered *alius* to the correct form *alii* and *fundatorius* to *fundatoris*.

Fiachra in his list of forty-one Derry 'saints', which seems to be made up, effectively, of any early named person whose death or burial is recorded or supposed to have occurred in Derry, together with a few individuals said to have been associated in some other way with the early medieval church there. The Four Masters record Fiachra's death at 620, but without any further explanation as to who he was. This failure to identify him might suggest an embarrassment about the survival of an alternative version of the story of the foundation of Derry: one which was quite different to the legendary but 'official' version.

If Fiachra was involved in the establishment of Derry, when was the church there founded and did Columba have any role, even as an 'other founder' himself? There is no evidence available, but a number of indicators might suggest a fruitful avenue for speculation. Fiachra belonged to the second generation after Columba. His patronymic as outlined in the various annal references shows that he was a grandson of Columba's first cousin, Ainmere mac Sétnai. We do not know what age Fiachra was when he died in 619, but we might speculate that he founded Derry say about thirty to forty years prior to his death, or sometime from around the year 579. Such a date would fit with the suggestion made above that Derry was founded as a new Cenél Conaill 'border' church following the latter's victory over the Cenél nEógain at the Battle of Druim Maic Erce in 578. In addition, some late sources such as an appendix to the Middle Irish Life of Colum Cille and Manus Ó Domhnaill's *Betha Colaim Chille* have an episode in which the saint comes to Derry after the so-called Convention of Drum Cett (Herbert 1988, 268; O'Kelleher and Schoepperle 1918, 368–9; Lacey 1998a, 186). The story is not historical – that is, there is no contemporary evidence to substantiate it. But it is quite possible and even probable that Columba could have come to Derry around the time of the convention, the historicity of which (whatever about its date or agenda) is not in question. Derry is about fifteen miles – a day's walk, at most; less by boat – from what is said, traditionally, to be the site of the convention, the Mullagh Hill just outside Limavady (fig. 10). We know that Columba's second cousin, the king Áed mac Ainmerech, was a beneficiary of the convention, or 'conference of kings' as Adomnán called it. After the convention, Columba could have returned to Derry with Áed whose fortress, according to the legends, was said to be located there? Perhaps, partially as an act of thanksgiving, Áed could have made the site over to the church – in fact to his nephew Fiachra. Columba, who by then was a senior clerical figure normally resident in Iona, could have played some sort of witnessing or secondary role, although the surviving evidence does not require his presence or participation in any sense.

But what was the date of the Convention of Drum Cett? There are considerable differences of opinion about that, both in the ancient texts and in the

10 The Mullagh to the south-west of Limavady. According to tradition (and the seventeenth-century writer John Colgan), this was the location of the Convention of Drum Cett.

commentaries on them by modern scholars. Sharpe, for instance, has suggested that it probably took place somewhat later, perhaps about 590, rather than the 575 date of the annals (Sharpe 1995, 312–13; Meckler 1997).[11] The real purpose of the Convention was obscured until recently by a welter of highly entertaining but clearly fictional legends that were developed around the surviving memory of it. It is now widely agreed, however, that the main purpose of the meeting, which was probably arranged by Columba acting as some sort of diplomatic go-between, was so that his relative king Áed mac Ainmerech and king Áedán mac Gabráin of the Scottish Dál Riata could discuss their mutual interests and strategies, perhaps especially the use of the latter's sea-going fleet. That political and military alliance was most probably put together in opposition to the king of the Ulaid,[12] the highly ambitious Báetán mac Cairill who was possibly also king of Tara at the time (Mac Niocaill 1972, 77–8; Byrne 1973, 111). If that was the real purpose of the Convention, then it had to have taken place before the death of Báetán in 579. Thus, the suggestion that Derry was founded in connection with the Cenél Conaill victory at the Battle of Druim Maic Ercae and close to the time of the Convention of Druim Cett supports a date of 578 or 579, which is roughly forty years prior to the death of Fiachra mac Ciaráin.

If the widely accepted legend of the foundation of the monastery of Derry by Colum Cille is to be dismissed, then can it be explained how and why, and maybe even when, this 'official' version came into existence and the role played by Fiachra was eclipsed? Surely Fiachra, even if he was only 'the other founder' of Derry (along with Columba?), was buried in an honourable and remembered location in the church cemetery. How was it that all memory of

11 The Mc Carthy synchronisms would correct that date to 573.   12 Modern historians usually reserve the term Ulaid at that stage of history for the various peoples and kingdoms east of the Bann.

him seems to have disappeared in Derry? Whether the church of Derry was founded by Columba as tradition claims or by Fiachra mac Ciaráin as is suggested by the evidence, it seems abundantly clear that it was established by the Cenél Conaill, to which both those individuals belonged. Although they give his name and the year in which he died, neither the Annals of Ulster nor the Annals of the Four Masters, both of which ultimately derive for that period from what might be called Cenél Conaill sources, contain the additional information about who Fiachra was or why he was important enough to have his death recorded. It is only by accident that those details were preserved in the various sets of annals compiled later in the south of Ireland and in the midlands, away from the influence of the Derry and Cenél Conaill propagandists. It is very difficult to resist the conclusion that those responsible for preserving the 'official' history of Derry, from at least the tenth century onwards, were extremely reluctant to give Fiachra the credit he was due, whatever his precise role. Such historical evidence as exists for the identity of its founder – as opposed to the legends – supports Fiachra's claim, not Columba's. The 545 entry in the Annals of Ulster is no more than a piece of propaganda. It was probably inserted in the annals around the twelfth century by those seeking to boost the fortunes of Derry through linking its foundation story with Columba who, by then, was honoured as a famous saint, rather than with Fiachra – effectively, a nobody. Almost all surviving tradition is definite that Derry was the first of the saint's foundations and the one dearest to his heart, but such stories are the product of that church's propagandists of times much later than the sixth century. There is no historical evidence of any kind that Columba founded the monastery of Derry!

TABLE 3. Genealogy of Fiachra, the 'founder' of Derry.

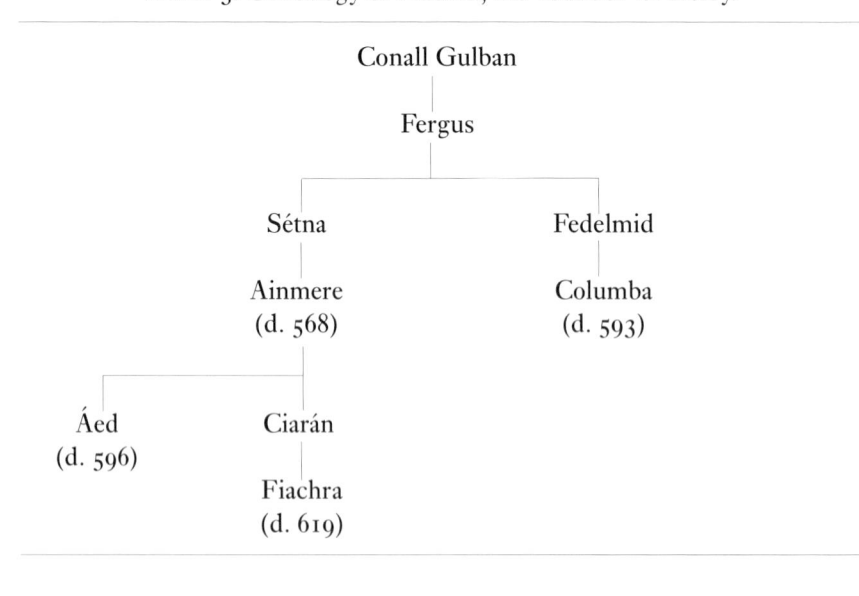

```
                    Conall Gulban
                         |
                      Fergus
                _____|_____
               |                 |
             Sétna             Fedelmid
               |                 |
            Ainmere            Columba
            (d. 568)           (d. 593)
         _____|_____
        |             |
       Áed          Ciarán
     (d. 596)         |
                   Fiachra
                   (d. 619)
```

*Daire Calgaich and the Cenél Conaill*

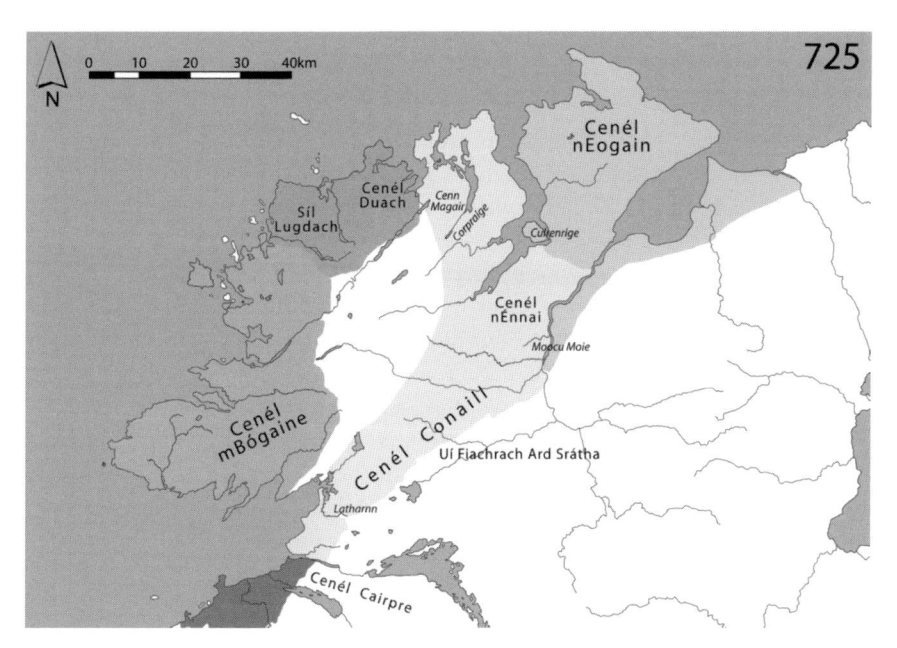

11 Generalized map of the kingdoms of Donegal, *c*.AD725. The Cenél Conaill have reached the greatest extent of their expansion – from the River Erne in the south to the Fanad and Rossguill peninsulas in the north-west. The Cenél nEógain have begun to expand east of the Foyle.

Derry was certainly not the first and best-loved of Colum Cille's monasteries that we find in the later legends and in the large amount of propaganda poetry of the eleventh or twelfth centuries. Apart from the reference to Fiachra's death, there is no further mention of Derry in the surviving annals for the seventh century, which would be unusual to say the least if it was close to the heart of the founder of Iona, where the annals of the time were actually being compiled. There is a mention in the Annals of Ulster for 669 that has been taken in the past as referring to Derry. It occurs in a marginal verse at the entry recording the death of Máel Fothartaig mac Suibne, king of Uí Tuirtre.

> No dearer to me
> is one king rather than another
> since Máel Fothartaig was taken
> in his shroud to Daire.

There is no obvious reason why Máel Fothartaig would have been buried in Derry. The Uí Tuirtre belonged to a completely different political context to the Cenél Conaill. They had their own royal and Christian burial places. The name Daire certainly does not require to be identified with Derry. It is much more likely that the name refers to one of the numerous locations with a 'derry' name in Uí Tuirtre territory, now in east Co. Derry (Lacey 1999, 139).[13]

The annals record the death in 724 of Caech Scuili the *scriba* of Derry (AU). The name of this person is unusual and not easily explained. The first part Caech probably means something like 'blind' or 'one-eyed' (*RIA Dictionary*, col. 10, 93). The meaning of Scuili is not immediately obvious, but seems to suggest something like 'scholar' or 'scholarly'. A *scriba*, of course, was not a scribe in the sense of an ordinary copyist of manuscripts, but a senior cleric, 'someone learned in the law; ... the law of the Bible', who often acted as an ecclesiastical judge (Charles-Edwards 2000, 265 and 269). Caech Scuili was almost certainly a high-ranking Columban church official and scholar whose working life need not have been confined to Derry. He lived, for example, around the time of the composition of the influential *Collectio Canonum Hibernenses* – 'possibly the earliest, systematic presentation of Christian law in Latin' (O'Loughlin 2005, 63). The *Collectio* had several Columban connections. The work, which is attributed to two compilers – Cú Chuimne of Iona and Ruben of Dairinis – was clearly a collective product that may have involved other anonymous contributors. Although there is no specific evidence to support it, it is certainly possible that Caech Scuili could have had some involvement with that work.

The only other reference to Derry in the annals for the eighth century is under 788, when it was burned. The circumstances of that particular incident are not further elucidated, but the very fact that it was recorded suggests a deliberate rather than an accidental event. If it was deliberate it is very likely that it was connected with the contemporary campaign of attack by the Cenél nEógain on the Cenél Conaill. This would culminate in the Battle of Clóitech (Clady on the River Finn, Co. Tyrone) in the following year, 789. That battle would see the Cenél Conaill massively defeated by the Cenél nEógain king, Áed Oirdnide, driven out of their homeland north of the Barnesmore Gap and deprived of any further role in the over-kingship of Donegal, as well as in the kingship of Tara. The burning of the Columban (for which, read 'Cenél Conaill') church at Derry in 788 was most probably part of that campaign. Apart from a brief reference to an incident in 833 when, significantly, the Cenél nEógain defeated the Vikings there, we have no more references to Derry for about a century. It may be that the fire of 788 more or less destroyed the settlement.

If these annalistic notices can be taken as a gauge of its significance, Derry appears to have been a fairly quiet, relatively unimportant Columban monastery for the first three centuries or so of its existence. No contemporary references at all survive for the sixth century. There is only one probable

13 Ciarán Devlin noted, although without citing a reference, that Fr Walter Hegarty had previously 'suggested that Derryloran [Co. Tyrone] might be more likely' (1983, 33).

reference for the seventh century – in 619 recording the death of Fiachra, and two – the death of Caech Scuili in 724 and the burning in 788 – for the eighth century. Those few references as well as the mentions in Adomnán's *Vita Columbae* are just sufficient to let us know that throughout that period the monastery continued to survive as a Columban church located on the northern boundary of Cenél Conaill's territory, which, in a way, it was probably specifically founded to mark. Despite the claims made for it by later Columban 'historians' and propagandists, to quote Dumville, Derry 'hardly loomed large in the perceptions of early annalists at Iona' (1999, 100).

There is one other (fictional) mention linking Derry, Iona and Columba that could be quite early – it occurs in the Life of St Colmán Ela. Colmán Ela belonged to the sixth and early seventh centuries. Allegedly he came from what is now Co. Antrim, but he is mainly associated with Lynally (Co. Offaly). A Life of the saint in Latin belongs to a distinct collection of such texts in the Codex Salamanticensis, which are known as the O'Donohue group. There is an academic controversy about the date of those texts. Pádraig Ó Riain argues that they date to the late twelfth century at the earliest (2013, 49), whereas Richard Sharpe believes that they date to as early as the eighth century, or AD800–50 at the latest (1991, 329). In the Life of Colmán Ela, there is a miracle story about Derry – which, needless to remark, is not historically true (Heist 1965, 213–14 §13; Ó Riain 2011, 204–5). Colmán is said to have visited Iona and was given an altar cruet by Colum Cille. The cruet was accidentally left behind on Iona, but later turned up miraculously beside the altar of a church in Derry (Daire Calach < Calgaich). If the O'Donohue texts are as early as Sharpe believes them to be, then, apart from the indirect references in Adomnán's *Vita Columbae*, this story – which, itself seems to be in part based on Adomnán's reference to Colmán's visit to Iona – is the earliest literary account we have that links Colum Cille, albeit indirectly and fictionally, with Derry.

CHAPTER 4

# Derry and the Cenél nEógain

Around the beginning of the ninth century, there was a complete change in the politics of north-western Ireland. For the two hundred and fifty years previously, the kingdom of Cenél Conaill had been the dominant force there. The Cenél Conaill had provided most if not all of the over-kings of what would later become Co. Donegal, including that part of Co. Derry – mainly the urban area of Derry city itself – on the west bank of the Foyle. Several of those kings had gone on to be recognized as kings of Tara, indeed a number were even described – in a highly inflated way – as 'kings of Ireland'. After the disastrous Battle of Clóitech in 789 when they were heavily defeated by the Cenél nEógain, the Cenél Conaill were excluded from overall power in the north-west and confined to Donegal south of the Barnesmore Gap. The Cenél nEógain took their place as rulers in most of the previous Cenél Conaill territories north of Barnesmore (including the settlement at Derry), as overlords in the north-west and as the candidates from that area for the kingship of Tara. In addition to those local changes, by 800 the 'foreigners' or Vikings had arrived as a significant additional factor in Irish political life. Their involvement would have some consequences for Derry, but not many, as we will see.

What was happening in Derry itself at this time? The place had suffered a significant disaster when it was burned in 788. We have no further direct information about that incident, but it must have been fairly serious to have been recorded in the annals. The settlement, whatever its size then, must have been very badly damaged if not totally destroyed, because, as will be seen below, we hear almost nothing more about it for almost another century. Derry is only mentioned twice in the annals for the ninth century (AU 833 and 882), and the first of those references may be purely incidental.

In 833, the Annals of Ulster records that 'Niall and Murchad routed the foreigners [*Gallu*, 'Vikings'] in Daire Calgaig'. A number of conclusions can be drawn from this short reference. Possibly, despite the conflagration in 788, some kind of settlement had re-emerged at Derry to attract the interests of the Vikings, although there is no specific evidence that Derry itself was their target. Even if the settlement had not yet fully recovered from the major fire of forty-five years earlier, as seems likely, the site itself may have proved attractive to the Vikings, just as it had done for all the previous people who had come to settle there over thousands of years. Secondly, the victors in 833 – although otherwise not identified by the annalist – were almost certainly the high-king

*Derry and the Cenél nEógain* 41

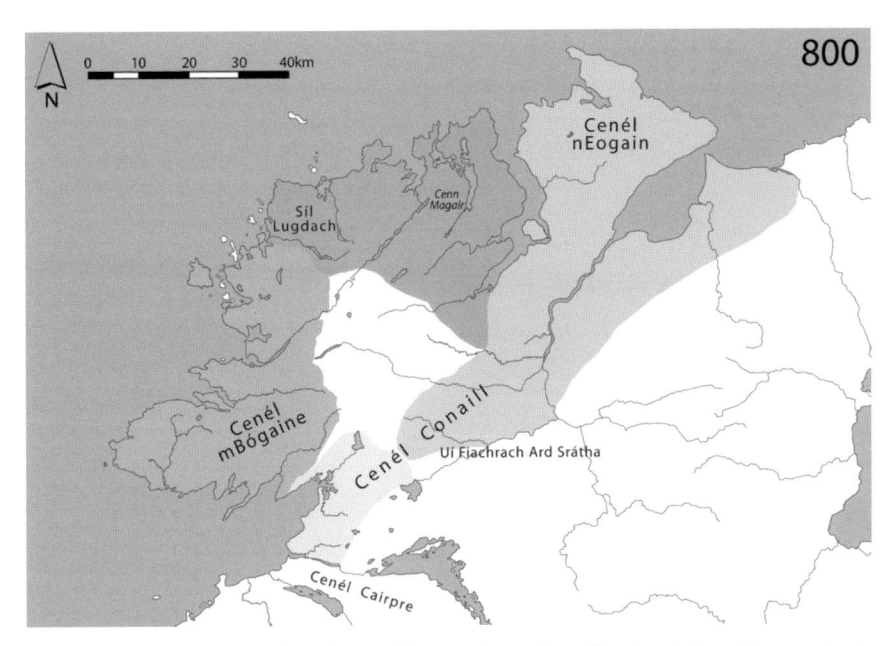

**12** Generalized map of the kingdoms of Donegal, *c*.AD800. The Cenél Conaill – massively defeated at the Battle of Clóitech in 789 – have been confined south of the Barnesmore Gap and their former territory to the north has been divided between the Síl Lugdach and the Cenél nEógain. Derry is now part of the latter's greatly expanding territory, with much of their new land located east of the Foyle (map by Robert Shaw).

Niall son of Áed Oirdnide, who would later become known as Niall Caille, and his cousin Murchad son of Máel Dúin. Murchad had formerly reigned as king of the Cenél nEógain, but he had been deposed and replaced by Niall in 823. Coincidentally, a secondary note added in the margins of the Annals of Ulster tells us that in the same year as his (presumed) victory at Derry, 833, Niall began 'to reign' as king of Tara.

The mention of both these men in connection with Derry, as opposed to any member of the Cenél Conaill, confirms that control and ownership of that settlement had changed hands, whatever its nature at the time. Derry was now definitely part of Cenél nEógain territory. Although the Cenél Conaill would not totally surrender their claims over Derry and would, at a later stage of the Middle Ages, engineer some sort of involvement there again, the Cenél nEógain would retain their leading association with that settlement for most of the remainder of the medieval period.

Apart from this 833 incident, there are no other entries about Derry in the annals until 882, when 'Muirchertach son of Niall, abbot [*abbas*] of Daire Calgaig, and other monasteries [& *aliarum civitatum*]', died (AU). There is no indication about which 'other monasteries' he was involved with, but – if it is not just a fictional propaganda claim – they probably were mainly in the north-

TABLE 4. Genealogy of Niall Caille and his cousin Murchad, and the probable pedigree of Muirchertach, the abbot of Derry who died in 882.

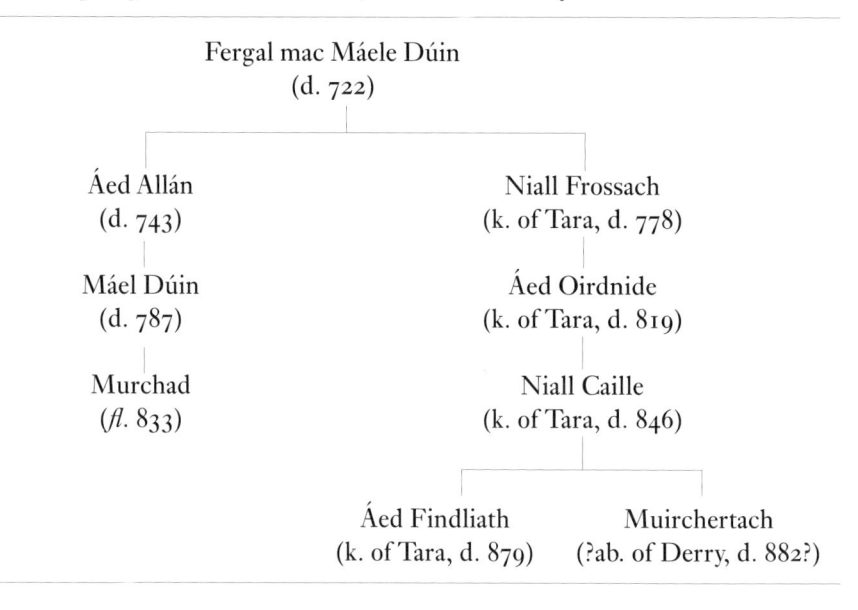

```
                    Fergal mac Máele Dúin
                         (d. 722)
                            |
         _____|_____
        |                                       |
     Áed Allán                            Niall Frossach
     (d. 743)                            (k. of Tara, d. 778)
        |                                       |
     Máel Dúin                             Áed Oirdnide
     (d. 787)                            (k. of Tara, d. 819)
        |                                       |
     Murchad                              Niall Caille
     (fl. 833)                           (k. of Tara, d. 846)
                                                |
                                   _____|_____
                                  |                           |
                             Áed Findliath               Muirchertach
                          (k. of Tara, d. 879)       (?ab. of Derry, d. 882?)
```

west of Ireland, largely on the Inishowen Peninsula. Muirchertach has not been identified positively himself, but one strong possibility must be that he was the son of the powerful Niall Caille (as shown on table 4). A Muirchertach who was the son of that Niall is recorded in the Cenél nEógain genealogies as giving rise to the Cenél Muirchertaich (O'Brien 1962, 135: 140a25). If the abbot Muirchertach son of Niall and the Muirchertach son of Niall Caille of the genealogies were the same person, whatever his clerical status, it does not appear that he was particularly celibate. Niall got his soubriquet 'Caille' subsequent to his death, which occurred when he drowned in the Calann river (Co. Armagh) in 846 (Byrne 1973, 221). It might be objected, therefore, that Muirchertach the abbot of Derry who died in 882 lived a little too long to have been the latter's son. However, we know that individuals associated with the church in early medieval times often lived much longer than their secular aristocratic relatives – largely because the latter experienced much more dangerous lives. In support of this identification, it can be pointed out that Áed Findliath, who definitely was Niall Caille's son – presumably his eldest – and who himself became king of Tara, had died only three years earlier than the abbot Muirchertach, in November 879 (AU).

Although no evidence has come to light so far about this, we should not underestimate the profound implications for Derry – in political and cultural as well as religious terms – if its abbot was the son of one king of Tara and the brother of another. Whoever that Muirchertach son of Niall was, his period as

*Derry and the Cenél nEógain* 43

13 'St Columb's Stone', Belmont House, Pennyburn. The name is probably a late addition derived from the saint's dominance in local folklore. Located on the south-eastern edge of Inishowen (although that is now obscured by modern urban development), the stone was probably a significant Cenél nEógain 'border' monument – perhaps featuring in their royal inauguration ceremonies.

abbot of Derry seems to signal some sort of significant change in that monastery; either in actuality or, at least, in the recording of events. The 882 record of his death sees the beginning of a sequence of references to 'heads' of the church there, which, at first glance at least, appears to be fairly complete; although, as we will see below, not all those references are what they seem.

In 908, the annals record the death of Diarmait, the *princeps* 'superior', 'head' or 'governor' of the church of Daire Calgaich. We have no other information as to who Diarmait was, but, given the circumstances, it is most likely that he belonged to the Cenél nEógain or, at least, had their patronage. From this time onwards, until the middle of the twelfth century, the heads of the church of Derry are always referred to in Latin as *princeps* or in Irish by the equivalent word *airchinnech*. Some apparent exceptions to that rule will be discussed as they arise below.

There is a record of the death in 921 of Cináed son of Domnall, who is described as '*princeps* of Daire Calgaig and Druim Tuama, and chief counsellor [*cenn adchomairc*] of Cenél Conaill of the North' (AU). Druim Tuama or Drumhome was a Columban church in south Donegal. In the early seventeenth century, John Colgan listed Cináed as one of his 'saints' of Derry with a feastday on 19 November. Colgan's claim was probably based on nothing more than the reference to Cináed in the annals that appeared to connect him with Derry. Certainly no other information about Cináed has come to light in

---

TABLE 5. The alleged pedigree of Cináed mac Domnaill, as outlined in the mid-twelfth-century MS Rawlinson B502. The dates of death in round brackets are derived from the annals, but those in square brackets are calculated backwards from Cináed on the basis of an average thirty-year generation gap. The result appears to be several generations too short, so we cannot be certain of the pedigree's accuracy – particularly the link between Domnall mac Áedo and his alleged son Colcu. Separate evidence seems to confirm that Domnall had a son Colcu (O'Brien 1962, 163: 144e24), but – arising from the dating discrepancy in the pedigree – it is a moot point if the latter was the father of Conchobor as is claimed here.

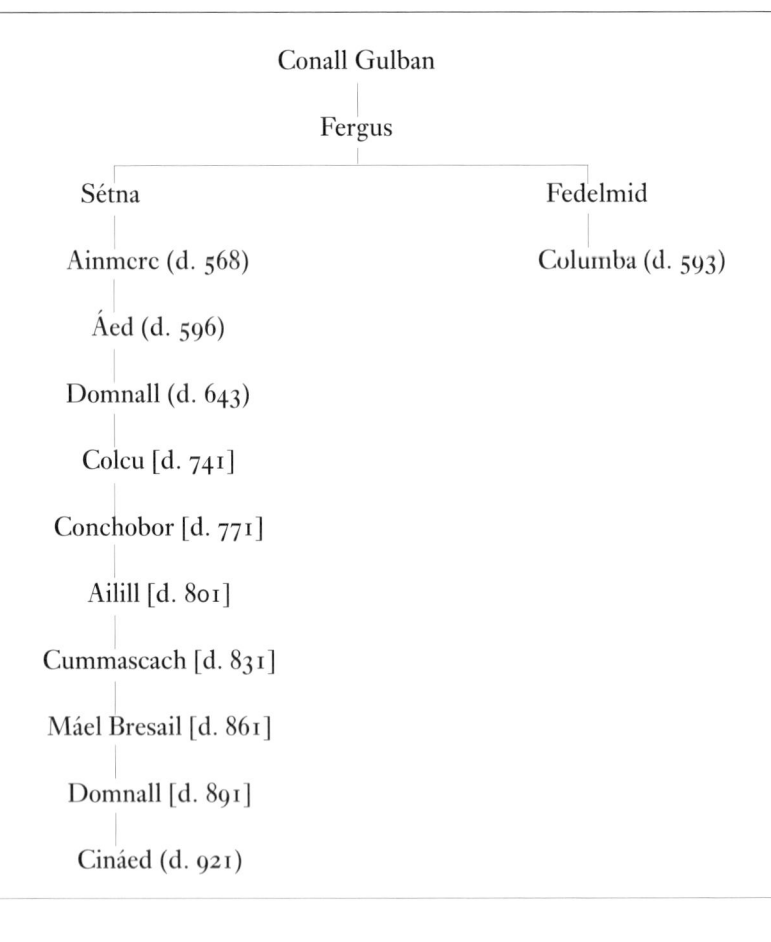

---

Conall Gulban
|
Fergus
|
┌──────────────┴──────────────┐
Sétna                        Fedelmid
|                              |
Ainmerc (d. 568)             Columba (d. 593)
|
Áed (d. 596)
|
Domnall (d. 643)
|
Colcu [d. 741]
|
Conchobor [d. 771]
|
Ailill [d. 801]
|
Cummascach [d. 831]
|
Máel Bresail [d. 861]
|
Domnall [d. 891]
|
Cináed (d. 921)

modern times and it is unlikely that anything more was available in Colgan's time either. Despite the title given to him in the annals, however, it is not certain that Cináed was a cleric of any kind, although he was clearly a very important man. Very unusually – that is, if he was a cleric – his personal pedigree is specifically recorded in the secular genealogies (table 5 and O'Brien 1962, 164: 144f18). It immediately follows that of Cathbarr Ó Domhnaill, the Donegal king of the following century who was responsible for the making of the shrine of the *Cathach*, the great Columban treasure that may itself have had a Derry connection, as we will see below (Ó Floinn 1995, 125). Later again, the *Cathach* was kept at Ballymagroarty, less than two miles from Drumhome.

According to his pedigree, Cináed claimed to be a direct descendant, eight generations later, of Áed mac Ainmerech, the sixth-century Cenél Conaill king who, in the legends, gave Colum Cille his fortress at Derry as the site for the latter's first monastery. The earliest surviving version of this 'official' account is to be found (as has been seen in ch. 2) in the prefatory material to the poem *Noli Pater Indulgere* in the *Liber Hymnorum*. The date of this written version is generally reckoned to be about the tenth or early eleventh century; Herbert says 'after 989'. However, it is at least possible that the story, as distinct from the surviving written account, belonged originally to the period around 921 when the grandiose title outlined above was claimed for Cináed. Few individuals besides Cináed would have had a better motive for embroidering the story of Áed granting Derry to Colum Cille.

In fact, it is very unlikely that Cináed was an official (senior or otherwise) in the monastery of Derry in any sense or, indeed, that he had any real governing connections with the place. Although originally the founders of the church at Derry, for almost a century and a half prior to Cináed's death his people, the Cenél Conaill, had been excluded from serious influence in the area in which Derry was situated (the former Cenél Conaill territory north of Barnesmore) and, almost certainly, from any office in that monastery itself. Cináed's claim to a role in Derry's affairs in his title (whatever about his connections with Druim Tuama, which seem much more likely) is probably no more than a nostalgic, propagandistic but anachronistic and futile, *soi-disant* assertion. By the beginning of the tenth century, it can hardly have been even a realistic ambition for any member of the Cenél Conaill to take up a governing office in Derry. It may be that Cináed, from his base south of the Barnesmore Gap (perhaps in the church at Drumhome), was one of the first to argue – for propaganda purposes – the theory of the foundation of the Derry monastery by the Cenél Conaill's most important saint, Colum Cille, or else that he had inherited that legend, which had been cultivated by his predecessors for exactly the same sort of reasons.

The two churches mentioned in Cináed's title – Derry and Druim Tuama – are the only two named churches in the wider 'Donegal' area mentioned by

Adomnán in the *Vita Columbae* of *c*.700. At least one of the purposes for mentioning them there was to indicate the northern and southern boundary markers of the Cenél Conaill's territory during Columba's later years and in the time of Adomnán (Lacey 2006, 158–9).

There is a reference to the death in 927 (*recte* 929) of Caencomhrac mac Maeluidhir who was described as abbot and bishop (*abb & epscop*) of the monastery of Derry (Daire Calcchaich) and steward of the Law of Adomnán (*maor cána Adhamnáin*). The account occurs only in the Annals of the Four Masters and there is little further information about Caencomhrac. His feastday was commemorated on 6 September (Reeves 1857, 393). If he was genuinely associated with Derry, almost certainly he would have belonged to the Cenél nEógain. However, his office as steward of Adomnán's Law suggests an association instead with the Cenél Conaill; in fact, Reeves shows his descent from the latter's alleged relatives, the Cenél mBogaine (1857, table facing p. 342). As we will see below, however, it looks as if the Four Masters, who were of course writing seven hundred years later, occasionally misread references to Daire [Eithne] – Kilmacrenan – as referring instead to Daire [Calgaich], so it is not certain that Caencomhrac was a Derry official.

There is an entry for 939 in the Annals of Ulster as follows: 'Fínnechta mac Ceallaigh, the *comarba* of Daire, died in Christ'. Again, although this entry has often been taken as referring to Derry, it is not all certain that the Daire in question here is Derry or, indeed, that it was a place of any sort. The term *comarba* – literally, 'heir of' – although certainly implying a position of clerical leadership, is usually associated at this stage with the cult of a person (that is, the heir of a particular 'saint') rather than with a place. However, the Four Masters in their rendering of this entry explicitly link Fínnechta with Derry 'Doire', adding that he was a 'bishop and adept [*saoi*] in the *Béarla Féine*' (AFM *s.a.* 937).[1] If the Annals of Ulster reference – which we must treat here as the superior evidence – does refer to Derry, then this is the first time (and one of the few instances) that the word *comarba* is used to describe the head of that monastery. Previously, the terms employed are *abb/abbas* or *princeps*. Subsequently, the term *airchinnech* becomes the norm.[2]

For the year 948 (*recte* 950), the Annals of the Four Masters have a reference to the death of 'Maelfinnen, learned bishop of Doire Chalgaigh'. Once again, this appears to be an error, as the more reliable (for this period) Annals of Ulster identifies Maelfinnen (Máel Finnáin?) as the 'bishop of Cell Dara' (Kildare). The latter entry continues 'Cleirchéne son of Conallán superior [*airchinnech*] of Daire Calgaich, rested in peace' (AU). Clearly the Four Masters (or their exemplars) omitted part of the text they were copying and

---

1 *Béarla Féine* was the somewhat obscure technical dialect or Irish language jargon used by the brehon law jurists.  2 Apparent exceptions to this are *abbas* (AU 975) and *comarba* (AFM 952, *s.a.* 950; AFM and AU 1025; and AU 1066). These will be discussed in detail below.

consequently mistakenly associated Maelfinnen with Derry. Cleirchéne, son of Conallán, definitely seems to have been the 'superior' of Derry.

Under the year 950, but properly corrected to 952, the Annals of the Four Masters records the death of Adhlann son of Éichneach son of Dálach, who is described as the *comharba* of 'Daire Colaim Chille'.[3] Adhlann belonged to the Síl Lugdach dynasty, which came originally – in the sixth and seventh centuries – from a small, almost certainly relatively impoverished, petty kingdom in the Cloghaneely area of north-west Donegal, but which had expanded its territory greatly during the eighth and ninth centuries (Lacey 2012). After the Battle of Clóitech in 789, the Síl Lugdach had acquired some of the former territory of the Cenél Conaill. They had also taken over some of the principal attributes of those people. Among the latter was a devotion to the cult of Colum Cille as propagated by the clergy of Kilmacrenan, their chief church (ibid.). It appears that the Síl Lugdach falsely incorporated the Columban patrimony as part of their own origin legends, on the pretext that they were descended from a sixth-century eponymous figure called Lugaid who, it was claimed inaccurately, had been a close relative of the saint (ibid.). Adhlann's grandfather Dálach was given the somewhat limited title of 'chief (*dux*) of Cenél Conaill' by the chroniclers when he died in 870 (AU).[4] Whatever about his maternal inheritance and despite a long-standing propagandistic tradition, it is extremely unlikely that Dálach – or his ancestors and successors – was genealogically part of the Cenél Conaill as is strongly argued in much of the later medieval literature. His son, usually known by the endearing form of his name as Éichnechán, was unambiguously claimed as king (*rex*) of the Cenél Conaill when his death was recorded in 906 (AU). That Éichnechán was Adhlann's father. John Colgan lists Adhlann as one of his Derry 'saints'.

Significantly, the reference to Adhlann is also the earliest use in the Annals of the Four Masters of the anachronistic name for Derry, Daire Colaim (or Coluim) Chille, rather than the older name Daire Calgaich. Was that done to imply that Adhlann himself had some heightened consciousness of the Columban connections? From at least the beginning of the ninth century onwards, the Síl Lugdach to which he belonged controlled the area of north-west Donegal extending from the Gweedore River around to the River Swilly – the area known later as Tír Luighdeach. At least in later times, there was a plethora of sites said to be associated with the early life of Colum Cille in that area: Cloghaneely, Tory, Gartan, Templedouglas, Kilmacrenan and many others. We have no source earlier than the mid-twelfth-century Middle Irish

---

3 Adhlann was a brother of the Domnall from whom descended the famous Uí Domhnaill family.  4 Despite the fact that the contemporary annals state that he was 'killed by his own people', Dálach was remembered fondly as a significant ancestor of several of Donegal's most important medieval families, most notably the Uí Domhnaill (O'Donnells). Such a contradiction could be explained if the people who killed him had been the real Cenél Conaill, furious at his theft of their dynastic title (Lacey 2012, 47).

Life that links Colum Cille with that area, with the possible exception of the explanation of the name Kilmacrenan. In the list of Columba's relatives (probably dating to about 700–50) attached to the B texts of Adomnán's *Vita Columbae*, there is a reference to one of the saint's sisters: *Mincoleth mater filiorum Ena[in]* 'Mincoleth the mother of the sons of Énán', who are said to have given their name to Kilmacrenan. If the etymology is correct, it would appear that the explanation of the place-name is the oldest genuine historical connection between Columba and the north-west of Donegal. Despite this lack of evidence, however, there are strong circumstantial reasons for believing that Columba was born and raised in the Gartan area (Lacey 2012, 102 and 190).

Adhlann son of Éichnechán – just as Cináed son of Domnall of a generation earlier – would have had special but different reasons for fostering the cult of Colum Cille in Derry, if it was the case that he was genuinely associated with that place. However, there is one problematic possibility that we cannot overlook. Derry and Kilmacrenan (Cill mac nÉnán), also known as Daire Eithne, shared the place-name element Daire or Doire. Other evidence suggests that this occasionally led to confusion – or even to deliberate distortion – in the sources dating from the later Middle Ages on (Lacey 2012, 48 and 53). This is particularly true of instances when the shortened forms of their names – Daire/Doire – were used without further identification. It is almost definite that some incidents and stories that have been interpreted as being connected with Derry should actually have been assigned to Kilmacrenan. This may well have been the case with regard to Adhlann (and maybe even to Caencomhrac mac Maeluidhir, discussed above).

The 952 record of Adhlann's death is the first time that the formula 'Daire Colaim Chille' (rather than Daire Calgaich or just Daire) is used in the Annals of the Four Masters. It must be remembered that, although that text was based on earlier documentation, it is not a copy of a contemporary evolving chronicle, as can be said, more or less, about the other annalistic compilations. The Annals of the Four Masters is a unified literary work composed in the early seventeenth century. Daire Colaim Chille is an anachronistic title for Derry for the middle of the tenth century; it is not used, for instance, in the (more contemporary) Annals of Ulster until the panygyric entry on the death of Domnall Ua Lochlainn in 1121, as we will see below. The original record from which the Four Masters or their exemplar took the details of the death of Adhlann probably referred simply to the unqualified place-name 'Daire', which was later expanded (without any specific evidence) to the form Daire Colaim Chille. That is certainly what happened for the only other entry in the Annals of the Four Masters prior to the twelfth century that employs the same formula. The Annals of Ulster records the death in 1025 of Máel Eóin Ua Toráin, '*comarba* Daire'. However, the equivalent reference in the Annals of the Four Masters expands the name Daire (with or without justification) to 'Doire

Colaim Chille'. Presumably on the premise that – since the sixteenth century at least – Derry has been considered a much more important place than Kilmacrenan, it looks as if previous unqualified instances of *Daire* or *Doire* were frequently interpreted by the Four Masters (and other authors down to the present day) as Derry.[5] This is what seems to have happened in the transmission of the record of Adhlann's death. It is much more likely that he was *comarba* of Daire Eithne – the church of Kilmacrenan – rather than of Daire Calgaich or Daire Coluim Chille – Derry.

The death of another *airchinnech* (superior) of Daire Calgaich, Cinaed Ua Cathmail, is recorded in 969 (AU). The Uí Cathmail were a Cenél nEógain family, whose name was later anglicized as Campbell or Caulfield, and who would settle in the Clogher area (Co. Tyrone) and adjacent parts of Fermanagh (Ó Ceallaigh 1951, 7, 55, 114). That a member of their family was a senior officer in Derry is fully consistent with the contemporary political situation. Preceding their notice of Cinaed's death, the Annals of the Four Masters (*s.a.* 967) note the death of Aenghas Ua Robhartaigh, anchorite (*ancoire*) of 'Doire Chalgaigh'.[6] We have no further information about who Aenghas was, but individuals with the Ua or Mac Robhartaigh surname would have many associations with Derry and the cult of Colum Cille in later medieval times. Their presence, for example, is memorialized in the name Ballymagrorty on the north-western outskirts of Derry and in the similarly named Ballymagroarty in south Donegal (where the treasure known as the *Cathach* of Colum Cille was kept). It is also reflected in the name of Magheraroarty on the Donegal coast opposite Tory Island, an area where there was a concentration of devotion to Colum Cille.[7]

The death of Fogartach, who is described as the abbot (*abbas*) of 'Daire', is recorded in 975 (AU). Again, we cannot be certain that Derry is the place intended, as no further identifying information is supplied. A little more can be gleaned from the death notice of Uisíne Ua Lapáin in 984 (AU), who is described as the *airchinnech* of Daire Calgaich. Whatever their genealogical origins, the Uí Lapáin were a family based close to Derry, with a settlement – probably a crannog – on the former Lough Lappan, now known as Portlough, five miles west of Derry.[8]

---

5 Another example of this is the reference to *Doire donn* in the poem 'Ard na scéla, a mheic na ccuach'. The modern editor of the poem, Margaret Dobbs, took it, almost certainly mistakenly, that this was a reference to Derry (1955, 33), whereas it is much more likely that Doire Eithne – Kilmacrenan – was the place in question (Lacey 2012, 48).   6 AFM adds that they 'died in the same month – *décc in aen mí*'; the latter clause was not translated by John O'Donovan.   7 The O'Roarty were coarbs and erenaghs on Tory according to an inquisition in 1609 (Ó Gallachair 1960, 278). We have no direct evidence that these families had connections with each other. See now Devlin 2013, 65–70.   8 In 959, Aengus Ua Lapáin died (AU); AFM (*s.a.* 957) adds that he was 'bishop of Raphoe', that is, presumably at the church there – not the diocese, which had not yet been formed. Another Aengus Ua Lapáin died in 1010 (AU) and a secondary interlinear note adds that he was 'king of Cenél nÉnnai' (see ch. 1).

14 The remains of the O'Doherty castle at Elagh, Co. Derry (although just inside the border with Donegal). The building is located on a high rocky (*aileach*) outcrop at one of the most southerly points of the Inishowen Peninsula, overlooking what was probably an ancient causeway across the marshy land of the Pennyburn Depression (still reflected in the nearby modern place-name 'Bridge End'). The site was probably the original Aileach of history, giving its name subsequently to the greatly enlarged Cenél nEógain kingdom (see also fig. 2).

In 990, Derry was plundered (*do argain*) by what the Annals of Ulster call 'the Danes' (*Dhanuraibh*), although elsewhere they are referred to just as *gallaibh*, 'foreigners' (AFM). In a very similar entry, the latter annals say that Derry was plundered again in 997. As this was not recorded elsewhere, it has been suggested that it is just a repetition of the 990 entry. Although we know from other sources that the Vikings were active in the Lough Foyle, Lough Swilly and Mulroy Bay areas (for example, Lacey 2012, 47–51), according to the surviving records, Derry itself, under the protection of the powerful Cenél nEógain, seems to have had very little interference from them, except for these references in the 990s and the battle at Derry in 833. The failure of the Vikings to establish themselves in Derry, however, may not have been to its long-term advantage. At other comparable ancient monastic sites where they settled, wealthy trading centres emerged that became the basis of many of the later prosperous medieval Irish towns. The success of the Cenél nEogain in keeping

*Derry and the Cenél nEógain*

the Vikings out of Derry may actually have contributed to its eventual marginalization.

The records for Derry during the eleventh century are very patchy. The deaths of four possible ecclesiastical officials are recorded, but we cannot be absolutely certain that any of them had a definite connection. In 1025 (AU), Máel Eóin Ua Toráin, who is described as the *comarba Daire*, died. As mentioned before, at this stage the term *comarba* is usually associated with the name of a saint rather than with a place, so it must remain an open question as to whether or not this reference applies to Derry.[9] The Annals of the Four Masters describing the same event refer to Máel Eóin as the *comharba Doire Colaim Chille*. There appears to be no reason why this particular form of the name was used, other than that the equivalent Annals of Ulster entry used the form *comarba Daire*. The use here of Doire Colaim Chille by the Four Masters appears to be simply an unsubstantiated seventeenth-century rendering of the eleventh-century indefinite name Daire. This is probably also the explanation for the use of Doire Coluim Chille in the 950/952 entry (AFM) discussed above.

In 1061 (AU), Muiredach Ua Maelcoluim, the *airchinnech* or 'superior' of 'Daire', died. In this instance, we can be reasonably certain that a place is intended. Muiredach's surname suggests an association with a Columban church, but there can be no certainty that the place in question was Derry, as we saw above that Daire Calgaich (Derry) and Daire Eithne (Kilmacrenan), each of them with varying Columban associations, have been confused – both accidentally and probably deliberately – by medieval and early modern chroniclers.[10] The death of another *comarba Daire* is recorded in 1066 (AU). An interlinear additional note to the main entry adds that his name was Dunchadh Ua Duimen,[11] but nothing more is known about him and, as above, it is not certain that a place, least of all Derry, is intended in the reference. On the 'nineteen of the Kalends of January' (AU)[12] – 14 December 1096 – the death of Eogan Ua Cernaigh the *airchinnech* of Daire is recorded. It is almost certain that the place in question was Derry, as a century later, in 1199, as will be seen below, his namesake and probable relative Gilla Críst Ua Cernaigh took over as *comarba* there.

Although founded by Cenél Conaill in the sixth century and remaining under their control until the end of the eighth century, throughout the ninth, tenth and eleventh centuries Derry had been part of the patrimony of the powerful Cenél nEógain. The territories of the latter had continued to expand

---

9 Máel Eóin may have been related to Máel Brigte mac Tornáin (d. 927) who, unprecedentedly, united the positions of *comarba Pátraicc* (abbot of Armagh) and *comarba Coluim Cille*, effectively removing the latter office from Iona to where it never returned (Herbert 1988, 74–6).    10 Edward Gwynn thought that a relatively obscure reference to Ua Maelcholuim in a poem about Ailech written probably between 1036 and 1056 might refer to this Muiredach (1924, 100–1, 401).    11 This seems to be the surname anglicized now as Devine, which is still common in the north-west of Ireland.    12 AFM says 'eighteenth'.

from what was their original Inishowen homeland across what are now Cos Derry and Tyrone and parts of Armagh and Fermanagh. Simultaneously, up to the beginning of the eleventh century, the Cenél nEógain had alternated with the equally powerful Clann Cholmáin (based in what would become Co. Westmeath) for the prestigious office of kingship of Tara. However, the growth of Cenél nEógain's power and territory was not an unmitigated blessing. By the beginning of the eleventh century, they were entering a period of decline. As Francis John Byrne said, 'It is clear that the Cenél nEógain were quite ineffective outside their immediate sphere of influence from 1036 until 1080' (2005, 857); he added: 'The Cenél nEógain may be said to have become victims of their own success' (ibid., 880). This was due to two factors: 'internal faction' and the 'over-extension of their lordship'. The internal factionalism resulted from the rivalry between their two emerging leading families: the O'Neills,[13] whose power-base was largely south and east of the Sperrins and who were linked with the church of Armagh; and the Mac Lochlainns, who retained the ancestral lands in Inishowen and controlled Derry.

Paradoxically, it was from the tenth century onwards – when the Cenél nEógain were in control of Derry – that the legend of its foundation by the great Cenél Conaill saint, Colum Cille, was recorded and elaborated. But was it the Cenél nEógain who were responsible for that? One cannot help thinking that the cultivation (and perhaps even the outright invention) of that legend might have been designed by the Cenél Conaill themselves, at least initially, as a propaganda bulwark against the advance of the Cenél nEógain into Derry. However, if that is what happened, then it backfired. It would be the Cenél nEógain family, the Mac Lochlainns, in the twelfth century who would reap the greatest benefits of the legend. The paradox is that, originally, that legend may have been cultivated, at least in part, to keep such people out!

---

[13] The plural of the anglicized surname O'Neill in Irish is Uí Néill. But that same name has a completely different meaning in early Irish history, referring to a wider dynasty that operated over much of the northern half of Ireland. For purposes of clarity, therefore, the anglicized version O'Neill is used here and below when referring to the mid-Ulster ruling family.

CHAPTER 5

# The Mac Lochlainns and Doire Coluim Chille

The twelfth century opened with Derry coming under attack, although the Annals of Ulster and the Annals of the Four Masters for the year 1100 record two slightly different versions of what appears to be the same event. The powerful northern king Domnall Ua Lochlainn[1] was in bitter conflict with many of the leading political figures throughout Ireland, most especially the Munster king Muirchertach Ua Briain. Domnall's aim was to achieve recognition as incumbent of the much desired but equally much contested office of high-king of Ireland. Domnall was almost certainly living or at least based in Derry by then.[2] Derry had become, in effect, the capital of the Cenél nEógain north of the Sperrins, particularly of their ruling family the Mac Lochlainns. The Annals of Ulster tells us that in 1100, as part of his war with Domnall, Muirchertach led an 'expedition' (*slógadh*) to the frontier of the latter's directly controlled territory at Assaroe on the River Erne (now Ballyshannon). Strictly speaking, south Donegal from the Barnesmore Gap to the Erne was the territory of the Cenél Conaill, but by that stage the latter were clearly subordinate to the all-powerful Domnall. Against all custom and tradition, Domnall would eventually intrude his own son Niall as king of the Cenél Conaill.

Muirchertach Ua Briain's expedition in 1100 was clearly part of a pincer strategy. The Annals of Ulster adds that the fleet (*longus*) of the Norse settlement at Dublin, which was subordinate to and allied with Muirchertach, attacked Domnall's home territory in Inishowen, but 'they were slaughtered, both by drowning and killing'. The Annals of the Four Masters record these two related events slightly differently.

> An army was led by Muirchertach Ua Briain, with the choice part of the men of Ireland about him, until they arrived at Eas Ruaidh. The Cenél Conaill assembled to defend their country against them; and they compelled Muirchertach and his forces to return back without booty, without hostages, without pledges … The great fleet of the foreigners was brought by the same Muirchertach, till he arrived at Doire; but they did not commit aggression or injure anything, but were cut off by [Domnall] Ua Lochlainn, both by killing and drowning.

---

1 The terms 'Ua' (Ó) or 'Mac' are effectively interchangeable in the Mac Lochlainn surname from this point onwards.   2 Ciarán Devlin suggested that Domnall actually lived at Enagh Lough, three miles north-east of Derry (2000a, 97).

15 The hill-top location of the Grianán of Aileach, four-and-a-half miles north-west of Derry. The latter, now greatly restored, stone monument – perhaps dating to about AD800 – is located at the centre of a series of earthworks that probably belonged to a hillfort of the Bronze or Iron Age. Almost certainly, this would have been a boundary marker of the Cenél nÉnnai and later the Cenél Conaill kingdoms before the area was conquered c.AD789 by the Cenél nEógain, who, may then have built the stone structure as a symbol of their new dominance over the north-west of Ireland.

This incident is the first mention in the annals of Domnall's direct involvement with Derry. Whether or not Muirchertach Ua Brian himself was actually present in Inishowen and Derry in 1100 – which seems unlikely despite the annal entry quoted above – he certainly came to the vicinity of Derry in the following year; allegedly destroying the great hilltop monument known as the Grianán of Aileach a few miles away (fig. 15). The Grianán had been a symbolic headquarters of Domnall Ua Lochlainn's people, the Cenél nEógain, probably for the previous three hundred years.[3]

Those events in 1100 and 1101 indicate Domnall's close association with Derry, although, like all medieval kings, he was actually constantly on the move, especially in the summer half of the year. From early in the twelfth century, we can see members of the king's extended dynastic line – the Cenél nEógain – being appointed to the various ecclesiastical offices in Derry. Domnall had come to power among his own people in 1083 following about half a century of Cenél nEógain decline. He was an extraordinarily dynamic chieftain who set about expanding his power base, intruding himself and his appointees wherever and whenever the opportunity arose. He was too much interested in contemporary power to be overly concerned about ancient Cenél Conaill claims on Derry.

3 Whatever its actual or symbolic function, the Grianán can never have been a normal dwelling place: see Lacey 2006, 310.

# The Mac Lochlainns and Doire Coluim Chille

TABLE 6. Genealogy of Mac Lochlainn kings involved with Derry. There has been a lot of controversy about the exact descent of Lochlann, the eponym of the Ua (Ó) or Mac Lochlainn surname. Lochlann's own name, seemingly meaning 'Viking', suggests some Scandinavian association. However, the main question at issue was whether he was descended, four generations later, from either of two contemporary Cenél nEógain kings: Domnall Daball (king of Ailech), who died in 915, or Niall Glúndub (king of Tara), who died in 919 and who was definitely the eponymous ancestor of the O'Neills of Tír Eógain. There is a substantial literature on this subject, but Donnchadh Ó Corráin (who cites the relevant publications) seems to have resolved the matter in favour of Domnall Daball (2001, 247–50), as in the table. This interpretation has implications for the descent (again as shown) of Ardgar (father's name not known) who was killed, according to the Annals of Ulster, by *muinnter Daire* 'the community of Derry' in 1124 (see below).

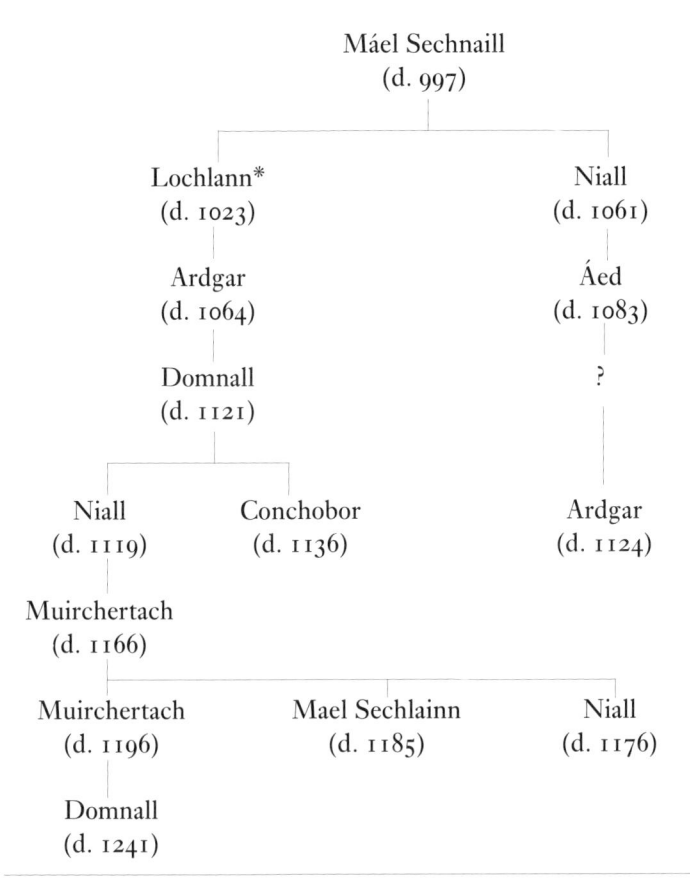

```
                        Máel Sechnaill
                           (d. 997)
                    ┌─────────┴─────────┐
              Lochlann*                Niall
              (d. 1023)              (d. 1061)
                 │                      │
              Ardgar                   Áed
             (d. 1064)              (d. 1083)
                 │                      │
              Domnall                   ?
             (d. 1121)                  │
           ┌─────┴─────┐                │
         Niall      Conchobor        Ardgar
       (d. 1119)   (d. 1136)        (d. 1124)
           │
      Muirchertach
       (d. 1166)
     ┌─────┼─────────────┐
Muirchertach  Mael Sechlainn  Niall
 (d. 1196)    (d. 1185)     (d. 1176)
     │
  Domnall
 (d. 1241)
```

(* *from whom the Ó or Mac Lochlainn surname derives*).

As part of his campaign to secure the high-kingship of Ireland, Domnall set about reorganizing the affairs of Derry. Cenél nEógain candidates were appointed to the senior positions there such as Congalach the son of Mac Conchaille, the *airchinnech* who died at ninety-four years of age in 1112 (AU). According to William Reeves, the Mac Conchaille family were a branch of the Cenél mBinnig segment of the Cenél nEógain (1857, 404 n. f),[4] many of whom – although originally having come from Inishowen – were by then settled along the west bank of the Lower Bann (Ó Ceallaigh 1951, 193 map 1). On 23 December 1134, Bé Bhinn, 'daughter of Mac Conchaille', almost certainly a close relative of Congalach, died with the title *banairchinnech* or 'female monastic steward' of Derry (AFM). She is the first named woman in the almost six hundred years of Derry's history.[5] There has been much discussion about the precise nature of Bé Bhinn's office as *banairchinnech*. It has been suggested, for example, as William Reeves pointed out in 1857, that she was merely the inheritor of the overseeing position previously occupied by Congalach.[6] But, as we will see below, Bé Bhinn's term as *banairchinnech* (whenever it began) would have overlapped with that of the famous male *airchinnech*, Gelasius, who occupied the position from around 1121 to 1137. While the absence of documentation makes it impossible to be definite, it looks as if there must have been a separate house of nuns at the time, of which Bé Bhinn was the abbess. Whatever its nature or affiliations at that time, this must have been the institution later recorded as the Cistercian *Conventus Sanctae Mariae*, which will be discussed further below.[7]

Domnall Ua Lochlainn must have been centrally involved in this consolidation of Cenél nEógain personnel in Derry. From his time forward (if not for the three centuries before when Derry was within their control), we have a stream of references connecting members of the Cenél nEógain with Derry. For instance, in 1122: 'Máel Coluim Ó Brolcháin, bishop of Ard Macha [Armagh], died on pilgrimage [*ina alithri*] in the hermitage [*i ndisiurt*] of Daire, with victory of martyrdom and repentance'.[8] He had 'assumed the bishopric' –

[4] However, in 1024 (AU), a Máel Dúin ua Con Chaille, king of Uí Nialláin (in Co. Armagh), was killed. This strengthens the suggestion of some sort of connection around this time between the churches of Armagh and Derry.  [5] And the only named woman connected directly with Derry mentioned in any of the sources for the period covered in this book, with the exception of an indirect reference to the 'concubine' Catherine O'Dogherty in 1397 (see ch. 8, below).  [6] Reeves 1857, 404. The Mac Conchaille family had other important connections with the church. Conchobor Mac Conchaille became prior of the house of Augustinian canons of SS Peter and Paul in Armagh – to which the Dubreclés in Derry would become affiliated – in the mid-twelfth century and later was appointed archbishop of Armagh. He died in Rome in 1176, 'having gone thither to confer with the successor of St Peter' (AFM). He was succeeded by Giolla an Choimhde Ó Caráin, bishop of Raphoe – who almost certainly also had Derry connections (Devlin 2000a, 100).  [7] The names of the places Galliagh (*Baile na gCailleach*) and Rosnagalliagh – from *cailleach*, 'nun' – in or close to the city, memorialize land owned by the nuns (Bryson 2001, 194, 196).  [8] AU. Tomás Ó Carragáin has made the interesting suggestion that 'the complex known as

*do gabail epscopoite* in 1107 (AU). Although we cannot be certain that Derry is the place referred to here, it does seem very likely. The Uí Brolcháin were a distinguished clerical family that also included scholars, poets and craftsmen.[9] They belonged to the Cenél Feradaigh who were settled in Tír Eógain and who in turn claimed to be part of Cenél nEógain (Reeves 1857, 405–6. See also Ní Bhrolcháin 1986 and Devlin 2000a, 98). As we will see below, a more prominent member of the Uí Brolcháin family would come to play a very significant role in the affairs of Derry in the second half of the twelfth century.

In 1124, 'Ardgar grandson of Áed ua Máel Sechlainn, heir designate [*rigdomna*] of Ailech was killed by the community [*muinnter*] of Daire for the honour of Colum Cille' (AU). Ardgar was a prominent member of the Cenél nEógain, and the reference to Colum Cille in his death notice probably confirms that Derry is the place in question. We do not know why *muinnter Daire* killed him, but almost certainly it was part of Mac Lochlainn internal secular politics. By that stage, the settlement in Derry would have played a crucial role in their various local and internal intrigues.

Domnall Ua Lochlainn himself had died in February 1121. His wife Bé Bhinn, 'daughter of Cennétigh Ua Briain', had died in 1110.[10] Domnall had been one of the most powerful men in the Ireland of his day. The Annals of Ulster has the following obituary for him:

> Domnall son of Ardgar son of Lochlann, over-king [*ardrí*] of Ireland, pre-eminent among the Irish in form and lineage, in sense and valour, in happiness and prosperity, in giving valuables and food, died in Daire Coluim Chille in the thirty-eighth year of his reign, the seventy-third year of his age, on Wednesday night, the fourth of the Ides [10] of February and the eighteenth [day of the moon], the feast of Mo Chuaróc the wise.[11]

the Dísert or Reiclés Coluim Cille in Kells [Co. Meath] incorporated a hospital as well as domestic buildings and an anchorhold' (2010, 267). Perhaps the Derry *dísert* did likewise. 9 AU. For further details about members of this family, see below. As well as being important in their own right, the Uí Brolcháin were also connected by marriage to the Clann Sínaich, the powerful family that, from the tenth century to 1134, had secured control of the patrimony of Armagh as well as many of its ecclesiastical appointments. Referring to the great poet Máel Íosa Ó Brolcháin, Muireann Ní Bhrolcháin commented: 'caomhnaíodh ginealach an teaghlaigh agus nochtadh síolrú Mhaoil Íosa ní amháin ó Chinéal Eoghain ach a gaol leis an gcine eaglasta ba cháiliúla agus ba chumasaí i gCúige Uladh – the family's genealogies were preserved and demonstrate Máel Íosa's descent not only from the Cenél nEógain, but his relationship with the most famous and most powerful ecclesiastical family in Ulster [Clann Sínaich]' (1986, 13). The same could be said of all members of the Uí Brolcháin. 10 Cennétig, who died in 1084, was a great-grandson of Brian Boru. For a while, he had been intruded by Domnall Ua Lochlainn as king of the ostensibly Cenél nEógain petty kingdom of Telach Óc as part of the latter's conflict with the emerging O'Neill family (see Hogan 1940). 11 John O'Donovan highlighted a minor confusion about the specific date of Domnall's death, insisting that the annals should have

Domnall died (and was almost certainly buried) in Derry, but it seems obvious that he had many other associations with that settlement and that his influence there must have been enormous, even if we cannot recover the detailed evidence for that now. In a poem in the Book of Fenagh, he is described as *Domnall debthach Daire* 'the contentious Domnall of Derry' (Hennessy and Kelly 1876, 282–3). Many of the recorded events of his career are centred on Derry or the territories governed from there. It seems as if he had been living in Derry or its vicinity for much of his later years at least. The Annals of Ulster obituary says that Domnall died in Daire Coluim Chille, 'Derry of Colum Cille'. This is the first contemporary use in those annals of that name. Its use there, rather than as a straightforward place-name, has a literary or cultic character to it; in some ways it is analogous to the way we would now talk about Joycean Dublin or Dickensian London.

Although not yet specifically dated, around the eleventh and twelfth centuries a large collection of texts purporting to have been written by or about Colum Cille came into circulation. Many of those have a Derry theme: arguing that Derry was Colum Cille's first church, the one most loved by him, the one he was saddest to leave when the time came for him to go to Iona. Words are put into the mouth of the saint in verses that are blatantly propagandistic on behalf of the Columban monastery of Derry.

> And, oh! were the tributes of Alba mine,
> From shore unto centre, from centre to sea,
> The site of one house, to be marked by a line,
> In the midst of fair Derry were dearer to me.
>
> That spot is the dearest on Erin's ground,
> For its peace and its beauty I gave it my love;
> Each leaf of the oaks around Derry is found
> To be crowded with angels from heaven above.
>
> My Derry, my Derry, my little oak grove,
> My dwelling, my home, and my own little cell;
> May God the Eternal, in heaven above,
> Send woe to the foes and defend thee well.[12]

---

cited the 'fifth of the ides' and that the latter fell on 9 February (AFM, ii, 1012). AFM also adds that Domnall was 'the most distinguished of the Irish for personal form, family, sense, prowess, prosperity and happiness, for bestowing of jewels and food upon the mighty and the needy, [and he] died at Doire Coluim Chille, after having been twenty seven years in sovereignty over Ireland [*uas Erinn in ríghe*], and eleven years in the kingdom of Aileach'.
[12] The translation here is by Douglas Hyde. Alba, of course, refers to Scotland.

**16** The dioceses of the north-west of Ireland as determined at the Synod of Rath Breasail in 1111. The dashed line represents the supposed northern boundary of the Cenél nEógain diocese.

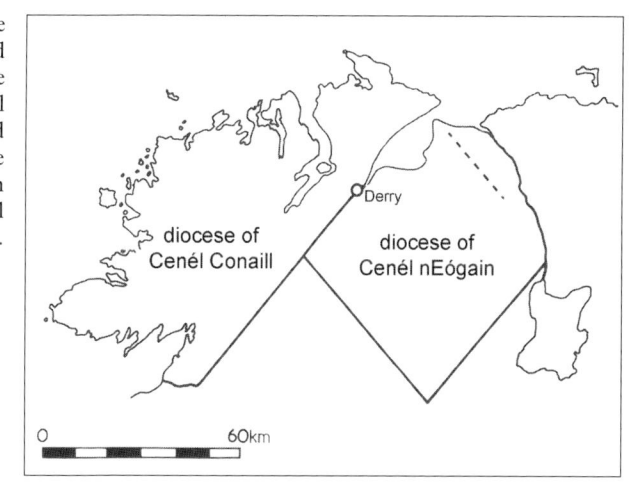

Since at least the tenth century, when the *Liber Hymnorum* preface to the poem *Noli Pater Indulgere* had been composed, the belief that Colum Cille had been the original ecclesiastical founder of the monastery of Derry had been propagated and cultivated. As we have seen, the impetus for the elaboration of that claim, paradoxically, may have been Cenél Conaill propaganda in opposition to the new Cenél nEógain rulers of Derry. By asserting that Derry had been founded back in the sixth century by the most important of their saints, the Cenél Conaill could justifiably claim that it still belonged by right to them in the tenth, eleventh and twelfth centuries – even if that claim was contradicted by contemporary political realities. However, if this is even part of the explanation for the explosion of Columban literature about Derry around this time, it backfired. It was the latter-day rulers – the Cenél nEógain – who fully developed the Columban legend and made the most use of it.

One of the earliest hints about this Cenél nEógain versus Cenél Conaill conflict over Derry may be the indecision regarding the naming of Derry or Raphoe as the seat of a Donegal (or Cenél Conaill) diocese at the Synod of Rath Breasail (near Borrisoleigh, Co. Tipperary) in 1111 (fig. 16). There has been much discussion about the decision to have an all-Donegal diocese,[13] as also the location of the seat of that diocese. It seems that the true explanation of the conundrum lies in the age-old conflict between the two dynasties.[14] Although the church of Derry had been in origin a Cenél Conaill foundation – irrespective of whether or not Columba himself had been involved in its

---

13 There was no concept at the time of what we would think of now as Co. Donegal. That territory was divided among various competing polities.   14 Ciarán Devlin suggested that the all-Donegal diocese may have been formed to 'mirror' the realm of Domnall Ua Lochlainn's son, Niall, who had been intruded as king of Cenél Conaill in 1101 (2000a, 97). But most authorities argue that the latter did not happen until *c.*1113, that is, after the declaration of the diocese (Ó Corráin 1972, 148; Flanagan 2005, 926).

establishment – and its legends and propaganda all underlined those Cenél Conaill connections, by 1111 it was definitely part of the Cenél nEógain patrimony.

Bishops had always been part of the Irish church, but their functions had developed somewhat differently to that in other parts of Christendom. Bishops ruling the adjacent area or 'diocese' from their episcopal seats in cities (for the most part founded originally by the Romans) had been the norm throughout Christian Europe. By and large, Ireland had not been influenced in that respect by the Romans and there were no cities. The role of bishops in Ireland was confined largely to spiritual and sacramental duties rather than as general overseers of the local church and governors of its properties and wealth. Greater exposure to Continental practices, however, as a result – for example – of increased pilgrimage to Rome and other sacred destinations abroad, led to demands for similar practices in Ireland. In addition, there was a contemporary general reform movement in the wider church, particularly under Hildebrand, Pope Gregory VII. There also seems to have been a desire among leading Irish ecclesiastics to move the church away from the direct control of the ruling secular families, although, paradoxically, the assistance of those leading dynasties such as the Mac Lochlainns was essential for effecting the necessary reforms.

The new diocesan system was brought about in Ireland mainly by two synods or councils of the leading churchmen and laity: at Rath Breasail in Munster in 1111 and at Kells (Co. Meath) in 1152. At Rath Breasail, the island was divided north and south into two ecclesiastical provinces, 'Armagh' and 'Cashel'. Each province would contain twelve dioceses. Among the dioceses in the north relevant to Derry were to be those based on the episcopal 'seats' at Armagh, Ardstraw (most of northern Cenél nEógain territory, later to be part of the diocese of Derry), Clogher and Connor. Revealingly, the synod decided that either Derry or Raphoe could be the seat of a diocese that included most of what we now think of as Co. Donegal (including of course the area known from the seventeenth century onwards as the Liberties of Londonderry – that part of Co. Derry on the west bank of the Foyle).

The boundary points actually listed for the Donegal diocese were: from Eas Rua to Srubh Broin and from Carn Glas to Srubh Broin – from Assaroe (on the Erne) to Stroove (in north-eastern Inishowen), and from the Beltany Stone Circle (on Tops Hill, just outside Raphoe) to Stroove.[15] Crucially, this diocese

15 All three named boundary points are more or less in a straight line. The apparently superfluous reference to Carn Glas was to confirm that the Cenél nEógain-controlled territory west of the rivers Foyle and Finn – Mag nItha and adjacent territories – were excluded from the 'Donegal' diocese. That demarcation was continued in the later arrangements for the boundary between the dioceses of Derry and Raphoe. It persists to this day, resulting in an area of east Donegal between the Finn and Tops that belongs to the diocese of Derry rather than, as one might expect, to the diocese of Raphoe. Tops is only 1.5 miles south of Raphoe, but the actual boundary between the two dioceses at this point – the

included the Inishowen Peninsula and Derry itself, both of which would later be hived off to a separate northern Cenél nEógain diocese. The latter originally represented the area directly controlled by the Mac Lochlainns; it would eventually become known as the diocese of Derry. At Rath Breasail, however, as well as the territory west of the Foyle, other parts of what would later become attached to the northern Cenél nEógain (Derry) diocese were allocated to separate dioceses. The area between the Bann and the northern end of the Sperrins was allocated to the diocese of Connor, but most of the territory was allocated to the diocese of Ardstraw (McErlean 1914; Devlin 2000a). Later, the seat of the Ardstraw/northern Cenél nEógain diocese was moved to Machaire Ráith Lúraigh (Maghera, Co. Derry). It would not be until the middle of the thirteenth century that it was finally settled at Derry itself.

The measures adopted at the Synod of Rath Breasail – with some amendments – were further adopted and given papal approval at the Synod of Kells in 1152. Muiredach Ua Cobthaig, the bishop of the Cenél nEógain diocese (what would later evolve into the diocese of Derry as we now know it), was in attendance, but there is no record of a bishop attending to represent the Donegal diocese that would later evolve into the diocese of Raphoe (Holland 2005).[16]

Derry had developed into a busy settlement by this period, with an obvious secular as well as a monastic life. For instance, we have a record that on 30 March 1135 'Doire Cholaim Chille with its churches [*co na theamplaibh*] and houses was burned' (AFM).[17] The same annals record that it was burned again in 1149, but we know very little about the physical nature of the settlement there at that time. We will return to a discussion about that in ch. 6.

In 1126, Fionn Ua Conaingen who had been '*airchinnech* of Doire for a time' died (AFM). We do not know anything more about Fionn: who he was or why he had occupied the office of *airchinnech* only 'for a time'. But he must have been replaced in 1121 (see below) by the important Cenél nEógain cleric variously known as Gilla Meic Liac or Gelasius.[18] However secularized the role of *airchinnech* had been previously, it seems clear that from early in the twelfth century at least – with the various reforms – it was a fully ecclesiastical office, that is, the clerical abbacy of a monastery. In 1137, Gelasius was promoted: 'A change of abbots [*abbadh*] at Ard Macha, i.e. the *airchinneach* of Doire in place of Niall son of Aedh' (AFM). Gelasius had been the senior cleric – the *airchinnech*/abbot – in Derry for the previous sixteen years, which means he must have taken up the office in 1121.[19] His transfer to Armagh meant that as

---

relatively insignificant stream known as the Swillyburn – runs between them (see Lacey 2006, 122–3). **16** See below for more information about Muiredach. There are various lists of the medieval bishops connected with Derry and limited biographical notes; see especially Leslie 1937 and Byrne 1989. For more detail on some of the medieval bishops of Derry, see Devlin 2000b, 114–33 and 2013, 249–87. **17** The so-called Miscellaneous Irish Annals just say '*tempull* – church' (Ó hInnse 2004). **18** Devlin (2000a, 99) notes that Gelasius was descended from the powerful Cenél nEógain king, Áed Allán (d. 743). **19** The report of

well as being abbot there he had become the *comarba* or 'successor' of St Patrick, the most senior position in the medieval Irish church. Evidently, he had been centrally involved with the ecclesiastical reform movement that had been developing in the Irish church since the beginning of the century.[20] Direct evidence is non-existent, but Derry must have been one of the main centres of that movement, although we have no documentation to demonstrate what that actually meant.

In 1150, there was another significant change in the monastery of Derry. Máel Íosa Ua Branain, the '*airchinnech* of Doire Coluim Chille, [and] head of the happiness and prosperity [*cinn sonasa & sobharthain*] of the north of Ireland, died' (AFM).[21] The Uí Branain, who had various other connections with Derry as will be seen below, belonged to the Cenél Tigernaich segment of Cenél nEógain (Reeves 1857, 408). Máel Íosa was replaced in Derry by Flaithbertach Ó Brolcháin, another senior Cenél nEógain ecclesiastic. Flaithbertach, who was described in the annals for 1163 and 1164 as the 'son of the bishop' (AU), was probably the son of Máel Coluim Ó Brolcháin, the Armagh bishop who had died while on pilgrimage in Derry in 1122.[22] Unusually, Flaithbertach was not accorded the title *airchinnech* of Derry like his predecessors; instead he would be known (eventually at least) by the much more prestigious title of *comarba Coluim Cille*.[23] For about 220 years previously, that title and the authority over the Columban *familia* in Ireland that went with it had been the prerogative of the senior cleric in Kells (Co. Meath).[24] By the middle of the twelfth century, however, the influence of Kells and the secular polities surrounding it were in decline because of complicated local political reasons that will not be examined further here (see Flanagan 2005). All this disruption provided an opportunity for Derry to take over the Columban leadership role (Herbert 1988, chs 8 and 9).

We do not know how or why the decision to transfer this power from Kells to Derry came about. If there had been a general council or meeting of the Columban churches to arrive at a decision by consensus, then we have no

his death on 27 March 1174, at 87 years of age, says he was sixteen years *i n-abdaine Coluim Cille i n-Daire* (AU), thus equating the roles of abbot and airchinnech.  20 For the twelfth-century reforms, see Hughes 1966, ch. 24; Flanagan 2010.  21 Reeves, citing the Book of Lecan, fo. 193, noted the death of Erchelaidh, *abbas de Daire* in 1147 (1857, 405). A similar reference had been cited anonymously (but presumably by John O'Donovan or George Petrie) in the 1837 *Ordnance Survey memoir* (Colby). I know of no other information about Erchelaidh or how to explain what his function might have been. It is possible that he preceded Máel Íosa as *airchinnech* or that a different Daire was intended.  22 Another Ó Brolcháin, Máel Bhríde, was also described as *epscop Arda Macha* – bishop of Armagh – when he died in 1139 (AFM).  23 We know from various sources that the *comarba* was also the abbot of the Derry monastery. For example, in 1198, 'Gilla Mac Liac Ua Branain resigned the *comurbuis* and Gilla Crist Ua Cernaigh, by the choice of the clergy and laity of the north of Ireland, was ordained in his stead in the abbacy [*abdaine*] of Colum Cille' (AU).  24 Previous to that, of course, it had been the prerogative of the abbot of Iona, but had passed to Kells through the *Comarba Pátraicc* in Armagh (Herbert 1988, 74–6).

record of it. Clearly, the move was supported (see below) by the leading churchman in the country – Gelasius. However the change came about, in 1158 at the Synod of *Brí Mic Thaidhg*, Flaithbertach's position was given formal recognition and his role as what seems to have been a mitred abbot, with a status equivalent to that of a bishop, was proclaimed:

> There were present twenty-five bishops with the legate of the successor of Peter [the papal legate], to ordain rules and good morals. It was on this occasion the clergy of Ireland, with the successor of Patrick [Gelasius], ordered a chair, the same as every bishop for the successor of Colum Cille, Flaithbertach Ó Brolcháin, and the chief abbacy [*ard-abdaine*] over all the churches [of Colum Cille] throughout Ireland.
>
> (AU)

Flaithbertach's promotion would have been supported also by Derry's most important secular patron, Muirchertach Mac Lochlainn, grandson of the famous Domnall. Muirchertach had been born about 1091. His father Niall, Domnall's son, who died in 1119, had also been a powerful Cenél nEógain leader. Throughout the 1130s and 1140s, Muirchertach had fought his way to power, encountering various internal and external set-backs along the way.[25] By 1156, he had achieved recognition as king of Ireland 'with opposition' (Ó Corráin 2001, 241). In 1161, there was 'another hosting' by Muirchertach:

> into Meath, into an assembly of the Men of Ireland, both laics and clerics [*fer n-Erenn eter loechu & cleirchiu*] at Áth na Dairbrighe [Dervor near Kells, Co. Meath], so that he received the pledges of them all. It is on that occasion the churches of Colum Cille in Meath and Leinster were freed by the successor of Colum Cille, namely, by Flaithbertach Ó Brolcháin, and their tribute and jurisdiction were given to him, for they were subject before that.
>
> (AU)

Flaithbertach lost no time. That same year he went on a visitation to the Osraige (effectively, Co. Kilkenny). The tribute due to him was 'seven score oxen: but it is their value that was presented there – namely, four hundred and twenty ounces of pure silver: to wit three ounces for every ox' (AU). Charles Doherty has drawn attention to this particular visitation, with its similarity to the claims made on the king of the Osraige by Colum Cille himself in the late fictional account of the Convention of Druim Cett found in the introduction to the *Amrae Coluimb Chille* in the early twelfth-century manuscript Rawlinson

---

25 For the detail of Muirchertach's complicated career, see the valuable essay in O'Byrne 2005.

B502 (1982, 328). According to various versions of the story, one of the issues dealt with at the convention was the freeing of a young Osraige prince, Scandlán son of Colmán (or Cenn Fáelad), who was being kept hostage by the Cenél Conaill high-king Áed mac Ainmerech, Colum Cille's close relative. Colum Cille is said to have negotiated Scandlán's release. Therefore – according to the abbreviated version in the earlier introduction to the *Amrae* in the *Liber Hymnorum* – 'there are due eight score plough-oxen still [that is, at the time of the composition of the 'introduction'] to the congregation of Hi' [Iona, for which read the Columban *familia*] from the Osraige' (Bernard and Atkinson 1898, 54).

As has been pointed out in ch. 2, Herbert argued that the introductory material in the *Liber Hymnorum* was probably composed in the late tenth century. At that time, Kells functioned as the Columban headquarters in Ireland. By 1161, when Flaithbertach went to the Osraige, however, Derry had become the Columban headquarters. In the version of the story in the appendix to the Middle Irish Life of Colum Cille (Herbert 1988, 246 and 268), Scandlán goes to Derry after his release.[26] That version also mentions *an mórbachall* 'the great staff', which Scandlán takes from Derry to the Osraige. It was probably some kind of relic crosier with a Columban connection kept in the Kilkenny area. The story in the Middle Irish Life is not so crude as to portray Colum Cille making specific demands on the Osraige, but it does show how Scandlán's freedom came about and how he enjoyed great hospitality in Derry afterwards – the reciprocal obligations did not need to be spelled out. It is possible that this appendix dates to the time of the Osraige visit and that Flaithbertach had gone there immediately after the Dervor assembly, armed with this Kells Columban 'invoice' that he had acquired there.

This was not the first of Flaithbertach's profitable visitations; apparently he was assiduous in collecting whatever was 'owed' to Colum Cille. Immediately on taking up office in 1150 he had made a *cuairt* or official visitation throughout the territories of the Cenél nEógain in mid-Ulster.

> And he obtained a horse from every chieftain, a cow from every two biatachs [big farmers], a cow from every three freeholders and a cow from every four *díomhaoin* [tenant farmers?], and twenty cows from the king himself [plus] a gold ring of five ounces, his horse and his battle-dress.
>
> (AFM 1150).

He made a similar tour through Síl Cathasaigh (mid-Antrim) the following year, when he got 'a horse from every chieftain, a sheep from every hearth

---

26 This extra section occurs only in the *Leabhar Clainne Suibhne* and National Library of Scotland versions (Herbert 1988, 212, 239, 244–7, 265–9).

**17** Detail from Francis Neville's 1690 map of the Siege of Derry. The map shows (*top right*) 'St Collomkills 3 wells' and (*bottom left*) 'The foundation of the old cathedrall or long [round] tower with the church yard'. The cathedral is shown as having had a cruciform plan.

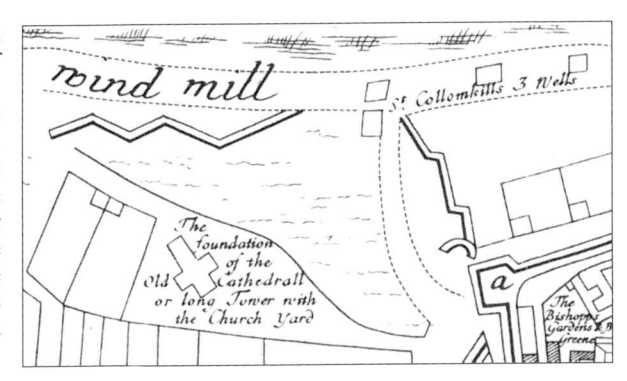

[house], and his horse, battle-dress and a ring of gold (in which were two ounces) from their lord'.[27] Two years later, he visited the Dál Coirpre and the Uí Echach Ulad (Co. Down). Again, he received a horse from each chieftain and a sheep from each house, a *screaball* (a unit of precious metal), a horse and five cows from the lord – Ua Duinnsléibhe – and an ounce of gold from his wife (AFM 1153).

Flaithbertach had also commenced a radical reorganization of the physical layout of the monastery and the surrounding secular settlement shortly after becoming *comarba* in Derry. No doubt he used the various tributes to Colum Cille that he had collected to support his operations. He commenced a number of building projects. As early as 1155, he had made a 'door' for the *Tempull*.[28] The recording of that event suggests that it must refer to the insertion of a monumental doorway – possibly in the latest Hiberno-Romanesque style and perhaps similar to the roughly contemporary doorway inserted into St Oran's chapel on Iona.[29] One of the most significant of these projects occurred in 1162 when Flaithbertach, with the help of 'the king of Ireland' Muirchertach Mac Lochlainn, separated the ecclesiastical precincts from the secular areas of the township that had grown up around the ancient monastery. He had to demolish

---

27 AFM 1151. The Síl Cathasaigh belonged to the Uí Tuirtre, a population group that lived along the east side of the Lower Bann but which originally had been settled along the west shore of Lough Neagh, between the Moyola and Blackwater rivers (Lacey 1999, 122, 138).
28 Presumably this is the building referred to as the *Tempall Becc* ('small church') in 1185 (AU). 29 Fisher 2005, 85. There are a number of church ruins in Co. Derry (at that time Cenél nEógain territory) that incorporate architectural details that can be broadly dated to this period also: at Banagher, Bovevagh and Dungiven (Anon. DOENI, 1983, 125–8; Rowan 1979, 293–4). During the rebuilding of the abbey church at Iona in the fifteenth century, a Donald Ó Brolcháin, stone-carver, inscribed his name on the capital of one of the pillars at the church crossing (RCAHMS 1982, 24). The anonymous author [Ian Fisher?] adds: 'The similarity of the south presbytery-window [in the Iona Abbey church] to the tomb-canopy above an effigy of West Highland type at Dungiven, Co. Londonderry, is so marked that the latter may be attributed to an Iona mason, and very possibly to Donald Ó Brolcháin himself, since a branch of that family was established in the Ballinascreen area near Dungiven' (ibid.).

over eighty houses in the process. He then constructed a stone wall around the monastery and declared a malediction on anyone who would violate it.[30]

His most important building achievement in conjunction with the same king was the construction of the *Tempull Mór* or 'great church', which was completed in 1164. This would become one of the most famous churches in the north-west of Ireland and in the following century it would be re-dedicated as the cathedral of the diocese of Derry (fig. 17).

Flaithbertach's success in reorganizing the affairs of the Columban churches in Ireland generally – apart from his work in Derry – was noticed in some unexpected quarters. This created something of a dilemma.

> [T]he leading members of the monastery of Iona, i.e. Augustin, the 'high' priest, and Dubhsidhe the Lector, and the head of the anchorites, Mac Gilladuff, and the head of the *Céile Dé*, Mac Forcellaigh, and the seniors of the monastery in general, came to meet the *comarba* of Colum Cille, Flaithbertach Ó Brolcháin, [to invite him] to take the abbacy of Iona, with the consent of Somerled [Lord of Argyll] and the men of Argyll and the Hebrides; but the *comarba* of Patrick [Gelasius] and the King of Ireland, [Muirchertach Mac] Lochlainn, and the chiefs of Cenél nEógain prevented it.
>
> (AU 1164)

Derry was burned 'for the most part' in 1166, including the Dubreclés. The account in the Annals of Ulster is somewhat odd in that, with the exception of one verb, the entire entry is in Latin.[31] It finishes by noting: *quod non auditum est ab antiquis temporibus* '[this is] something unheard of from ancient times' (AU). It is not precisely clear whether the latter phrase refers to the burning of Derry in general or of the Dubreclés in particular. Although in later times that institution was understood to have been Colum Cille's original Derry monastery, this seems to be the very first reference to it by that name, certainly in the annals.[32] But, far from being the sixth-century monastery, could the Dubreclés have been a relatively new foundation – or re-foundation – perhaps on the ancient site? At some stage in the twelfth or early thirteenth century, like many similar ancient Irish churches, the monks of the reformed Columban community of Derry adopted the rule of St Augustine. Their monastery became a house of Arroasian Augustinian canons regular, subject to the abbey of SS Peter and Paul in Armagh. The question is: when did this happen and was Flaithbertach involved?[33] The Augustinians had been recognized officially

---

30 See ch. 6.  31 By this stage, most of the annals are in Irish, with only some stock phrases in Latin. The 1166 entry about Derry reverses this.  32 There is a reference to the Dubreclés, cited above, in an appendix to the Middle Irish Life of Colum Cille. See below for the possible date of this additional text.  33 The speculation that follows owes much to a discussion with Gilbert Márkus on Inchcolm Island near Edinburgh in July 2012.

as an order about the middle of the eleventh century and by 1125 they had houses in England and Wales. Their introduction to Ireland seems to have been by St Malachy (archbishop of Armagh, 1132–6) perhaps a few years before 1130. The Augustinian abbey in Armagh was probably founded in 1126 (Gwynn and Hadcock 1988, 146–7). In 1140, while on his way to Rome, Malachy visited the Augustinian house at Arrouaise in France where the canons had adopted a stricter rule than elsewhere. Malachy subsequently encouraged the spread of the Arroasian observance in Ireland and the abbey of SS Peter and Paul in Armagh adopted that rule. Derry would at some stage become subject to that house according to the register of Archbishop John Bole in the mid-fifteenth century (ibid., 169). Most authorities assert that the monastery in Derry did not become Augustinian until c.1230 (ibid., 153). However, given Derry's long-standing close contacts with the reforming ecclesiastical authorities in Armagh, it is certainly possible that Flaithbertach's reformed house in Derry had adopted the Arroasian rule much earlier – perhaps as early as his own arrival there as abbot in 1150. Although the Augustinians wore white habits, they also adopted the use of black cloaks. Could this be the meaning of the word *dub*, 'black', in Dubreclés, which so far has eluded all attempts to explain it? We will return to the subject of the Augustinians in Derry below, but one thing is clear: innovators everywhere often attempt to represent the changes they seek to make as a return to 'roots' and a restoration of tradition.

About the same time that Derry was being reorganized physically and institutionally by Flaithbertach, its 'historians' set about realigning the intellectual framework against which its monastery could be seen as the most important of the Columban churches in Ireland. Herbert has shown that between 1150 and 1182 – and almost certainly before the 'Norman invasion' in 1169 – the text known as the Middle Irish Life of Colum Cille was written in Derry;[34] in fact it is the oldest book we know of to have been written in Derry.[35] Although various other texts about Columba had been composed since Adomnán wrote his work in the late seventh century, many of those had been based on abridgments of the latter. The Middle Irish Life containing slightly different material – although clearly heavily dependent on Adomnán's work – is nevertheless, in Herbert's words, 'a new literary creation'. It was written as a homily to be preached on the occasion of the saint's feastday, 9 June.

> Christians celebrate the festival and commemoration of Colum Cille's death on the fifth of the Ides [9] of June as to the day of the month every year, (which is) on this day today ... At that time every year, Irish

[34] 'Middle' here refers to the form of the language in which it is written – Middle Irish.
[35] Herbert 1988, where there is a full text, translation, notes and discussion. See also Bannerman 1993, 41, where the author argues for an Armagh provenance. However, that suggestion has not been widely accepted.

scholars give a brief account of the holy Colum Cille's nobility of kin and ancestry, and furthermore of the wonders and innumerable miracles which the Lord performed for him here in this world, and of the culmination and excellent ending with which he finally crowned his victorious career, attaining his real home and his true native land, the abode of Paradise in the presence of God for ever.

(Herbert 1988, 251)

One of the most important theses in the Life is that Derry was the first monastery founded by Colum Cille and, therefore, the one most loved by him. If that premise was accepted, there could be little objection to Derry assuming the leadership of the confederation of churches associated with the saint. The Life sets out the story of the foundation of Derry by a very young Colum Cille, but it also claims, for example, that he was involved in the foundation of the monastery at Kells (Co. Meath), although there is no doubt that it was not established until the years 804 to 807 (AU; also Herbert 1988, 68–70). The story of the Columban foundation of Derry is no more reliable; it is a fiction designed to bolster the new role of leadership of the Columban *familia* for the monastery there through the device of linking it with the cult of the famous saint.

The anonymous author uses Adomnán's older Latin Life, but, unlike that text, it reshapes its material into a linear chronological narrative. It gathers relevant information together from the scattered approach of Adomnán and creates a continuous story, highlighting some of Adomnán's episodes, simplifying and clarifying others, apparently deliberately leaving some things out, supplementing others and transferring the locations of some events from Scotland to Ireland. Kathleen Hughes, for example, said of the Middle Irish Life's simpler and more direct treatment of the story of the white horse that comes to sympathize with Colum Cille shortly before his death: 'it is all in Adamnán [*sic*], but muffled in words' (1972, 236).

The Middle Irish Life, as is appropriate for the story of an exile, takes as its opening Biblical text the Lord's advice to Abraham: 'Leave your country and your land, your kindred and your own patrimony for my sake, and go into the country which I shall reveal to you' (Gen 12:1). There follows the story of the saint's birth and early life, and then an outline of his career as a founder of monasteries in Ireland is set out in the form of a journey around the country. Colum Cille is said to have founded many monasteries, but just twelve are named: Derry, Raphoe, Durrow, Kells, Clonmore (Co. Louth), Lambay, Swords, the unidentified *Druim Monach*, Moone, Assylin (Co. Roscommon), Drumcliff and Tory. A notable absence for whatever reason – almost certainly political – is a mention of the saint's connections with Kilmacrenan (Co. Donegal). There is, however, a suggestion of his involvement in the foundation of the famous monastery at Monasterboice (Co. Louth), otherwise connected with St Buite. That story is quite unhistorical, but it possibly reflects connections of some sort between Monasterboice and the *familia* of Colum Cille (for which read, Derry) in the eleventh and twelfth centuries. The two saints were linked: Buite was said to have died on the day that Colum Cille was born.[36]

Colum Cille is depicted throughout the Life as a spiritual model for his followers. Herbert says that 'it caters for the demands of biography and edification, while also presenting twelfth-century aspirations in terms of the sixth-century lifetime of Colum Cille'. A story in the Life sets out to explain how one of the greatest treasures of Derry, the *Soiscél Martain*, came to be there.

> On a further occasion [Colum Cille] went from Derry to Martin's city of Tours, and brought back the Gospel which had been on Martin's breast in the grave for a hundred years, and he left it in Derry.

St Martin, the fourth-century bishop of Tours in northern France, was remembered for introducing monasticism into western Christianity. The Irish church had a particular monastic character, so St Martin's cult was widespread in Ireland, not least in the churches associated with Colum Cille. The Life of Martin by Sulpicius Severus was widely known in medieval Ireland and had been used as a literary model by Adomnán as well as by other Columban writers. One of the high crosses on Iona was named after St Martin, and in medieval Derry there was a graveyard (AU 1204) and a holy well (see below) dedicated to him. We might presume that some of the clearly fictional traditions associating Colum Cille and Tours might derive from slightly garbled stories associating him with Tory Island. The rendering of the name Tours in Irish as *Torinis* looks suspiciously like the similar name of Tory and could easily have been the cause of confusion, not to mention facilitating the deliberate exercise of poetic licence.[37]

The *Soiscél Martain* was lost in the year 1182, when Domnall the son of Áed Ua Lochlainn went with a Cenél nEógain army to fight the 'foreigners' [*gallaibh* – the 'Normans'] at the Battle of Dunbo (now in north Co. Derry). The 'foreigners', who won the battle, carried off the *Soiscél Martain* as a trophy. It seems that it was being used then as a battle talisman in much the same manner that the *Cathach* – a late sixth- or early seventh-century manuscript of the Psalms – was used in later times.[38] This has led to a suggestion that the *Soiscél Martain* and the *Cathach* were actually one and the same

---

36 For some discussion about these connections, see Ó Riain 1985a, 121–6.   37 'Toraighe, and sometimes called Toir-inis, i.e. the island of the tower' – John O'Donovan (AFM, III, 1202, 132 n. x).   38 By tradition, the *Cathach* was said to have been written in Colum Cille's own hand. The attribution can be neither proven nor disproven, although the manuscript is roughly of the correct period (see, for example, Herity and Breen 2002).

manuscript (Ó Floinn 1995, 125). The leading ecclesiastical family on Tory Island were the Ó Robhartaighs, who may have been connected to the similarly named family at Ballymagrorty just outside Derry. There was also a Mac Robhartaigh family in south Donegal, where the *Cathach* was kept in the later Middle Ages.

The 'king of Ireland', Muirchertach Mac Lochlainn, was familiar with the use of such Columban relics. To say the least, he led an adventurous and dangerous life. In 1166, his luck ran out when even his own people, the Cenél nEógain, abandoned him at a place called Fidh Ó nEchtach (The Fews, Co. Armagh).[39]

> So there fell in that place Muirchertach (son of Niall) Ua Lochlainn, arch-king of Ireland. And he was the Augustus of all the north-west of Europe for valour and championship. And a few of Cenél nEógain were killed there [along with him], namely, thirteen men. A great marvel and wonderful deed was done then: to wit, the king of Ireland to fall without battle, without contest, after his dishonouring the successor of Patrick and the Staff of Jesus and the successor of Colum Cille [Flaithbertach Ó Brolcháin] and the *Soiscél Martain* and many clergy besides. Howbeit, his body was carried to Armagh and buried there, in dishonour of the successor of Colum Cille with his Community [*sámudh*] and Colum Cille himself and the head of the students [*toisech mac léighind*] of Daire fasted [made a ritual hunger strike] regarding it [the insult to Derry], for his being carried to burial [in Armagh].
>
> (AU)

Despite the fact that Muirchertach had fallen foul of the church – as the annals show, he had broken a solemn promise guaranteed by various clerics and relics including those from Derry – the authorities there were still furious that the 'king of Ireland' had not been returned for burial in his home place. Muirchertach's death – apart from the absence of his grave – must have been a huge blow to Derry in every respect. We have no way of knowing what patronage or 'business' he brought to the settlement, but it would be wrong to underestimate them. As a demonstration of the fall in status of the Cenél nEógain world and of Derry as a principal part of it, the following year, 1167, the new 'king of Ireland', Ruaidhrí Ó Conchobhair (O'Connor) of Connacht, led a huge colourful expedition of nobles to the north of Ireland to impose his authority. As the Annals of Tigernach described it,

---

39 He had 'blinded' – perhaps meaning 'castrated' – the east Ulster king Eochaid Ua Duinnsléibe in contravention of public oaths to protect him taken on the most important holy relics in the country and before the leading churchmen.

> A hosting by Ruaidhrí Ó Conchobhair, high-king of Ireland, and by the kings of Ireland, i.e. Dermot McCarthy, king of Desmond, and Muirchertach O'Brien, king of Dál Cais, and the kings of Leinster and Osraige with their great muster, and Dermot O'Maelseachlainn, king of Meath, and Tigernan O'Rourke, king of Ui Briúin and Conmaicni, and O'Carroll, king of Airgialla, and Ua Eochada, king of the Ulaid, with his mighty gathering; and all those kings were assembled together. Thirteen battalions they were of footsoldiers and seven of cavalry; and they reached Armagh and remained there for three nights awaiting the Cenél Conaill and the great fleet [the Norse of Dublin?]. They came round Ireland [by sea] till they reached the harbour of Derry and they went by sea and by land throughout the territory of the Cenél nEógain under cliffs and woods ... And [the Cenél nEógain] gave eight hostages to the king of Ireland.

Derry had never seen anything like it (nor has it since). The elaborate cavalcade demonstrated that the high-kingship of Ireland had passed away from the Cenél nEógain and from Derry. It would never return. To confirm that situation, in the following year,

> The chieftains of Cenél nEógain and the *comarba* of Derry came into the house of [submitted to] Ruaidhrí O'Conchubair, king of Ireland, at Athlone; and they carried [away] gold, raiment, and many cows with them to their houses.
>
> (AFM)

One of Muirchertach Mac Lochlainn's principal clerical supporters and colleagues had been Muiredach Ua Cobhthaigh, the bishop of the Cenél nEógain diocese that would eventually evolve into the diocese of Derry. He is said to have been an Augustinian canon (Leslie 1937, 1). We do not know when he was appointed, but he was present at the Synod of Kells in 1152. He is also recorded as being a witness to the foundation charter of the Cistercian abbey of *Viride Lignum* in Newry c.1156–7 (ibid.; Gwynn and Hadcock 1988, 142; Simms 1999, 153); Muirchertach Mac Lochlainn was the abbey's lay founder. According to papal documentation dated 31 May 1247, it was Muiredach who transferred the seat of the Cenél nEógain diocese from Ardstraw to Machaire Ráith Lúraigh, Maghera, Co. Derry (Gwynn and Hadcock 1988, 93). A notable sculptured lintel above the west door possibly marks the elevation of the church there to cathedral status. Muiredach is said to have done fealty to the king of England, Henry II, in 1171 or 1172, when the latter was in Ireland. Muiredach was referred to in the contemporary documentation as *ep. Tarensis*, that is *episcopus Darensis*, 'bishop of Derry' (ibid.; Byrne 1989, 280 n. 15). The

Annals of the Four Masters and the Annals of Loch Cé described him on his death in 1173 (certainly exaggeratedly) as bishop of Derry and Raphoe. The more reliable Annals of Ulster give him the following elaborate obituary:

> Muiredach Ua Cobhthaigh, bishop of Cenél nEógain and of all the north of Ireland, the son of chastity and the precious stone and the gem of purity and the shining star and the preserving casket of wisdom and the fruitful branch of the Canon and the fount of charity and meekness and kindliness and the dove for purity of heart and the turtle for innocence and the saint of God among men, after ordaining priests and deacons and persons of every [ecclesiastical] grade besides – namely, seventy priests and after renovating many churches and after consecrating churches and cemeteries and after building many monasteries and regular churches and [performing] every ecclesiastical work besides and after bestowal of food and clothing to the poor, after victory and piety and penance and pilgrimage, he sent forth his spirit unto heaven in the Dubreclés of Colum Cille in Daire, on the fourth of the Ides [10th] of February ... Now, a great marvel was wrought on the night he died; the night was illuminated from Nocturn to the call of the cock and the whole world [was] ablaze and a large mass of fire arose over the place and went south-east and every one arose, it seemed to them it was the day. And it was like that by the sea on the east.

Perhaps it was a meteor that illuminated the heavens on the night Muiredach died. Amhlaim Ua Muiredaigh, 'bishop of Ard-Macha and Cenél Feradhaigh', died in 1185 at Duncrun (north Co. Derry).[40] The annals say that he was in his eighty-sixth year and that 'he was carried honourably to Daire of Colum Cille and buried at the feet of his father [*a athar*], that is, the bishop Ua Cobhthaigh', adding that the grave was beside 'the small church' (AU). The relationship of these two men is not clear. Apart from the confusing difference in surnames, the Irish word *athar* could refer here to Amhlaim's 'spiritual father'. At the time of Muiredach's death in 1173 – although we do not know the latter's age – Amhlaim would have been about 73 himself. This would seem to preclude a father–son relationship with Muiredach.

Muiredach's death had been another major blow to Derry, with the removal of such an eminent local figure. Although we cannot prove it, it seems likely that he actually lived in Derry, at least for much of his episcopate. His death was followed quickly, in 1174, by the loss of another influential Derry patron, Gelasius the archbishop of Armagh. But worse was to come the following year, 1175.

---

40 F.J. Byrne says that he 'succeeded Muiredach Ua Cobthaig ... as bp of Ráith Lúraig/Derry, but ... appears to be reckoned as coarb of Patrick in the Book of Leinster list' (1989, 241 n. 31).

Flaithbertach Ó Brolcháin, successor of Colum Cille, tower of wisdom and hospitality, a man to whom the clergy of Ireland gave the chair of a bishop for wisdom and for his excellence and to whom was offered the succession of Iona, died piously, after choice tribulation, in the Dubreclés of Colum Cille. Gilla Mac Liac Ua Branain was instituted in his stead in the succession of Colum Cille.

(AU)

Flaithbertach was probably one of the most important people ever to live in Derry. Clearly, he had been embarked on creating a new institutional future for the Columban *familia*, with Derry as its spiritual and – from his perspective – historically appropriate headquarters. But he was too late. In 1169, one of the most momentous events in the history of Ireland had occurred, the arrival of the Anglo-Normans in Leinster. Among other things, that event was to have profound implications for the *familia* of Colum Cille, because many of the most important Columban churches were located in areas that quickly came under the control of the 'invaders' (Herbert 1988, 122). Together with the great twelfth-century ecclesiastical reforms – such as the changeover to a formal diocesan system – the impact of the Anglo-Normans dealt a final blow to the possibility of the Columban confederation reorganizing along the lines of the Continental religious orders like the Augustinians or the Cistercians, if that is what Flaithbertach had intended. In 1176, Kells was destroyed. In 1179, control of the Columban monastery on Lambay off the coast of north Co. Dublin was transferred to the canons of the church of Dublin. The church of Sord Coluim Chille (Swords, Co. Dublin) was also transferred to the control of the archbishop of Dublin, while Moen Coluim Chille (Moone, Co. Kildare) became part of the possessions of the bishop of Glendalough. Durrow – the only church we can be certain that Columba definitely founded in Ireland – also quickly came within the Anglo-Norman sphere of influence. The character of the church at Raphoe had changed also when it became the seat of the Cenél Conaill diocese. When Gilla Mac Liac Ua Branain succeeded Flaithbertach as *comarba* in 1175, his title indicated little more than that he was abbot of the Dubreclés of Derry.

It was the ultimate paradox. For some time, Derry had been attempting to cultivate a reputation of pre-eminence among the Columban monasteries. In the first half of the twelfth century, it had been at the forefront of moves to bring the Irish church fully into line with the rest of Christendom, drawing it away from the more exotic eccentricities of 'Celtic' monasticism – some of which may have been set in train by Columba himself in the sixth century. Just at the point when Derry's claims to primacy came to be recognized, the world it sought to lead collapsed about it – partly from the forces that it itself had set in motion.

There was one final show of strength. About the year 1200, Reginald son of Somerled of the Isles founded a Benedictine abbey and an Augustinian nunnery on Iona. Bethóc – Somerled's daughter – became prioress of the nunnery, which possibly had connections with similar institutions in Ireland. Some of the architectural details on the surviving early parts of the building are comparable with contemporary buildings in Ireland.[41] In December 1203, a letter from Pope Innocent III to its abbot, Celestinus, took the newly established Benedictine abbey under papal protection. Unlike the nunnery, which was located about five hundred yards to the south, a huge new abbey building in the contemporary European style was commenced for the Benedictines on the site of the ancient Columban monastery. There was fury in Ireland about this, as recorded in the annals for the following year.

> A monastery was built by Cellach [Celestinus] ... in the centre of the enclosure [*ar lár croí*] of Iona, without any right, in dishonour of the Community [*muinnter*] of Iona, so that he wrecked the place [*in baile*] greatly. A hosting, however, was made by the clergy of Ireland, namely, by Florence Ua Cerballáin, bishop of Tír Eógain [equivalent to the diocese of Derry] and by Mael Ísu Ua Dorig [O'Deery ?], that is, bishop of Tír Conaill [equivalent to the diocese of Raphoe], and by the abbot of the monastery of Paul and Peter in Armagh and by Amalgaidh Ua Fergail, abbot of the monastery of [*abad Reiclesa*][42] Doire, and by Ainmire Ua Cobhthaigh and a large number of the community [*muinnter*] of Doire and a large number of the clergy of the north [of Ireland], so that they razed the monastery, according to the law of the Church. That Amalgaidh aforesaid took the abbacy of Iona by selection of foreigners [the Norse of the Hebrides] and Gaidhil.
>
> (AU 1204)

These building operations on Iona (or 'destruction', depending on your point of view) must have been facilitated by the death in the previous year of Domnall Ó Brolcháin, who was described then as 'prior' of Iona (AU 1203). The expedition by this united bloc of northern Irish clergy proved to be no more than a futile attempt to stop the development of the new monastery and install the abbot of Derry (*comarba Coluim Cille*, as he would have seen himself) in charge there. Amhalgaidh Ua Ferghail's authority could not have lasted for long, if at all; there is no further mention of it. The Benedictine abbey was completed shortly afterwards and expanded greatly over time, particularly in the fifteenth century. It still stands as the main architectural

---

41 For example, with some architectural details at Jerpoint Abbey, Co. Kilkenny, and Dunbrody Abbey, Co. Wexford (RCAHMS 1982, 161–3; see also Fisher 2005, 87).
42 Presumably the same institution as the Dubreclés.

feature on the island, largely obliterating – as the clergy of the north of Ireland had feared it would – almost all of the remains of the early Christian monastery.[43]

The account of the expedition to stop the building of the new abbey is the last mention of Iona in the Irish annals, except for one passing reference in 1249. There continued to be some contacts, however, of which one of the most intriguing from a Derry perspective is the fifteenth-century inscription recording the work of 'Donald Ó Brolcháin' on one of the pillar capitals in the Iona abbey church, which has been mentioned above.[44]

After 1220, there are no further references in the annals to the *comarba* of Colum Cille in connection with Derry. As we will see in ch. 8, in 1397, when it was visited by the archbishop of Armagh, John Colton, we hear of the 'monastery of the Canons Regular [Augustinians], called the Black Abbey [*Cella Nigra*] of Derry'.[45] Like many similar ancient Irish churches, at some stage in the twelfth or early thirteenth century,[46] the Columban community of Derry had fully adopted the rule of St Augustine. It became a house of Augustinian canons of Arrouaise, subject to the abbey of SS Peter and Paul in Armagh. It survived in that fashion throughout the later Middle Ages, until the English conquest of Ulster and the dissolution of the monasteries in the Gaelic territories in the late sixteenth century.

The formal position of the *comarba Coluim Cille* as leader of the saint's *familia* was terminated with the end of the *familia* itself. When we next hear of this title, it is being used more generically, in connection with several of the individual old Columban churches. The *comarba* of Colum Cille at Drumcliff who died in 1252 was 'the richest and most prosperous man of his time in Ireland and the most esteemed, most charitable and most generous'. When Manus Ó Domhnaill was 'inaugurated' as chieftain of Tír Chonaill in 1537, it was 'by the successors [*comharbaibh*] of St Colum Cille with the permission and by the advice of the nobles [*maithe*] of Cenél Conaill, both lay and ecclesiastical' (AFM). The former were almost certainly the clergy of Kilmacrenan, perhaps supported by ecclesiastics from other older Columban churches.[47]

Between 1166 and 1175 – with the death of Muirchertach Mac Lochlainn, Muiredach Ua Cobhthaig, Gelasius and finally Flaithbertach Ó Brolcháin – Derry lost all the members of that great coalition of leaders, benefactors and supporters that had brought the settlement to the forefront of religious and political affairs in Ireland. Although initially there seems to have been little impact, the real effect was in the long term. In addition, Mac Lochlainn power generally began to fade after Muirchertach's death, giving way eventually to

---

43 For a full description of the surviving remains, see RCAHMS 1982. For a review of the history of archaeological excavation on Iona, see O'Sullivan 1999.  44 RCAHMS, 106–7, 144.
45 Reeves 1850.  46 The precise date is not known, but see discussion above, pp 66–7.
47 John O'Donovan argued that these included the bishop of Derry (AFM, V, 1439–40).

the supremacy in Cenél nEógain of the O'Neills. Events in other parts of the country also, particularly the arrival of the Anglo-Normans, exacerbated the process of marginalization of Derry that had already been set in train. But, for at least another half century or so, the effects would not be felt to any great extent. If anything, Derry was still to experience its medieval heyday, although, in reality, that would also be its 'swansong'.

CHAPTER 6

# The medieval settlement: its layout and structures

The ecclesiastical settlement of Derry was located on a hill on the west bank of the River Foyle. The original hill, which can be reconstructed more or less from modern contour maps, was effectively an island, largely cut off on its western side by an abandoned but still marshy former river channel that could only be crossed by two or three artificial causeways or bridges. That 'island' was about two hundred acres and its highest point, on its north-eastern side, rose to about 120 feet above sea level (fig. 18). The river as it passed the hill was fast-flowing, about forty feet in depth and over a thousand feet wide. It was still tidal as it passed the hill (and for another twenty miles or so inland). It seems that the local inhabitants made no distinction between the river and its associated lough, seeing the whole thing – from the outlet to the ocean right up to the junction of the rivers Finn and Mourne – as the one combined natural feature, known to them as Loch Feabhail.[1] A lot of the strand and floodplain of the river close to the modern city centre has been reclaimed incrementally since the seventeenth century, so that its present appearance and dimensions differ notably from what they would have been in medieval times. Up to the seventeenth century, the river came right up to what are now the city walls in Shipquay Place. There was no bridge across the Foyle prior to the eighteenth century and the river could be crossed in medieval times only by ferry, connecting on the east bank with the road that wound its way across northern Ireland to join the famous Slighe Midhluachra (Ó Lochlainn 1940, 472).

By comparison with the surrounding countryside today and as reported by Elizabethan observers around 1600, the parts of the hill not built over seem to have been good agricultural land. There was clearly an impressive grove of oak trees growing on the island, which gave the place its root name, *Daire*. That grove was protected well into late medieval times by a range of folk beliefs that linked the trees with the settlement's patron saint, Colum Cille. Some of the stories about those trees seem to suggest that they were guarded also by what were probably even more ancient taboos that, although partly disguised with a Columban 'veneer', had probably originated in pre-Christian times. According to Manus Ó Domhnaill:

---

[1] However, Adomnán c.700 uses the word *flumen* 'river' in a reference to the Foyle near Derry.

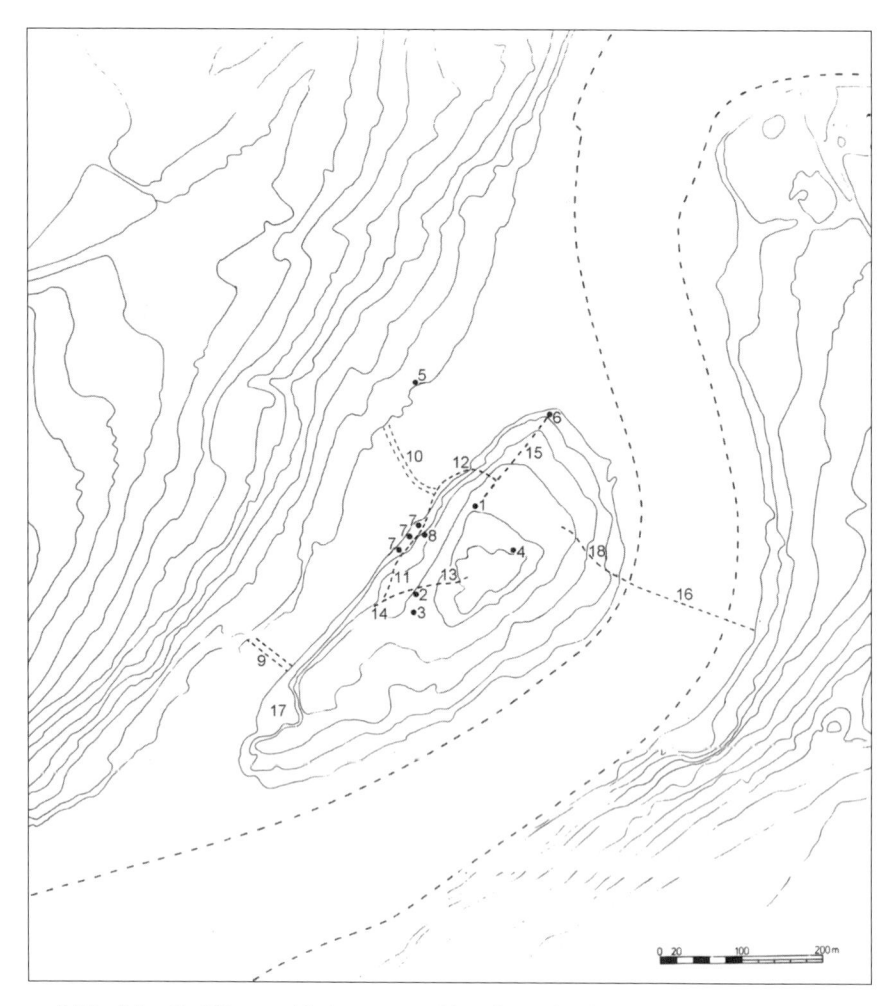

18 The 'island' of Derry with the suggested locations of various medieval structures and places. The numbers are keyed to the descriptions in the main text (see pp 86–92).

Colum Cille loved Derry very much and he was reluctant to cut or fell the grove of trees there. For, on account of the proximity of the wood, when he was building the oratory that is now known as the Black Church he could not find an appropriate space so that its altar would be facing towards the east. And so much did he not want to cut the trees that he ordered that the side of the church should face east. The proof that the altar where he himself said mass was on the side, is clear to all today [1532] from the situation of the church. But he left instructions to his successors that any tree that fell by itself, or was blown down by the wind in that place, should be left uncut for nine days and then it was to be shared out among the people of the settlement, both good and bad. A third of it was to be saved for the visitors in the guest-house and a tenth was to be given to the poor. And this is the verse he made after going into exile in Scotland, showing that there was nothing worse for him than the cutting of the trees in Derry:

> Though truly I'm afraid
> Of death itself and Hell,
> I'm frankly more afraid
> Of an axe-sound, back in Derry.
>
> (Lacey 1998, 54)

As we have seen, the earliest surviving written account of Colum Cille's alleged foundation of Derry occurs in the preface to the poem *Noli Pater Indulgere*, itself said to have been composed by the saint to protect the trees of Derry. Slightly contradicting this, however, is the legend in the same preface of Colum Cille burning the place before establishing his church there. The latter story might be a reflection of some ancient rite of exorcism – or at least of a later perceived need that there should have been some form of ritual cleansing to mark the site's transition from pagan sanctuary to Christian church. Whatever the origins of the beliefs about the 'sanctity' of the trees of Derry, clearly they were exploited in medieval times in order to protect the property rights of the monks arising from them. For instance, the Annals of the Four Masters has a curious entry for the year 1188, relating to an incident that seems to confirm the power of Colum Cille's alleged taboo.

> Domhnall Ua Canannáin wounded his foot with his own axe at Derry, as he was cutting a piece of wood, and he died of the wound, in consequence of the curse [*eascainne*] of the community [*sámhtha*] of Colum Cille.

Manus Ó Domhnaill records another Derry tree story:

> There was a special yew tree in front of the Dubreclés where Colum Cille and the saints used to say their office. There were a thousand angels keeping guard above that yew; as Colum Cille himself said in these verses:
>
>> This is the 'Yew of the Saints',
>> Where ten hundred angels fair,
>> Would come to me, together,
>> Side by side, above it there.
>>
>> Dear to me that yew tree;
>> Would that I were near that place,
>> At the entrance to the Black Church,
>> On the left, a thing of grace.
>>
>> (Lacey 1998, 104)

In the probably twelfth-century sentimental verses put into the mouth of Colum Cille when he was said to be leaving Ireland for Scotland, the saint is depicted as returning to the topic of his special attachment to the trees of Derry.

> Derry of oaks, let us leave it,
> Tearful with gloom and with sorrow,
> Leaving here, broken-hearted,
> To go to the land of the strangers.
>
> Beloved tree-grove, out of which I was sent,
> Banished, though still without guilt.
>
> (Lacey 1998, 106)

The annals record the accidental destruction on several occasions in the twelfth century of some of those trees, recording the incidents as both natural as well as human disasters. In 1146,

> a great wind storm occurred on the third day of December, which caused a great destruction of woods throughout Ireland; it prostrated sixty trees in Doire Coluim Chille, and killed and smothered many persons in the church [*cill*].
>
> (AFM)

The *cill* in question was presumably, at least in part, built of wood. Again in 1178 a violent windstorm occurred causing great destruction of trees – apparently especially of oaks: 'it prostrated one hundred and twenty trees in Doire Coluim Chille' (AFM). The destruction of 180 (presumably, mature) trees on the hill of Derry in a space of just over thirty years gives us some indication of how significant and extensive the grove of trees there was. Apart from the legends, the fact that these incidents were recorded is surely testament to how seriously the disasters were perceived locally, and how greatly the trees were prized.

Adomnán was the first person to leave us any indication of the physical nature of Derry when, in the *Vita Columbae* written about 700, he told us that there was already by his time (and probably by the time of Columba, a century previously) a church (*eclesia*) and a, presumably Christian, burial place (*sepulchrum*) there. He also seems to indicate that its port (*portus*) was well established by then as a place of embarkation and landing on journeys between Ireland and Britain. After Adomnán, there are no further records of physical structures in Derry for about three hundred years, although the annalistic references to individuals and events there clearly imply buildings of various sorts.

## The medieval settlement: its layout and structures

The preface to *Noli Pater Indugere* claims that the poem was composed at 'the door of the hermitage' (*dorus disirt*) of Daire Calgaich. The date of that text is generally reckoned to be late tenth or early eleventh century. The Annals of Ulster says that in the year 1122 the bishop Máel Coluim Ua Brolcháin 'died on pilgrimage (*ina ailithri*) in the hermitage (*i ndisiurt*) of Daire'. Again, we have no specific information about the nature of the disiurt, but physical structures are clearly implied.[2] The so-called Miscellaneous Irish Annals records that in 1135 'Derry, including houses (*tige*) and church (*teampull*) [was] burned'. The Annals of the Four Masters describing the same event has the plural 'churches' (*co na theamplaibh*). The same annals claim that Derry was burned (*losccadh*) again in 1149. According to the Annals of Ulster, in 1166 'the greater part of Daire Coluim Chille was burned (*cremata est*), and the Dubreclés was burned (*do loscadh*)'. In the medieval literature, the Dubreclés was believed to have been the church originally founded by Colum Cille. Whatever the nature of the building or its actual age, it seems that it – or at least its site – was already fairly old by the mid-twelfth century.[3] We are not given any further information about the causes of those fires and, while the wooden buildings in medieval settlements were vulnerable to accidental burning, there were also acts of deliberate violence. In 1177, for example,

> Niall O'Gormley, king of Fir Magh Itha and Cenél nÉnnai, was killed by Clann Diarmata [Clondermot, on the east bank of the Foyle opposite Derry] in the centre of Daire Coluim Chille, and a house was burned on him so that he came out from it and was killed at the door of the house. However, Donnchadh Ó Caireallan chief of Clann Diarmata made peace with Colum Cille and with the Community [*muintir*] of Derry on behalf of himself and his son and his grandsons – to wit, the monastic service [*mainchene*] of himself for ever and of his son and his grandsons and his posterity to doom unto Colum Cille and unto the Community of Daire and [gave] a ballybetagh [of land] in the neighbourhood of Domnach Mór [Donaghmore in east Co. Donegal]. And the *Mac Riabhach* ['gray son'], that is, the best goblet that was in Ireland, was given to the Community of Daire, in pledge for three score cows. And [he agreed] to make a house for the cleric whose house was burned upon O'Gormley and to pay him all the chattel that they burned about him. The Clann Diarmata also made peace on their own behalf.
>
> (AU)

---

2 See above, pp 56–7 n. 8, where it was suggested that the *disiurt* might have included a hospital of some sort.   3 See above, pp 66–7. Presumably the actual building would have been reconstructed, probably many times, since the original foundation.

The house in question here belonged to a cleric. As well as monastic communal dwelling places, there must have been other houses belonging to or at least lived in by clerical officials. At an Inquisition in 1609, the jurors found that 'tyme out of mynde' the bishop of Derry had occupied 'one house or castle, with a garden plott thereunto adjoyninge, scituate on the south side of the cathedral church nere the longe [round] tower'. The bishop also had an orchard on the north east side of the island for which he paid the Mac Lochlainn erenagh ten 'white' [silver?] groats annually. Houses, apparently for the use of lay people rather than clerics, are referred to a number of times in the annals for the twelfth and thirteenth centuries. For example, in 1214 the Ó Catháin chieftain and the Fir na Craibhe 'came to Daire to seize a house against the sons of Mac Lochlainn' (AU). In 1162,

> Total separation of the houses from the churches of Derry was made by the *comarba* of Colum Cille (i.e. Flaithbertach [Ó Brolcháin]) and the king of Ireland i.e. Muirchertach Ua Lochlainn, in which were demolished more than eighty houses and the cashel [enclosing stone wall] of the centre was built by the *comarba* of Colum Cille who pronounced a malediction on anyone who would transgress it.
>
> (AU)

It is not absolutely clear what Flaithbertach was doing, but it seems that he was separating the lay and ecclesiastical areas of the settlement, and notably enclosing his own monastery with a stone wall [*caisil in erlair*]. He augmented the protective qualities of that wall with the malediction. We may get some idea of what he was trying to achieve by comparing the massive cashel enclosure around the monastic settlement on Inishmurray, Co. Sligo (O'Sullivan and Ó Carragáin 2008, esp. 66-9) and the stone gateway at Glendalough, Co. Wicklow (Leask n.d., 30-2).

Flaithbertach was clearly involved in a major reform of Derry, both physically and institutionally. As well as changes to its layout, he was evidently also intent on beautifying its buildings. In 1155 (AU), he made a door for the *Tempull* in Derry. The recording of that event surely suggests the insertion of a monumental doorway, possibly in the latest Hiberno-Romanesque style along the lines of the details added around much the same time to the relatively nearby churches at Banagher, Bovevagh and Dungiven in Co. Derry. In 1192, the Ó Catháin chieftain and his wife similarly presented a 'door' to the refectory (*dorus proinntigi*) of the Dubreclés.

The annalistic references are ambiguous about the number of separate churches in Derry at any particular time during the Middle Ages, but, as with other similar monastic 'cities' such as Clonmacnoise and Devenish, we can assume that there was certainly more than one such building. In fact, by the late twelfth century there seems to have been at least four separate churches in Derry: (i) the Dubreclés monastic church (also seemingly called the reclés – AU 1204 – unless the latter was a separate building which seems unlikely); (ii) the *Tempull Mór* (for which see below); and (iii) the *Tempull Becc* (AU 1155? and 1185). Although we have no specific references to it, there was presumably also a separate nuns' church (see ch. 9, below). There were also other sacred 'spaces' and 'monuments'. For instance, in 1204 Derry was burned from the graveyard (*relic*) of St Martin to the well (*tíbrait*) of St Adomnán (AU).

The settlement at Derry is described as a *civitas* in 882 (AU), as a former *rígdún* 'royal fortress' and a *cathair* in the Middle Irish Life of Colum Cille, and as a *baile* in some of the additions to that text (Herbert 1988, 229–31). In 1173 (AU) and 1212 (AU) and in Manus Ó Domhnaill's *Betha Colaim Chille* (written in 1532), it is also referred to as a *baile*. The precise nature and size of that settlement at the various stages of its development eludes us, but, presumably, the fact that eighty houses were demolished in 1162 must imply that a lot more than that number were left standing or were rebuilt shortly afterwards. What is clear is that by the late twelfth century, Derry was much more than a simple religious community. It had probably not been such for several centuries at least. The evidence, although meagre, suggests that lay people as well as the clerics were living and going about their ordinary domestic business in Derry. If not a town in the full medieval sense, then we are surely permitted to describe Derry – in the twelfth and thirteenth centuries at least – as a township.

A number of entries in the 1160s – that is, after the commencement of Flaithbertach Ó Brolcháin's reorganization – mentions the *sámad* ('community') of Colum Cille in connection with Derry (AU 1163, 1164, 1166). The annals seem to be making a distinction with the *Muinnter Daire*, which is also mentioned several times (AU 1124, 1177 (3 times), 1204, 1214, 1220 (5 times)). Although the Irish word *muintir* may have derived from the Latin *monasterium*, implying a distinct ecclesiastical – indeed 'monastic' – community, by the twelfth century it seems as if its meaning had widened to include the inhabitants of the settlement generally, both lay and clerical.[4] *Sámad Coluim Cille* on the other hand seems to indicate the specifically Columban monastic community.

Between 1177 and 1261, the annals record a long series of incidents in Derry of a strictly secular nature: murders (1177, 1213, 1214, 1261); blood feuds (1177, 1180); thieving (1196, 1215); an execution (1196); a possible rape (1223); the deliberate burning of a house (1177); pilgrimages of lay aristocrats (1188, 1215); and a marriage arrangement (1259). There were also at least four separate visits by groups of Normans to Derry during this period (1197, 1198,

---

4 See *RIA Dictionary*, 470, col. 191, *muinter*; for *sámad/sámud*, see 521, col. 5.

1212, 1213), involving the plundering of the settlement. It is almost certain that the Mac Lochlainn family – right up to those of its members who claimed the title of 'king of Ireland' – had been living in Derry or its vicinity from at least Domnall Ua Lochlainn's reign at the beginning of the twelfth century. We have seen how the high-king Muirchertach Mac Lochlainn was actively involved in the 1160s reorganizing the settlement and erecting new structures that, presumably, were suitably 'grandiose' (relatively speaking) in character. In 1196 (AU), his son, another Muirchertach, was buried in Derry – as the latter's great-grandfather, Domnall, almost certainly had been – and there are several other references to the family's involvement with the settlement. The identification of a Mac Lochlainn ('Loughlina' < Lochlinnach) as one of the two 'herenaghes' of Derry mentioned in the 1609 inquisition (see below) suggests that the family maintained a presence in Derry throughout the whole of the late medieval period, although evidently in somewhat more reduced circumstances than when their ancestors could claim the title of 'king of Ireland'.

We have very little information about the economic basis of the settlement. Obviously natural resources such as the land and its crops, the oak-grove itself and the fisheries on the Foyle and other local rivers would have contributed to the economy. The seventeenth-century inquisitions show that the ecclesiastical institutions on the island owned various parcels of land,[5] some at quite a distance. A document dated 11 October 1603 mentions

> Clancolumbkille [Glencolumbkille] 5 qrs [quarters of land] – the fishing of the bay or port called Tellin [nearby Teelin] in McSwine Banagh country – the 4 qrs of Gartan; [belonging to] the estate of the late monastery or house of canons of Collumkille de Derry; rent £2.
>
> (*CPRI* James I, 8 quoted in Manning 2002, 46)

In 1215, Áed Mac Lochlainn made a foray (*crech*) against the *comarba* of Colum Cille and stole a herd of cattle (AU). The Annals of the Four Masters adds that 'before the expiration of the year afterwards', Áed was killed 'through the miracles of God and Colum Cille'. The *cuan*, 'harbour', or *portus* of Derry is mentioned several times throughout the Middle Ages, and an entry in the Annals of Loch Cé for 1217 seems to suggest the possibility of sea-going fishermen from there, or at least from its vicinity. In the mid-twelfth century, Flaithbertach Ó Brolcháin raised large amounts of revenue from visitations to the Columban churches and other related locations throughout Ireland. Presumably, some of the wealth he collected went into supporting his major

---

5 See, for instance, the map of and commentary on some of those parcels of land: Appendix 1 in Bryson 2001, 194–6.

building operations in Derry. Entries in the annals suggest that patronage, offerings and compensations made by kings and local aristocrats formed a sizeable element in the wealth of the settlement. For example, in 1177, as mentioned above, Donnchadh Ó Caireallan confirmed the monastic service (*mainchene*) of himself, his son and grandsons forever to Colum Cille and the Community of Derry. He also donated a ballybetagh of land close to the church at Donaghmore (in the fertile countryside of east Donegal), as well as 'the best goblet (*corn*) that was in Ireland' as a pledge for three score cows. That object and four more of 'the best drinking horns [or 'chalices'] in Ireland' were stolen from the altar of the *Tempull Mór* in 1195 (AU). The treasure (*seód*) of the 'people of Derry and the north of Ireland', stolen from the monastery church (*teampall an Recclesa*) by the Normans in 1213 (AFM), had possibly been lodged there for safe-keeping. There is a reference in a late twelfth-century Dublin Roll of Names to a *Robertus de Deri*. Whereas neither the place of origin nor the occupation of Robertus is certain, it is possible that he was a Derry merchant of some sort.[6] Unfortunately, the earliest evidence for a commercial transaction in the settlement – the fictional purchase of drink in a tavern – does not occur until the early sixteenth century (see ch. 9).

Derry appears to have been settled continuously – admittedly with some ups and downs – from at least the middle of the sixth century down to the end of the sixteenth, when it passed into the English sphere of influence.[7] During that long period, the settlement underwent many changes. Virtually none of that is reflected above ground today. The building of the various English fortifications from 1600 onwards and the burning by Sir Cahir O'Doherty in 1608 of the first small chartered city there ensured that little of ancient Derry was left by the time that plantation Londonderry was being laid out from 1610 onwards. Neither has very much archaeological evidence come to light. A section of the seventeenth-century city walls on their western side is said to have been constructed from the debris of the destroyed medieval buildings. It may be significant that this section was not fronted by an external ditch, the fill from which was used elsewhere to form the earthen rampart at the core of the stone walls. However, a ditch would not be *as* necessary along that stretch because of the steepness of the hillside, and detailed examination and restoration work on the walls over many decades has failed to identify any pieces of medieval cut stone.

It is still possible to recover some idea of the location and nature of at least some of the major buildings – and perhaps even of some of the 'streets' – of

6 Gilbert 1870, 16. I am grateful to John Bradley for this reference.   7 Although for roughly a century, from a major fire in 788 until 882, there are effectively no references to the life of the settlement (see ch. 4, above). It may have been so severely damaged in 788 – coincidentally also losing its major Cenél Conaill patrons at the time – that it was effectively abandoned for a while.

the medieval settlement, although the precise evolution of the settlement over time is another matter.

1 The Dubreclés, *Cella Nigra*, house of Canons Regular or abbey or monastery of Colum Cille is mentioned in a wide range of sources between 1166 and 1609 in contexts that indicate that the same institution is being referred to. Various translations and explanations of the name have been suggested down the years. Above, it was suggested that it might derive from the black cloaks worn by the Augustinian canons. A recent suggested translation is 'black ascetic complex of Columba' (Ó Carragáin 2010, 267). The same author notes:

> The Duibreiclés may have been built, or rebuilt, to house associative relics [of Colum Cille] that embodied the site's new-found authority [following the transfer to Derry of the successorship of Colum Cille]. As Aidan MacDonald has suggested, these may have included what seems to have been Derry's most prized relic: the book known as the *Soiscéla Martain*.[8]

Despite the fact that its church had probably been built and reconstructed – both in wood and in stone – several times since the sixth century, not to mention the question of who actually founded it, the medieval Dubreclés was still believed to have been Colum Cille's original monastic church.[9] An appendix to the Middle Irish Life of Colum Cille mentions the *crann caingel* of the Dubreclés, which Herbert translated as the 'chancel screen' (1988, 246, 268).[10] A refectory is mentioned in 1192 (AU), confirming that by then at very least it was definitely a community house. An unidentified *cellóir mór* is mentioned in an annal entry for 1214 (AU). His role was probably that of manciple or cellarer, responsible for the acquisition of provisions for the monastery. In 1397, there were 'suitable chambers' there for the accommodation of John Colton, archbishop of Armagh, and his attendants, and a refectory and dormitory for the canons. In 1532, Manus Ó Domhnaill refers to a cemetery (*reilg*), a guest-house (*tigh na n-aidhedh*), and a special yew tree in front of the entrance. As we

---

8 Ibid., 268: MacDonald 1999, 263–4. From various references to it from the late tenth century onwards, another important relic in Derry in medieval times was the object known as St Mo Bíí's belt. We do not know exactly what this was, but presumably it was similar to the surviving Moylough Belt Shrine. 9 For this kind of thinking about ancient sacred sites, both in medieval Ireland and in similar cultures, see Ó Carragáin 2010, especially the section 'Churches as associative relics', 149–56. For a modern example in Derry itself, see the section on the Long Tower church in ch. 10, below. 10 The appendix has not been dated, but above I have suggested a connection with events in 1161.

saw above, he records a legend that because of the disposition of the trees in Colum Cille's time the altar of the Dubreclés was positioned on the side of the church facing east – presumably rather than in the usual narrow end, as 'is clear to all today [in 1532]'. The church, together with what were probably ancillary buildings, is shown on several early seventeenth-century maps. It used to be the received wisdom that the abbey church was renovated for use by the first English settlers in Derry, prior to the construction of St Columb's Cathedral (1628–33). However, Henry Jefferies has argued recently that that church was in fact a new building (1999, 175, 196; 2000, 146).[11] Various replacement churches have occupied the general site since then, including the present St Augustine's Chapel of Ease.

2 The *Tempull Mór* was erected in 1164. The entries in the annals are somewhat contradictory, but suggest a length of between 80 and 90 feet (AU, AFM). Given the contemporary links between Derry and Armagh, Ó Carragáin has suggested that this church might have been 'consciously designed to be a respectful margin shorter than Armagh's [much older] *damliac mór*', which he argues was 100 feet long (2010, 63).[12] An annal entry for the previous year, 1163, records the building by 'Flaithbertach ... and by the Community [*Sámad*] of Colum Cille in the space of twenty days' of a lime-kiln whose dimensions are given ambiguously as 'sixty feet on every side'.[13] Most commentators have suggested that the lime-kiln was built in preparation for the construction of the *Tempull Mór*.

The church was built under the patronage of Muirchertach Mac Lochlainn, who was involved with a number of other major ecclesiastical building projects. These included the architecturally revolutionary new Cistercian monastery at Mellifont (Co. Louth), which was consecrated in 1157. Neville's map of the Siege of Derry *c*.1690 shows the ruins of the *Tempull Mór* as a cruciform structure (Thomas 2005, map

---

11 In support of this, Jefferies quotes from a 1607 survey by George Montgomery, the first Protestant bishop of Derry: 'In the same city is the church of St Augustine, near the governor's house, which is newly built though still without a roof. In times past, there used to be a church in the grounds of the house' (2000, 146). Contradicting this somewhat, and supporting the traditional interpretation, the State Papers for July 1608 reveal that when Derry was burned by Cahir O'Doherty the previous April, the church 'was not fired' probably 'in devotion to their solemn Collam Kill, the patron of that place' (see below, ch. 10). The resolution of this conundrum may be that the new church was raised out of the ruins of the old one.   12 Given the suggested ideal external breadth-to-length ratios for Irish churches as 1:1.5 (Ó Carragáin 2010, 63), it is likely that the *Tempull Mór* was about 54 to 60 feet wide.   13 AU. This is the first use of the term *sámad* in connection with Derry. This, too, is the entry that identifies Flaithbertach as the 'son of the bishop Ó Brolcháin'. Both expressions are repeated in 1164.

11; see fig. 17, above). The presence of transepts in a twelfth-century Irish church would be very unusual; they could have been added later or there may have been an attempt in Derry to replicate, for example, the plan of the church at Mellifont. An obscure reference to *cloc in tempaill* (usually translated as 'the [top] stone of the church') in 1164 (AU) and the recording of the collapse of its *beand* ('peak') on 8 February 1250 (AU) could possibly indicate that, at least originally, the church may have had some sort of stone roof.[14] The reference would surely have been to the *cloigtech* if the round tower or another belfry structure was intended. In 1247, the *Tempull Mór* became the cathedral of the diocese of Derry when the bishop's seat was moved there from Maghera. It was also the church of the parish to which it gave its name in the anglicized form Templemore. It was there that Archbishop Colton officiated during his visitation in 1397 (see ch. 8). In 1469, the church was 'all but roofless', in need of repair and lacking in 'chalices, books, vestments and other ecclesiastical necessaries'. An indulgence was granted to aid in its restoration. Whether or not the restoration happened, in 1566 it seems to have been used as an ammunition store by the English forces that occupied the settlement. An accidental explosion is said to have damaged the building irretrievably. A small inscribed tablet in the entrance lobby of St Columb's Cathedral is said to have come from the *Tempull Mór* (fig. 30).[15] It is clear from Neville's map and other sources that the building was located in the general area now occupied by the Long Tower church complex – including the surrounding schools and graveyards.

3 The round or 'Long' tower or the 'high piramid or tourret of antiquity' is shown on several early seventeenth-century maps, but does not appear on the maps made at the end of that century. It was in the general vicinity of the *Tempull Mór*, almost certainly to the south of it.

4 A 'ruined chapel or house of nuns' is mentioned in three inquisitions held from 1602 to 1609. From the location given in 1609, it would seem that it can be equated with the church indicated on a number of early seventeenth-century maps and described by Docwra in 1600 as 'the walls of an old cathedral church', which he fortified because it

14 The suggestion might seem far-fetched; the widest surviving stone-roofed early church in Ireland is just over 17ft in breadth. The references might alternatively refer to a spire or steeple of some sort, perhaps like the small attached round tower on St Kevin's Kitchen at Glendalough.   15 It reads: *In Templo/Verus Deus/Est Vereque/Colendus* 'The true God is in the church and truly he is to be worshipped'. The lettering does not appear to be particularly Irish or medieval; however, it is possible that the stone was brought from the *Tempull Mór* and inscribed after its transfer.

was on the highest part of the hill. The reference to a cathedral is puzzling, as the *Tempull Mór* seems to have been destroyed in 1567 (see ch. 9). However, in 1590, an ordination was conducted in the *ecclesia cathedrali Derensis* (Martin, 1968). It is possible that the nuns' chapel served as a pro-cathedral during this period. It seems from Thomas Raven's map of the plantation city made in 1622 (Thomas 2005, map 9) that it was planned originally to build the new cathedral (St Columb's) lower down the hillside to the north-east, but by 1628 the present site was being built on. It is likely that the second site was chosen because of its long-established ecclesiastical connection. The nuns' chapel was on or near that site. The early seventeenth-century inquisitions identified it as a Cistercian house, *Conventus Sanctae Mariae* (Bryson 2001, 195–6). Although we know very little about it, it is said to have been founded by the O'Neills in 1218 (Hogan 1998, 128). Such a date would certainly be consistent with O'Neill influence in Derry. As outlined above, however, in 1134 Bé Bhinn Mac Conchaille, the *banairchinneach* of Derry, died. Almost certainly, she was the abbess of a convent of nuns. Just as the Columban monks of Derry adopted the Augustinian rule in the late twelfth or early thirteenth centuries, it may be that an older convent of nuns adopted the Cistercian rule in the early thirteenth century. Abbot Thomas Hervey of Mellifont (Co. Louth) is said to have reported the following to a General Chapter of the order in 1512:

> the total ruin and desolation of the nunnery of the Blessed Mary of Derry, which has for a long time lacked both an abbess and regular persons of the order. As a consequence, its income and revenues are put to profane and forbidden uses instead of being applied to the celebration of divine service and the utility of the order.
>
> (Hogan 1998, 128)

5  The 1609 inquisition refers to a 'priorie or religious house of begging friars of St Frauncis ... with a churchyard' on the north side of the bog near the island of Derry. There is no other evidence of a Franciscan house in Derry during the Middle Ages. Almost certainly, the reference should have been to the Dominican priory, which will be discussed in the next chapter.

6  A small tower house is shown on several early seventeenth-century maps. This belonged to the Uí Domhnaill and will be discussed in ch. 9.

*Medieval and monastic Derry: sixth century to 1600*

19 'St Columba's Well' in the Bogside. The late nineteenth-century cast iron pump is said to mark one of the three wells shown on Francis Neville's 1690 map (see fig. 17). John Bryson (pers. comm.) suggests that this is actually the site of St Martin's Well, with the locations of St Columba's (in the middle) and St Adomnán's wells slightly further to the west.

7 A well of St Adomnán is referred to in 1204 (AU), and a holy well miraculously initiated by Colum Cille and named after him is mentioned in the mid-twelfth-century Life and by Manus Ó Domhnaill. The sketch map of 1600 shows two 'fountaines of Collom kills well under the hyll'. Three more-or-less adjacent wells are marked on a number of other early maps (see fig. 17). Traditionally, those wells, which lay along one side of the street called St Columb's Wells (formerly, St

*The medieval settlement: its layout and structures*

**20** 'St Columb's Stone'. Since 1898, this bullaun stone has been built into a modern calvary scene in the Long Tower churchyard. It was formerly located in St Columb's Wells street, near the sites of the three holy wells (after Colby 1837, 26).

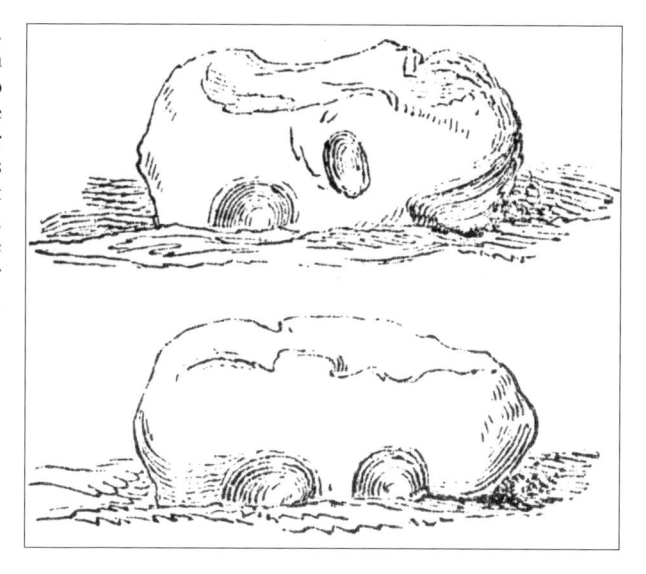

Columb's Lane), were dedicated to SS Colum Cille, Adomnán and Martin of Tours. Their general position is well known; one of them is still in existence and is marked by a nineteenth-century cast-iron pump (fig. 19).

8  A bullaun stone, which formerly lay in the middle of St Columb's Wells street, is now built into the base of a calvary sculpture at the Long Tower church, to where it was moved in 1897 (Lacey 2004, 40-2). It is known as St Columb's Stone. There are three hollows on the visible face and apparently two more on the back. The smallest visible hollow may be of recent origin, as it is not mentioned in a description of 1837 (Colby, 26).

Two of the causeways shown on Docwra's 1600 map crossing the bog on the west side of the 'island' would seem from a general correlation of the early maps with the modern topography to correspond with Brandywell Road (**9**) and Fahan Street (**10**). The latter joined up on the 'island' side with St Columb's Wells street (**11**), which led south in the general direction of the *Tempull Mór*, although lower down the hillside. Another passage probably led from the causeway north-east up the hillside – possibly along the line of the present Fahan Street (**12**). Although interrupted by the seventeenth-century city walls and more recent redevelopment, it would seem that the line of the original Long Tower Street (**13**), rising from the *Tempull Mór* area, would have connected in medieval times with the churches on the higher part of the hill – the Dubreclés and the nuns' church. In 1532, Manus Ó Domhnaill refers to a miracle that happened at an apparently well known place in Derry called *an t-iompódh desiul*, ('the right turn'). Ó Domhnaill says it was south-west of the *Tempull Mór* (see ch. 9). This would seem to have been in the vicinity of a now destroyed junction of St Columb's Wells street and Long Tower Street (**14**). In 1600, what appears on the maps as a curving street (**15**) led from the castle up the hill to Docwra's Great Fort, within which was the Augustinian foundation. It is likely that that street followed an earlier pathway, which itself may have been a pilgrimage route (see ch. 9). Bridge Street, which curves down the hillside on its north-eastern side, led to the seventeenth-century ferry quay on the bank of the River Foyle. The latter was probably the location of the earlier medieval ferry (**16**). Manus Ó Domhnaill also refers to a place called *port na long*, which would seem to equate with the 'Ship quay' area of the plantation city (ch. 9). In the seventeenth century and earlier, this would have been located on the river's edge; the area has been reclaimed since. Manus Ó Domhnaill said there was an altar (*ulaidh*) there that marked the start of the pilgrimage route (see ch. 9). The quarry that still exists (**17**) is likely to be the one referred to in 1600 by Docwra, which itself had probably been in use since ancient times. Finally, one of the orchards, which figured prominently in the events of the Siege of Derry in 1689, was located on the north-east side of the island (between the city walls and modern Orchard Street). It was at very least in that general area that the pre-1600 bishops rented an orchard from the Mac Lochlainns. We know that the Mac Lochlainns were responsible for the northern end of the island, as they sold land there later in the Middle Ages for the building of the tower house to be discussed in ch. 9.

CHAPTER 7

# Derry in the late twelfth and early thirteenth centuries

From many references, it is obvious that there was an advanced school and a busy scriptorium in Derry during the second half of the twelfth and early part of the thirteenth century, at least. An anonymous *toisech mac léighind Daire* 'leader of the students [literally, "sons of learning"] of Derry' is mentioned in 1166 (AU). Whoever that person was, he was sufficiently important for his 'fasting' (hunger strike) protest at the burial of Muirchertach Mac Lochlainn in Armagh to have been noted by the annalists, as we saw above. Although such officials probably existed at other times, between 1162 and 1220 the annals refer specifically to four different lectors (*fir léighinn*) and two different senior lectors (*ardfir léighinn*) in connection with Derry.[1] The lectors included Cathasach Mac Comhaltáin, a 'distinguished scholar' (*saoi toghaidhe*), who died in 1162 (AFM); Maelíosa Ua Muiredaigh, who died in 1185 at a 'venerable old age' (*seandataigh thoghaidhe*) (AFM);[2] and Maolcainnich Ua Fercomais who drowned in 1189 while crossing the narrow strait between Magilligan Point and Inishowen at the entrance to Lough Foyle (AU).[3] A lector called Eoin is mentioned in 1220, but, as will be seen below, he may have actually been a senior lector. In addition, two different senior lectors are mentioned. In 1207, the *ardfer léighinn* Domnall Ua Muiredaigh died and Muirchertach Ua Millugáin was chosen in his place (AU).

The Annals of Ulster has a long entry for the year 1220 that refers to a number of the offices in the settlement at the time. The entry also allows us a glimpse of some of the internal politics of the settlement, involving the resolution of tensions between the local lay people, the nobility, the clergy and the different offices of the monastery and church there.

> Fonachtan Ua Bronáin,[4] successor [*comarba*] of Colum Cille rested in peace [died]. And there ensued contention between the Community

---

1 We do not know what subjects they taught, but it may be relevant to note that it is around this time that universities were beginning to emerge on the Continent from their originally monastic contexts. 2 His namesake and almost certainly his relative, Amhlaim Ua Muiredaigh, described as bishop of Armagh and Cenél Feradaigh, died that same year (in his eighty-sixth year) at Duncrun in north Co. Derry, but was buried in Derry itself (AU). 3 The Uí Fercomais belonged to the Clann Diarmata branch of the Cenél nEógain (see AU 1197). By this time, the latter were settled on the east bank of the Foyle opposite Derry. 4 A Maolcolum Ua Bronáin, *airchinnech* of the Columban church on Tory Island, died in 1202 (AFM).

93

[*Muinntir*] of Daire and the Cenél nEógain, respecting the selection in his stead. It is this was done then: the Community of Daire chose Mac Cathmail into the succession and Áed O'Neill[5] and the Cenél nEógain chose Flann Ó Brolcháin.[6] After that, moreover, there ensued contention between the Community of Daire and Ó Brolcháin and Ó Brolcháin was put out of the succession. After that, moreover, the Community of Daire and the Cenél nEógain chose Muircertach Ua Millugáin, namely, lector [*fer léighinn*][7] of Daire, into the succession. And he had the lectorship [*firusléighinn*] and the succession [that is, was *comarba* and lector jointly] for a year or a little more. And there ensued contention between Goffraigh Ua Daighri, namely the *airchinnech* of Derry and Ua Millugáin, that is, the abbot [*comarba*] respecting the lectorship, so that they appealed to the judgment of the successor of Patrick [the archbishop of Armagh] and he made peace between them. And John [Eoin] son of the [late] Lector[8] was chosen into the Lectorship, according to the successor of Patrick and the successor of Colum Cille and the Community of Daire besides.

One of the fascinating things about this entry is that it gives us some idea about the process of selecting the *comarba* of Colum Cille, whose 'national' role may have been diminished by 1220 but who was still abbot of the Columban monastery in Derry. There is no reference, as we might expect there would be, to the *Sámud Choluim Cille*, the saint's 'community', who may have been Augustinian canons by the time. Instead, we are told that at first it was *Muinnter Daire* – an ambiguous phrase that seems to encompass at least some of the lay as well as the clerical residents of the settlement – who made the choice. Their selection was rejected by Áed O'Neill and the Cenél nEógain (an undoubtedly secular body), whose candidate was also rejected, eventually. The two groups – *Muinnter Daire* and the Cenél nEógain – then agreed on a joint candidate. Although the annals are discreet, it seems obvious that this was anything but a polite, smooth and altruistic process. An entry in the annals for 1198 seems to confirm that this was the type of 'electoral' process normally engaged in. In that year, Gilla Críst Ua Cernaigh was 'ordained' as *comarba*

---

5 The most powerful Cenél nEógain chieftain at the time.  6 Evidently, Flann was installed.  7 This should be *ardfer léighinn* – see the reference to AU 1207 above, where Muirchertach succeeded Domnall Ua Muiredaigh with that specific title.  8 The word 'late' is a modern editorial addition. The identity of the person in question is not certain, but he may have been the son of the former lector, Muirchertach Ua Millugáin. The translation here is as given in Hennesy and MacCarthy 1887–1901. However, the Irish language text has *Eoin, mac in fhir léighinn*. The latter phrase could actually represent the contemporary form of the surname later anglicized as McErlean. Eoin may have been in reality a 'senior' lector, as he certainly succeeded Muirchertach Ua Millugáin, who had that title. The terms *fer léighinn* and *ardfer léighinn* seem to be fairly interchangeable, however, possibly indicating the absence of a strict hierarchy.

*Coluim Cille, ar togha loech & cleirech Tuaisceirt Erenn* 'by the choice of the laity and clergy of the north of Ireland' (AU). On its own, this entry might be dismissed as a formulaic trope but its literal meaning seems to be fleshed out by the 1220 details. It is also evident from the information recorded for 1220, as well as other references, that despite the undoubted reforms of the previous century, certain offices were still the prerogative of particular families.

Only a tiny portion of the literary works produced in Derry in the Middle Ages has survived. We know, for instance, that an exemplar of a portion of the Annals of Ulster was being compiled there between about 1190 and 1220.[9] But it is very unlikely that a set of annals was commenced at that time, as it were, out of the blue and continued for just about thirty years. Although it has not survived, logic dictates that there must have been a much more extensive Derry chronicle. It is certainly possible, for example, that the entry for the year 545/6 purporting to record the establishment of the monastery of Derry, derives from such a chronicle, irrespective of when that particular entry would have been inserted. Part of the genealogical material in the Book of Lecan is said to derive from, among other sources, the Book of Derry (Dobbs 1921, 308).

It is most probable that at least some of the large collection of poems and verses as well as other tracts relating to Colum Cille were compiled in Derry around this time, including of course the Middle Irish Life of the saint. Previous authors have suggested that two of Ireland's oldest and most treasured manuscripts, the *Cathach* and the Book of Durrow, could have been made in Derry. This is most unlikely, but the *Soiscél Martain*, 'Gospel of St Martin' (of Tours) – a treasure of Derry in the twelfth century – must have been a comparable illuminated manuscript and may have been the Cathach.

Manus Ó Domhnaill's *Betha Cholaim Cille* of 1532 gives the fullest account of the slightly inconsistent legends that rationalized the presence of that manuscript in Derry.

> At the time of his own death, Saint Martin [of Tours] predicted the coming of Colum Cille, long before he was born. This is what he said: 'Let my book, the book of the Gospel, be buried with me and put on my breast in the tomb. For a holy blessed boy will be born in Ireland and half of his name will come from heaven in the figure that John saw resting on Jesus in the River Jordan at the time he baptized him [a dove], and the other half of his name will come from the church. He will come here a hundred years from today[10] and will open my tomb and find my book there, and God will have protected it so that no dirt or stain will come on

---

**9** Daniel Mc Carthy argues for *c.*1196–1218 and that the *airchinnech* Máel Íosa Ua Daighri may have been specifically responsible for this, augmenting the Derry entries in the existing chronicle and continuing it up until the time of his own death in 1218 (2008, 238–41, 244). **10** In fact, Martin died *c.*397, whereas Columba lived between *c.*520 and 593.

any letter of it. He will bring it to Ireland and the *Gospel of Martin* will be the name of that book in Ireland forever'.

(Lacey 1998, 23)

Later in the *Betha*, Ó Domhnaill returns to the subject:

> Then Colum Cille went on a pilgrimage to Tours of Saint Martin. He went to the flagstone beneath which Martin was buried. He lifted the stone from the tomb and he found a book of the gospels upon Martin's neck. Martin and that book had been buried in the earth for a hundred years, but God had preserved the book for Colum Cille so that it was no better on the first day it was made than at that time. And by the will of God and of Martin, Colum Cille took that book back with him to Derry, as Martin himself had promised at the time of his death ...

(Lacey 1998, 59–60)

Later again, Ó Domhnaill outlines a more detailed legend as to how Colum Cille acquired the manuscript.

> Then they went to Tours. The people of the city did not know where Martin was buried. When they heard that there was nothing on earth or in heaven hidden from Colum Cille, and that he was a 'seer' of the heavenly Lord, they offered him a lot of gold and silver as well as other gifts to have him reveal to them where that burial was. 'I'll not take gifts of gold or silver from you', said Colum Cille, 'but I'll reveal Martin's burial to you if I can get the other thing that is in the grave along with the body'. The people of the city gave him assurances and oaths about that. Colum Cille revealed the burial then. Opening it, they found a mass-book, and Colum Cille said that it was that book that he himself was looking for and that it was for it that he had made an agreement with the people of the city. The population of the city considered breaking their word with him and not giving him the book. They said that he would not get the book unless he left permanently with them some holy person that was along with him. He left holy Macarius with them according to the order of the pope to serve the office of bishop for them, for they were at that time without a bishop. They gave the book to Colum Cille.

(Lacey 1998, 136)

As has been suggested above, these fictional literary connections between Colum Cille and Tours are most likely garbled recollections of the (equally fictional) links between the saint and Tory Island.

By the end of the twelfth century, Derry was at the centre of a number of complicated family and dynastic conflicts that dominated the secular and ecclesiastical politics of the north-west of Ireland. In the first place, there were the ancient rivalries between the Cenél nEógain, the Cenél Conaill and the Síl Lugdach, all of whom had various claims on the legends and cult of Colum Cille and, therefore, on Derry. Within the Cenél nEógain, there was rivalry between the Mac Lochlainns and the O'Neills. Within what might be called the Cenél Conaill proper, there was rivalry between the Uí Máel Doraidh and the Uí Canannáin. Within the Síl Lugdach, who by this time also saw themselves (almost certainly falsely) as Cenél Conaill, there was rivalry between the emerging Uí Domhnaill and Uí Dochartaigh. All these families – and others – had varying degrees of interest in influencing and controlling the affairs of Derry. An added element to this mixture of intrigue and rivalry was the arrival of the Anglo- (and Scottish-) Normans who clearly also – at least to some extent – took an interest in Derry. To make the picture even more complex in this context, individuals and their supporters often stepped outside their immediate family and dynastic loyalties to ally themselves with the external enemies of their own internal enemies.

The Mac Lochlainns of Derry had been especially powerful throughout the west of Ulster and beyond for most of the twelfth century. Towards the end of the century, however, their domination was challenged within Cenél nEógain by the O'Neills. But other leading families were also becoming involved with Derry. In 1180, we hear for the first time of the involvement of a family apparently new to its affairs. The Annals of Ulster for that year says 'the son of Aindiles Ua Dochurtaigh was killed by the son of Maghnus Ua Cellacáin', but the Annals of the Four Masters say that Aindiles Ua Dochartaigh (not his son) died in Derry. It is not clear if two separate events were intended. The significance of the Uí Dochartaigh connection with Derry at this time is that they belonged to the Síl Lugdach. Having engineered a false genealogical link with the Cenél Conaill and with the encouragement of the clergy of Kilmacrenan, the Síl Lugdach developed a distinct interest in the promotion of Colum Cille's cult for their own propaganda purposes (Lacey 2012).

Derry had been founded in the sixth century as a Cenél Conaill church, but the latter had lost control of it at the end of the eighth century (ch. 4, above). From then on, Derry was a Cenél nEógain centre, most especially in the twelfth century when it became the *caput* of the Mac Lochlainn kings. Paradoxically, it was the Cenél nEógain in the mid-twelfth century – particularly Muirchertach Mac Lochlainn and Flaithbertach Ó Brolcháin – and not the Cenél Conaill who raised Derry to its highest status in the Columban world. Up to the death of Máel Íosa Ua Branain in 1150, the *airchinnech* was the most senior official of monastic Derry, the abbot. Under Flaithbertach, his successor, Derry became the headquarters of the Columban confederation and its senior ecclesiastic was styled *comarba Coluim Cille*. However, the post of *airchinnech* continued as a separate office. Significantly, that office was held from before 1180 – when the *airchinnech* Mac Craith Ua Daighre died – apparently to the end of the Middle Ages, when the English arrived, by the Uí Daighre family, although, as we will see below, they had to share the position probably from the mid-thirteenth century onwards.[11]

The genealogical connections of the Uí Daighre (anglicized as O'Derry or O'Deery) are not absolutely clear, but all the indications are that they did not belong to the Cenél nEógain; it is more likely that they were at least associated with the Cenél Conaill.[12] The first mention of them in the annals is in 1062 when Máel Ruanaid Ua Daighre 'chief confessor [*primanmchara*] of the north of Ireland' died (AU). The notice of his death immediately follows that of the clearly Cenél Conaill cleric, Gilla Críst Ua Máel Doraidh, *comarba Colaim Cille* 'both in Scotland and Ireland'. An Amhlaim Ua Daighre died on pilgrimage in Iona in 1188; almost certainly he had some association with the Derry *airchinnech*. In 1609, an inquisition in Derry – the jurors for which included a Donogh O'Derry – found that 'O'Derry was the herenagh of the abbot of Collumkill [that is, of Derry] within the diocese of Rapoe' (see below). We have documentary proof that the Uí Daighre monopolized the position of *airchinnech* of the Columban (Augustinian?) monastery of Derry until at least 1233.[13] This seems to represent something of a compromise in terms of the ancient Cenél Conaill versus Cenél nEógain rivalry about the control of Derry: the Uí Daighre (Cenél Conaill?) held the position of *airchinnech*, while the office of *comarba* was held by members of a variety of Cenél nEógain families as we will see below. If such a compromise was adopted, then it appears to have coincided with a renaissance of Cenél Conaill power in the secular sphere, itself coinciding with the decline of Mac Lochlainn power.

Prior to the ninth century, the Cenél Conaill proper had been a very powerful dynasty whose direct rule and influence had extended over much of modern Co. Donegal. But from *c*.789 they were confined south of the Barnesmore Gap and expelled from their ancient church at Derry. By the

---

11 The name of Balloughry townland, just south-west of Derry, is derived from Baile Uí Dhaighre. There may be one (doubtful) exception to this rule that the family had an unbroken hold on the office of *airchinnech*. Reeves noted the death in 1202 of Maelfinin Mac Colmáin, *electus in prioratum de Daire*, but cites no historical source (1857, 409). I have found no corroboration for Reeves' claim. It is not clear what role, if any, Maelfinin played in Derry, but, as will be shown below, the office of prior seems to have been equated there around this time with that of *airchinnech*. The reference may have been to another Daire.   12 T.O. Clancy drew attention to the early ninth-century abbot of Iona, Diarmait, who was referred to as the *alumnus* ('foster son' or 'pupil') of Daigre (AU 814), suggesting the possibility of a link with the later Uí Daighre family of Derry (2003–4, 217–18).   13 Mac Craith was followed for the next forty years by Máel Íosa, who died on 8 December 1219 (AU). He, in turn, was followed by Goffraigh, who died in 1233. It is very likely that another Ua Daighre followed immediately, but the situation was about to change somewhat, as we will see below.

twelfth century, rivalry for their kingship was contested between the Uí Cannanáin and Uí Máel Doraidh families. About 1167 or 1168, Flaithbertach Ua Máel Doraidh took power within Cenél Conaill, as it happens shortly after the death of Muirchertach Mac Lochlainn who had been Derry's great royal patron. Flaithbertach quickly became a dominant player in the politics of western Ulster. Apart from its general character as a significant 'prize', Flaithbertach would have been very aware of his own family connections with Derry and Colum Cille – the settlement's alleged 'founder'. In fact, the Uí Máel Doraidh claimed direct descent from Áed mac Ainmerech, the Cenél Conaill king who it was said (almost certainly correctly) had donated Derry to the church in the sixth century (O'Brien 1962, 164: 1443e41). We do not know when Flaithbertach began to take a specific interest in the affairs of Derry, but an entry in the annals for 1197 indicates some existing involvement there, as well as other interesting incidental details.

> Mac Gilla Eidich of the Ciannachta [valley of the River Roe, Co. Derry] robbed the great altar of the *Tempull Mór* of Daire Colum Cille and took the four [*recte*, five] best goblets [*corn*, 'drinking horns' or 'chalices'] that were in Ireland therefrom, including the *Mac Riabhach* ['gray son'] and the *Mac Solus* ['bright son'] and the goblet of Ua Máel Doraidh and the *Cam Corainn* ['the twisted (thing) of Corann'] and the goblet of Ua Dochartaigh. Moreover, he broke off and took away from them their jewels and their setting. But, on the third day after their being stolen, the treasures and he who stole them were found out. And he was hanged (namely, at the Cross of the Executions [*Crois na Riag*]) in reparation to Colum Cille, whose altar was profaned there.
>
> (AU)

There is a very strong likelihood that the Ua Máel Doraidh *corn* was a gift from Flaithbertach. The Ua Dochartaigh *corn*, likewise, was probably a gift from one of Flaithbertach's principal allies in that family, Echmarcach. Flaithbertach's reign certainly coincided with a renewed Cenél Conaill involvement in Derry, such as the incumbency of the Uí Daighre in the *airchinnech*'s position. A less permanent but nonetheless revealing involvement is recorded in the annals in 1188 when Domnall Ua Canannáin injured his foot with an axe, while cutting firewood in Derry despite the protective taboos on its trees. He died immediately 'by a miracle of Colum Cille' (AU). In that same year, Flaithbertach had killed his own internal opponent Ruaidhrí Ua Canannáin, the former king of Cenél Conaill whose position he had usurped twenty years earlier.

In 1196, the Mac Lochlainns suffered another major set-back – further weakening their position – when their king, Muirchertach, was killed in an internal Cenél nEógain dispute 'and he was carried to Daire of Colum Cille and was buried honourably' (AU).

There is a long account in the Annals of Ulster for 1197 of events associated with Derry that culminated in the death of Flaithbertach Ua Máel Doraidh and his Ua Dochartaigh successor. This is the first time that the so-called Anglo-Norman invasion of Ireland seems to have impacted directly on the settlement there. John de Courcy had begun his conquest of east Ulster, allegedly on behalf of the king of England but mainly for himself, about twenty years earlier. Operating ruthlessly and with almost total independence, he gradually extended his sway around the north coast.

> A hosting by John de Courcy with the Foreigners of Ulster to Ess craibhe [The Cutts on the River Bann near Coleraine], so that they built the castle of Cell-Santain [Mountsandel] ... Moreover, in that castle was left Roitsel Fitton [and] a force along with him. Then Roitsel Fitton came on a foray to the Port of Derry, so that he pillaged [i] Cluain Í and [ii] Enach and [iii] Derc bruach.[14] But Flaithbertach Ua Máel Doraidh ... overtook them with a small force ... so that he inflicted defeat upon them on the strand of the [N]uathcongbhail[15] [and] they were slaughtered ... through a miracle of [Saints] Colum Cille and Cainnech and Brecan [whose churches] they pillaged there.
>
> Flaithbertach Ua Máel Doraidh, that is, king of Cenél Conaill and Cenél nEógain and Airgialla, defender of Tara and royal heir of all Ireland ... died after choice tribulation in Inis Saimer [a small island in the Erne estuary, just below Ballyshannon], on the fourth of the Nones [2nd] of February [1198], in the thirtieth year of his lordship and in the ninth and fiftieth year of his age. And he was buried honourably in Druim Tuama [Drumhome in south Donegal]. And Echmarcach Ua Dochartaigh [took] the kingship of Cenél Conaill immediately. And he was but a fortnight in the kingship when John de Courcy came with a large force under him past Toome into Tír Eógain. From there to Ardstraw; after that, around to Derry, so that they were five nights therein.[16] They go then to Cnoc Nascain ... [a hill near Lough Swilly]. But the Cenél Conaill, under Echmarcach Ua Dochartaigh, [came] to attack them and gave them battle, where two hundred of them [the Irish] were killed, around their king, that is, Echmarcach ... And they [the English] harried Inishowen and carried great cattle-spoil therefrom.

14 (i) Now the site of St Brecan's Church at Clooney in the Waterside area of Derry (see chs 8, 9), and churches at (ii) Enagh Lough and (iii) Gransha – all on the east bank of the Foyle close to Derry.   15 The estuary of the Faughan River, just east of Enagh Lough, where it flows into Lough Foyle. It appears from the annals that the Normans were being assisted by the un-named son of Ardgal Mac Lochlainn. Katharine Simms argues that the Mac Lochlainns allied with de Courcy 'in an unsuccessful effort to reinstate themselves with English help' (1999, 154).   16 AFM says: 'a week and two days'.

As the entry noted, the 'foreigners' led by de Courcy himself were back in Derry in 1198. They only withdrew when Áed O'Neill – who by then had effectively taken the leadership of the Cenél nEógain from the Mac Lochlainns – attacked the Norman bases at Larne in east Ulster. Despite the fact that they were very active throughout eastern, northern and mid-Ulster at this period, there are no further reports of Norman involvement in Derry for over a decade. In 1212, however,

> Thomas Mac Uchtrach with the sons of Raghnall Mac Somhairle, came to Daire of Colum Cille with seventy-six ships and the town [*baile*] was greatly destroyed by them and Inishowen was completely destroyed by them and by the Cenél Conaill.

The background to this incident was that King John had given highly speculative pioneering grants to members of the south-west Scottish Fitz Roland or de Galloway family – known in Irish sources as Mac Uchtrach. The family were allies of King John; Thomas was earl of Athol. Among Thomas' grants in Ulster was the 'cantred of Talachot' > Telach Óc (McNeill 1980, 14–15). That land was Tullyhogue (Co. Tyrone), which was 'sacred' to the O'Neills – the place where their chieftains were inaugurated. By this time, Áed O'Neill was leader of the Cenél nEógain and was also claiming to be king of Cenél Conaill (AU 1212), hence the alliance of the latter with Mac Uchtrach and their attack on the ancestral Cenél nEógain lands of Inishowen.

The grant to Fitz Roland had also included O'Neill's 'share of "the vill of Derekoneull" (i.e. Doire Colm Chille …)'.[17] The annals record Mac Uchtrach returning to Derry the following year:

> Thomas Mac Uchtrach and Rory Mac Raghnaill [Mac Somhairle] plundered Derry completely and took the treasure [*sét*] of the community [*muinntere*] of Derry, and of the north of Ireland besides from out of the midst of the church of the monastery [*teampall in reiclesa*].
>
> (AU)

The Annals of the Four Masters says they brought the booty to Coleraine, where Mac Uchtrach had a castle. However, Mac Uchtrach was unable to sustain his conquests and we hear no more about direct involvement of the Normans in the Derry area for the best part of a century.

When Flaithbertach Ua Máel Doraidh died in 1198, he was succeeded as king of Cenél Conaill – if only for just over a fortnight – by his close ally,

---

17 Simms 1999, 155. The reference to O'Neill's 'share' of Derry may indicate that there was already a concept of the partition of the 'island' between Cenél nEógain and Cenél Conaill (see below, pp 105, 109).

Echmarcach Ua Dochartaigh. As mentioned above, the Uí Dochartaigh were a Síl Lugdach family, actually unconnected with the Cenél Conaill although – for propaganda purposes and probably as far back as *c*.800 – their genealogies had been manipulated to reflect otherwise (Lacey 2012, 34–6, 68–9). Their ancestors had come originally from north-west Donegal, but they had later expanded to the better lands east of the central Donegal mountain ranges. By the twelfth century, the Uí Dochartaigh were established in the territory of Ard Midhair, an area that seems to have been south of the River Swilly towards Lough Finn and just across the Bluestacks from the real Cenél Conaill. When his death was recorded under 1199, Domnall Ua Dochartaigh was described as 'lord [*tighearna*] of Cenél nÉnnai and Ard Midhair' (AFM). The territory of Cenél nÉnnai was north of Ard Midhair, just west and south of Derry. The Uí Dochartaigh had presumably expanded into that much better land during the Cenél Conaill renaissance under Flaithbertach Ua Máel Doraidh, who had been allied with Echmarcach Ua Dochartaigh. They would later expand northward again into Inishowen, but not until the mid-fourteenth century. On the other hand, any ambitions of an Uí Dochartaigh kingship of Cenél Conaill – which had been realized for just a few weeks under Echmarcach – were immediately swept away by their internal Síl Lugdach rivals, the Uí Domhnaill. The first of the Uí Domhnaill to rule – from *c*.1200 to 1208 – was Éigneachán. We will return below to the Uí Domhnaill and what their rule meant for Derry. Whether they were ruled by Ua Máel Doraid, Ua Dochartaigh or Ó Domhnaill, the Cenél Conaill renaissance had various repercussions in Derry such as, for example, the incumbency of the Uí Daighre *airchinnechs*.

The last recorded *airchinnech* prior to Mac Craith Ua Daighre (who died in 1180) had been Máel Íosa Ua Branain of the Cenél nEógain. Máel Íosa had been abbot of the Columban monastery in Derry. He died in 1150, to be followed in the abbacy by Flaithbertach Ó Brolcháin. We do not know if the latter was styled *airchinnech* before he acquired the title of *comarba Coluim Cille*, which appears for the first time in the Annals of Ulster in 1155.[18] If the Annals of the Four Masters can be relied upon, in the interval since 1150 Flaithbertach was certainly *behaving* as *comarba*, making various visitations to other parts of the country and collecting the 'dues' owed to Colum Cille. It is not clear, therefore, when the role of *airchinnech* was activated again – this time as a Cenél Conaill office. We know that it happened sometime between Máel Íosa's death in 1150 and Mac Craith's death in 1180, apparently coinciding with the rise to prominence of Flaithbertach Ua Máel Doraidh.

Mac Craith was followed as *airchinnech* in turn by Mael Íosa Ua Daighre, who, when he died on 8 December 1219, was said to have been forty years in the office (AU).[19] Goffraigh Ua Daighre, who died in 1233, had followed as

[18] However, the title is used in AFM 1151 and 1153. Unfortunately, there is a lacuna in AU (a better witness to the original record) between 1131 and 1155. [19] See n. 9, above, for

*airchinnech* immediately on Mael Íosa's death (AU).[20] Thus, for at minimum the fifty-three years prior to 1233, the Uí Daighre (representing Cenél Conaill interests) had monopolized the office of *airchinnech* in what was strongly Cenél nEógain Derry. No more first names of *airchinnechs* are recorded in the annals, but, as will be shown below, the Uí Daighre (O'Deerys) continued in that role – although dividing it eventually with the Mac Lochlainns – right through the Middle Ages until the English conquest in 1600.

One of the additions to the Middle Irish Life of Colum Cille seems to be, in effect, the charter for the division of the two most senior monastic offices in Derry – *comarba* and *airchinnech* – between the Cenél nEógain and the Cenél Conaill; or at least a rationalization of that practice.[21]

> Colum Cille left Da Cualén, a cleric of his Community [*muintir*], as his successor [*ina comarbus*] in Derry. The latter was a cleric from his own native territory, and Colum Cille granted that the office of prior [*secnabuigecht*][22] of the same monastery [*bailí*] and the headship of its senior monks [*cendus a sruithe*] should be the prerogative of Cenél Conaill.
> 
> (Herbert 1988, 231 n. 2 and 257 n. 2)

We know very little about Da or Do Cualén – a 'saint' whose feastday was celebrated on 12 March (Ó Riain 2011, 270). There is absolutely no genuine evidence that he had any connection with Derry, most especially as its abbot, although such a possibility cannot be ruled out. It is not clear either in what sense he was believed to have been a cleric of Colum Cille's 'community'. The genealogies all associate him with the Cenél mBinnig section of Cenél nEógain, some of whose people, such as the Mac Conchailles, were definitely associated with Derry in the early twelfth century.[23] But a hint of what was believed about him around the same time may be that one of his grandfathers was said to have been called Colum (or Colmán 'little Colum'), while the latter's father – Da Cualén's great-grandfather – was said to have been called Crimthann (Columba's 'pre-Christian' name). To say the least, his pedigree looks a bit suspicious. Could it be that Da Cualén is a garbled form of the name Columba?[24]

Daniel Mc Carthy's suggestion that Mael Íosa was responsible for the compilation of the relevant exemplar of the Annals of Ulster. **20** He is referred to in an entry for 1220 (AU). **21** This extra section (quoted also previously in ch. 5) occurs only in the *Leabhar Clainne Suibhne* and National Library of Scotland versions (Herbert 1988, 212, 231, 257). **22** That is, in second position to the abbot (*RIA dictionary*: *secnapaidecht*, 532, cols 137–8). Significantly, it is not the most senior position, the *comarbus* ('successorship') or *abdaine* ('abbacy'), that is granted to Cenél Conaill. That office was firmly under Cenél nEógain control. **23** Dochualén m. Guaire m. Coluim m. Crimthaind m. Binnig m. Eogain (Ó Riain 1985b, 8:36). At an average generation length of thirty years, and placing Eogan around 450, this pedigree would suggest a *floruit* for Dochualén around 600, seemingly – although very tentatively – overlapping with Columba's dates. **24** For example, some

Nor is it clear in what sense Da Cualén was understood to have belonged to Colum Cille's 'own native territory'. By the twelfth century, the Cenél mBinnig were mainly located along the west bank of the Lower Bann; for that reason, Ó Riain suggested that the location of Da Cualén's *scrín* or 'shrine', although not yet specifically located, was 'probably somewhere in [Co.] Derry (within Ceinéal Binnigh)' (2011, 270). In earlier times, however, before the expansion of the Cenél nEógain, Cenél mBinnig would have been confined to Inishowen. This led Séamus Ó Ceallaigh to suggest that the Uí Fearáin, who were known as the 'people of the Shrine of Dá Chuailén', were settled in Inishowen (1951, 60–1). Ó Ceallaigh also linked the Uí Fearáin with a people settled at a place called 'Árd nGobhaill of Clann Chearnaigh beside Áth Meadhon', adding that 'unfortunately, all these items of nomenclature await identification' (ibid., 60). They still do! Perhaps significantly, however, there is a townland called Cloncarney about two miles east of the reputed birthplace of Columba, in the centre of the Gartan area, where all the monuments and sites associated with the early life of the saint still exist. Could this explain the reference to Colum Cille's 'own native territory' in the quotation above? It is not clear at all how a segment of Cenél mBinnig could have got possession of land in that area (or alternatively how people native to that area could have been genealogically linked to the Cenél mBinnig), but a further tentative clue to the explanation of the reference to Da Cualén may be found in the surname of the person who took the office of *comarba Coluim Cille* in Derry in 1198: Gilla Críst Ua Cernaigh.[25] Could he have been responsible for, or at least linked with, the reference to Da Cualén in the appendix to the Middle Irish Life?

Whatever the explanation, the evidence seems to indicate that before the end of the twelfth century a system of power-sharing had been worked out in Derry which meant that the office of *comarba* or abbot was held by a member of the Cenél nEógain, while the subordinate office of *airchinnech* – apparently equated with that of *secnab* ('prior') – was held by a member of the Cenél Conaill.

There had been contemporaneous changes in secular politics also, which had profound implications for Derry. Mac Lochlainn power had faded and by 1200 Áed O'Neill was the dominant chieftain in Gaelic Ulster. He was supported for much of his reign by the Uí Domhnaill in Donegal (both of them enemies of the Mac Lochlainns), whose power was rising around the same time. Áed had a varying, practical relationship with the English king and the Norman colonists. He died in 1230, but his son and heir, Domnall, was killed in 1235 by Domnall Mac Lochlainn, who sought to restore his family's

---

Cenél nEógain variant? See Ó Riain 1983, where he lists over twenty other variations of Columba's name. 25 A Gilla Críst Ua Cernaigh – who may or may not have been the same person – died as bishop of Connor in 1201 (AU). That diocese included Cenél mBinnig territory west of the lower Bann.

*Derry in the late twelfth and early thirteenth centuries* 105

**21** Map of the dioceses of Derry and Raphoe as they had evolved by the middle of the thirteenth century. Eventually, the 'island' of Derry itself would be partitioned between the two medieval dioceses: the northern end assigned to Derry and the southern end to Raphoe.

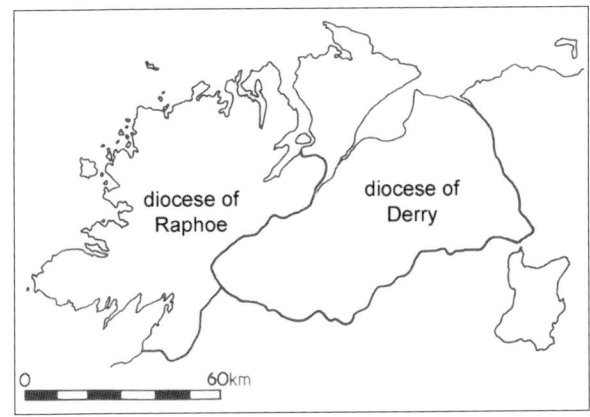

dominance. Domnall Mac Lochlainn succeeded, more or less, until the O'Neills, with the support of the Uí Domhnaill, massively defeated him at the Battle of Caméirge in 1241.[26] This signalled the end of the Mac Lochlainns as major players in Ulster politics. They held on to some land in their ancestral homeland in Inishowen and, as we will see, to a minor office in Derry itself. But from then on they were at the mercy of whoever controlled the north-west of Ireland. Derry would be greatly influenced by their fall from power; the decline in its fortunes from the mid-thirteenth century onwards certainly coincided with, and must have been linked to, the collapse of the Mac Lochlainns.

From then on – presumably with the agreement of the O'Neills – the Mac Lochlainns shared the subordinate office of *airchinnech* in Derry along with the Uí Daighre. An inquisition in 1609 recorded that:

> within the said iland of Derry, there were twoe herenaghes [*airchinnech*] belonging to the late abbot of Collumkill, the one called Loughlina [Lochlinnach = Mac Lochlainn] within the dioces of Derry [Cenél nEógain], and thother called oderry [O'Deery > Uí Daighre] within the diocese of Rapoe [Cenél Conaill].

This unusual partition of the hill of Derry itself derives, of course, from the ancient Cenél Conaill versus Cenél nEógain conflict. The division of the 'island' seems to have been into northern and southern sectors. Logically, in the context of Inishowen being part of the diocese of Derry, the northern end of the hill was probably in that diocese. Certainly, the Mac Lochlainn erenagh sold land to the Uí Dochartaigh at the northern end, probably around 1500, as we will see in ch. 9. Presumably, the southern end was in the diocese of Raphoe (fig. 21).[27]

---

**26** The site of the battle may be at Cummery, Erganagh townland, north of Omagh (see Simms 1999, 154, 170). **27** In the modern diocesan arrangements, all of Co. Derry west of

The division confirms the continuing interest of Cenél Conaill in Derry, although the seat of the Cenél nEógain diocese had been transferred there from Maghera (Co. Derry) in 1247 and confirmed by Pope Alexander IV on 4 November 1254.[28] That change took place during the episcopacy of Gilla an Choimded (Germanus) Ua Cerballáin, but was probably supported by the Cenél nEógain chieftain, Brian O'Neill (Simms 1999, 158). The confirming papal bull suggested that the bishops had actually been living in Derry 'as far back as the memory of man could reach' (Gwynn 1959, 97). Although the records are not clear, it seems that Germanus was Cenél nEógain bishop from *c*.1230 until his death in 1279 (Byrne 1989, 279). Some sources suggest that he was a Dominican.[29] If true, this would be significant. A report on the state of the Irish Dominican province was compiled by the prior provincial, Friar Ross MacGeoghegan, in 1622 (Ó Clabaigh 2012, 5). In it, he states that

> This is a most ancient province, in which there are thirty-eight priories, in addition to many residences and chapels, very many of which were founded and erected in the time of the most holy father Dominic, as a letter from the same St Dominic to the most illustrious Prince of Tyrconnell [Ó Domhnaill?] in favour and recommendation of two friars sent by him to Ireland confirms. That letter was preserved with the fullness of the friars' faithful veneration and singular devotion in our convent in Derry until it was lost as a result of fire and the devastation wrought by heretics recklessly oppressing the said convent and the friars living in it.

Colmán Ó Clabaigh says that a variation of the legend about this letter alleges that, after the destruction of the friary in Derry, it was then taken to Spain (presumably by the Uí Domhnaill) to a Spanish Dominican archive, where subsequently it was lost. Writing between 1948 and 1953, Benedict O'Sullivan OP argued that if the story of the letter had been true, 'it would make Derry the first Irish Dominican foundation' (Fenning 2009, 14–15). But both O'Sullivan and Ó Clabaigh are totally sceptical about a Gaelic origin for the Dominicans in Ireland. Ó Clabaigh claims that the legend was devised so

---

the Foyle is included in the diocese of Derry. The medieval boundary was probably the imaginary line connecting the summits of the range of hills running from Greenan Mountain across to Holywell Hill, and then on to Derry. The exact dividing line in Derry itself is difficult to work out. It can hardly have been the continuation of that line through the summit of the hill of Derry (more or less where St Columb's Cathedral now stands), as that would have left the *Tempull Mór* – the cathedral of the medieval Derry diocese (site of the present Long Tower church) – in the diocese of Raphoe.  28 Gwynn 1959, 97. For further details on the evolution of the Cenél nEógain diocese into the diocese of Derry, see Ó Canann 2009, 32 and now Devlin 2013.  29 Ibid.; Leslie 1937. But see O'Sullivan (in Fenning 2009), who does not seem to include Ua Cerballáin as a Dominican.

that 'the Irish friars were able to ignore the English roots from which they had in fact sprung' (ibid.).[30] O'Sullivan thought it much more likely 'that Blessed John of Vercelli who ruled the order (1264–83) at the time Derry [Dominican house] was founded may have sent a letter to O'Donnell' (Fenning 2009, 15). O'Sullivan says that at a chapter in Pisa in 1276 'permission was granted for another house [in Ireland] and this was, most probably, Derry, which was founded in 1274' (Fenning 2009, 44). St Dominic had died over fifty years earlier, in 1221. O'Sullivan also says that the Dominican Cairpre Ó Scuapa, bishop of Raphoe (1265–74), is likely to have played a role in the establishment of the Derry house while attending the Council of Lyon in 1274. The suggestion is that either Ó Scuapa himself wrote to Ó Domhnaill (and or possibly to Germanus Ua Cerballáin) or he persuaded John of Vercelli, whom he had met in Lyon, to do so, urging the foundation of the Derry priory. Ó Clabaigh repeats the general assertion that the Derry priory was founded in 1274 'possibly by Donal O'Donnell [Domnall Óg Ó Domhnaill], who was buried there in 1281' (2012, 11). The annals do record Domnall's burial *i mainister na mBráthair i nDoire Coluim Cille*, 'the friars' monastery in Derry' after the disastrous defeat of the Cenél Conaill by the O'Neills at the Battle of Desertcreat.[31]

It seems as if it was during the episcopacy of Bishop Germanus Ó Cerballáin that the Uí Domhnaill influence was consolidated in the settlement of Derry, although not necessarily with his full approval. Although the documentation is extremely limited, it looks as if it was Domnall Óg Ó Domhnaill who was largely responsible for this. He had come to power as chieftain of Donegal at eighteen years of age in 1258 on the death of his predecessor, Godfrey. Domnall Óg, who had been in Scotland, arrived back in Ireland in the midst of a war with the, by then, greatest enemy of the Uí Domhnaill, the O'Neills of Tyrone. He was clearly a leader from whom much was expected. Four hundred years later, the Annals of the Four Masters described his arrival as follows:

> Similar to the coming of [the mythical] Tuathal Teachtmhar over the sea from Scotland, after the extirpation of the royal race of Ireland by the Attacots,[32] was this coming of Domnall Óg, to consolidate the monarchy, to cement territories, and to defend his own country against foreigners, from the day on which he was installed in the lordship until the day of his death.

Almost certainly it was Domnall who founded the Dominican friary in Derry.

An inquisition of 1602 refers to an 'old and ruinous church or house of canon brothers' as being beside the 'island' of Derry. The 1609 inquisition

---

**30** In fact, similar stories were told about other Dominican foundations in Ireland (Fenning 2009, 14–15). **31** AFM *s.a.* 1281; AU *s.a.* 1278. **32** A mythical Firbolg people who are

records the existence of a 'priorie or religious house of begging friars of St Frauncis ... with a churchyard' on the north side of the bog near the 'island' of Derry. There is no other evidence, however, of a Franciscan house in Derry during the Middle Ages. Almost certainly, the reference should have been to the Dominican priory, *Mainistir na mBráthair*. This was the monastery shown on the north-west side of the bog on the map of Derry of 27 December 1600.[33] Its location outside the 'island' probably reflects contemporary political tensions, for example, between the Uí Domhnaill and the O'Neills. There may have been reluctance also on the part of the existing ecclesiastical entities on the island – the Augustinian Dubreclés, the Cistercian convent and the cathedral of the Cenél nEógain diocese of Derry – to allow the construction of the Dominican monastery within the main area of the settlement. Those tensions could be very destructive. As recently as 1261,

> Sixteen of the principal clergy of the Cenél Conaill, including Conchobar Ó Firghil [O'Friel] were killed by Conchobar O'Neill [chieftain of Cenél nEógain] and the Cenél nEógain at Derry. Conchobar Ó Neill was immediately killed, through a miracle of Colum Cille, by [Donn] Ó Breslein, chieftain of Fanad.
>
> (AConn.)

That same year, a vacancy had occurred in the bishopric of Raphoe when the Dominican Máel Pátraic Ó Scannail was appointed archbishop of Armagh. Most of the members of the diocesan chapter chose the current abbot of the Dubreclés in Derry, but there was a minority candidate (Gwynn 1959, 96–7). Because the conflict – which need not be dealt with otherwise here – was eventually referred to Rome, the resulting documentation allows us to know something about it. The candidacy of the abbot of the Dubreclés (which was not successful) was almost certainly an attempted clever manoeuvre by the Cenél Conaill, designed to regain more power for them in Derry. The conflict persisted. In 1318, there was another major battle: 'Seán mac Domnaill O'Neill was slain by Ó Domhnaill (Aodh mac Domhnaill Óg) in Derry ... and many others were slain and drowned' (AFM). The ancient rivalry seems to have been mitigated somewhat by the sharing of the monastic offices – originally of *comarba* and *airchinnech* or *secnap*, and later by the doubling of the position of *airchinnech* – and eventually by the actual partitioning of the island itself between the diocese of Derry and the diocese of Raphoe.

said to have killed all the Milesian royals and aristrocrats of Ireland. In the stories, Tuathal, whose mother had fled to Scotland, where he was born, returned as an adult, defeated the Attecots, restored the Milesians to power and was elected king of Ireland himself.   33 The 'foundations of the church' discovered in the Rossville Street, William Street and Abbey Street area in the early nineteenth century (Colby 1837, 26) probably belonged to that priory, although extensive trenching in the area in 1977 failed to find any traces.

*Derry in the late twelfth and early thirteenth centuries*

22 The coat of arms of the city of Londonderry. The top section derives from the arms of the city of London, while the bottom part is said to be the ancient insignia of Derry. Traditionally, the skeleton is said to represent Walter de Burgh, who was imprisoned and starved to death at Greencastle, Co. Donegal, in 1332.

In 1306, the bishop of Derry, Geoffrey Mac Lochlainn (1297–*c*.1315), sued the bishop of Raphoe, Enrí Mac in Chrossáin, for 'a messuage [farmhouse and associated outbuildings and yards] and ten carucats of land [possibly up to 1,200 acres of ploughland], and 1,000 acres of pasture' in Derry. Allegedly, the Cenél Conaill chieftain, Domnall Óg Ó Domhnaill, had 'unjustly deprived' Germanus Ó Cerballáin of these and given them to Fergal Ó Firghil (bishop of Raphoe, *c*.1275–99).[34] We do not know where exactly this land was situated, but at least part of it might have been at the southern, 'unbuilt-on', portion of the 'island'. The partition arrangement seems to have been institutionalized in 1322, if not before, from the return on lease of half the 'island' to the bishop of Raphoe by Richard de Burgh, earl of Ulster, who had previously acquired an interest there (Simms 1999, 164, 172 n. 74). In 1310, Edward II had established an inquiry to see 'whether or not the king or any other person would be prejudiced if he should grant to Richard de Burgh, earl of Ulster, that he might retain to himself and his heirs for ever the city of Derry'. In 1311, the king confirmed the grant of 'Derrecolumkille' and Lough Lappan (Colby 1837, 24). As Tom McNeill pointed out, de Burgh had

> obtained the king's pardon for accepting, without royal leave, land at Derry and Port Lough [Lough Lappan] from the bishop of Raphoe (the Cenel Connaill bishop) and other lands in Derry, Moville, Fahan and Inch from the [Cenél nEógain] bishop of Derry.
>
> (1980, 31)

In fact, Richard had got hold of the land through what Simms called 'extortion', probably with the intention of developing a Norman town at the port of Derry (Simms 1995, 186, 198 n. 16). Unfortunately, at least in some respects for its later history, de Burgh's planned town was never built. The

---

34 Colby 1837, 24 and references cited there.

only echo of this Norman interlude in Derry's affairs is said to be the skeleton on the city's coat-of-arms (fig. 22). By a tradition – the origins of which now seem to be lost – the figure is said to represent Walter de Burgh, who was imprisoned and starved to death in 1332 at the family fortress of Greencastle (Co. Donegal) at the mouth of Lough Foyle. After an uprising against the then earl, William the Brown, in 1333, the great castle was abandoned and the Normans withdrew from Inishowen. Gradually, the Uí Dochartaigh moved in and by the end of the fourteenth century they were rulers of the whole peninsula.[35]

35 According to AU, when Domnall Ua Dochartaigh died as arch-chief of Ard Midhair in 1339, 'there was little wanting from his having the lordship of Inis Eogain'.

CHAPTER 8

# Archbishop Colton's visit to Derry in 1397

Apart from the occasional reference to Derry in the annals and a few other scraps from miscellaneous ecclesiastical sources, we have very little in the way of solid evidence as to how the settlement itself functioned during the later medieval period. One source does give us such an insight. In the autumn of 1397, John Colton, archbishop of Armagh, made what has been mistakenly called a 'metropolitan' visitation of the diocese of Derry.[1] An account of that visit survives.

Colton was the only person in Irish history to have held the country's two most senior positions, secular and ecclesiastical. He was appointed archbishop of Armagh – head of the church – in 1381 and, for a time in 1382, he was also justiciar or head of the king of England's government in Ireland. His reason for visiting the diocese of Derry was that, due to a temporary vacancy in its bishopric, he came to exercise his substitute spiritual and temporal jurisdiction in accordance with ecclesiastical law. A diary of the journey was made by a secretary, Richard Kenmore, a notary public 'by apostolic authority'.[2] Although the text is concerned mainly with the official business transacted by the archbishop, the casual references to food, accommodation and travel arrangements give us a picture of some aspects of daily life in Derry and the surrounding areas that other medieval records do not convey. For this reason, it seems appropriate to quote extensive portions of it here.

On Monday 8 October 1397, the archbishop's party, including about fifteen other senior ecclesiastics and their attendants, set out on horseback from the church of Termonmagurk (Carrickmore in Co. Tyrone) in the archdiocese of Armagh. Clerics of both Gaelic Irish and Anglo-Norman origin, with 'their travelling furniture', were included; the cavalcade was probably intended to be an impressive manifestation of the power of the church. As the countryside had been settled in one form or another for thousands of years, we must presume that there were well-known roads and route-ways for them to travel on. We have no information about whether the archbishop's visit was expected or if he arrived unannounced; there was certainly no formal welcoming party for him when he first entered the diocese of Derry. The party passed over the

---

1 He did not come to act as archbishop – that is, in his 'metropolitan' capacity – but as the substitute bishop of Derry; see below.   2 The text was edited with numerous additional notes by William Reeves (1850). The extensive translated extracts below are quoted from J. Scott Porter (1853).

23 Map showing the route taken by Archbishop John Colton and his party during their visitation to the diocese of Derry in 1397 (*Ulster Journal of Archaeology*, 1853).

relatively desolate territory to the south-east of the Sperrins and eventually arrived into the diocese of Derry. It halted at the church of Cappagh (near Omagh, Co. Tyrone) so that the archbishop could be welcomed by the local erenagh (*airchinnech*) and announce formally the reasons why he had come.

The unusual scene at that tiny Tyrone church must have been as classic a confrontation between representatives of a colonial and a native culture as has been seen in any part of the world down the ages. On one side, there was the eminent aristocratic Englishman surrounded by his official entourage and the panoply of a prince of the church, a man who had been educated at Cambridge university, who had occupied the highest offices in the land – both secular and ecclesiastical, who was acquainted with the sophistication of the royal court – indeed who was himself a confidant of the king of England. On the other side, there was the erenagh of Cappagh – a country layman who was not sufficiently important to have even his name recorded – the secular guardian of a remote church in a remote part of Ulster. As Cappagh was too poor to lodge the archbishop's party, the cavalcade moved on to Ardstraw (Co. Tyrone).

Ardstraw cannot have had vastly better material facilities than Cappagh, but at least it had been the original 'seat' of the bishopric that had become the diocese of Derry. In accordance with the traditional custom of hospitality extended to the bishop of Derry when travelling about his diocese, the erenagh of Cappagh was obliged, at the expense of the parish, to convey to Ardstraw 'one fat ox for the use and supper' of the archbishop's party. The Ardstraw erenagh and parish had to provide for the other necessities of the visitors. The party stayed in Ardstraw overnight and presided at a religious service the following morning. It then proceeded via the church at Urney (where they stayed another night) and Leckpatrick (both now in Co. Tyrone) to Derry 'city', which they reached on 10 October. Any provisions or fresh horses that were required had to be provided, in accordance with tradition, by the local people. Kenmore was particularly careful to note that all these provisions were supplied by the local people free of charge. The route they chose is worthy of note. While a somewhat easier route would have been to proceed westward from Ardstraw, crossing the fordable River Finn and on to Derry along the west bank of the Foyle, that would have necessitated travelling for a short part of their journey through a portion of the diocese of Raphoe. Their chosen route – entirely in the diocese of Derry – meant that they had to be ferried across the more dangerous River Foyle on arriving at their destination. It would also have made a more impressive arrival.

> [T]he said Venerable Father, with his retinue, and with his baggage, proceeded towards Derry, and having crossed the river [Foyle][3] by means

---

3 It is interesting, as noted originally by Reeves (1857, 161), that this section of the Foyle was referred to by Kenmore as a river (*flumen*), just as it had been six hundred years earlier

of boats, advancing towards the city, Dr William M'Camayll [Mac Cathmail], dean of the cathedral church of Derry, with many others, clerks, friars and laymen, reverently came forth to meet the said Father, and conducted the said Father to the monastery of Canons Regular [Augustinians], called the Black Abbey [*Cella Nigra*] of Derry, and reverently lodged him and his attendants, and placed them in suitable chambers and place. He also procured and caused provisions in abundance to be supplied for the lord primate and his retinue, and for their horses, and that, even till the Saturday next following, *gratis*, and without expense to the said archbishop.

The following day, the archbishop resumed his duties as follows:

[T]he aforesaid Venerable Father, entering the choir of the church of the canons aforesaid [Augustinians], – after one mass solemnly sung, and another heard without singing, the aforesaid Venerable Father, sitting on his tribunal in the choir aforesaid, the canons of the said house having been summoned to his presence, the Venerable Father charged them that if they knew of anything relating to the state of government of the said house, which required reformation, they should declare it unto him.

The canons withdrew themselves and held a private meeting. When they returned,

[O]ne of them – constituted, as he asserted, the organ of the voices of the rest – complaining before the said Father, presented that a certain Hugh M'Gillivray [Mac Giolla Bhríde] O'Dogherty, a canon of their convent, and who, after the resignation of their monastery by a certain brother, Reginald O'Hegarty, their last abbot, had been, by consent of the convent aforesaid deputed as guardian of the said monastery, had usurped to himself the common seal of the aforesaid monastery, which according to the statutes of their order, ought to be, and had formerly customarily been, in the custody of the convent under three keys [that is, three separate key-holders]. Wherefore he begged, presenting in the name of the convent aforesaid, that a fit remedy should be provided for himself and the convent by the Venerable Father aforesaid. Which matter being propounded and heard, the said Venerable Father inquired of the aforesaid brother, Hugh M'Gillivray, the guardian, being then and there present, if the case were so or not. And when he answered and judicially

by Adomnán in the *Vita Columbae* (Anderson and Anderson 1961, 428–9). In Gaelic Irish sources, there does not seem to have been a concept of the River Foyle; Lough Foyle was thought of as extending right up to the junction of the rivers Finn and Mourne.

confessed that he had the said common seal, the said Venerable Father commanded him under the penalty of law, to deliver the same unto himself, the said Venerable Father, to be effectually kept until he should order something else to be done with it. Which brother Hugh, at the command of the said Venerable Father, delivered and yielded up the seal aforesaid to the said Venerable Father, before a full assemblage of clergy and people.

The archbishop kept the seal in his own possession until the following Sunday. That matter will be returned to below. Then, the spokesperson for the other monks

[P]roposed several complaints concerning the discipline of the said house, praying the said Venerable Father to constitute and ordain certain definitions on and concerning all of them; and so prayed [agreed] all the canons then standing by: and also the dean of the cathedral church of Derry, and many other clergy of the diocese of Derry then standing by, presented the same prayer [request]. And the said Venerable Father, assenting to their supplications, did afterwards constitute certain ordinances and definitions, concerning the state and discipline of the said house.

A few days later while visiting the church at Banagher (near Dungiven, Co. Derry), the archbishop delivered a new set of rules for the monks. We are surely entitled to draw inferences about the past behaviour of the monks from the details of these regulations.

John, by divine permission, archbishop of Armagh, primate of Ireland, guardian of the spirituality and temporality, and of the spiritual jurisdiction of the bishoprick of Derry, said bishoprick being deprived of the benefit of its pastor, to his beloved brethren, Hugh M'Gillivray O'Dogherty, the abbot [elected 12 October; see below], and to the convent of the Black Abbey of Derry, health, grace and benediction.

Whereas we have judged it right and proper, to make certain constitutions and definitions, concerning the state and government as well of your persons as your place aforesaid, we now transmit the same unto you, here expressed, firmly enjoining you, in virtue of your obedience sworn unto us that you observe them in and through all things entirely and faithfully, under pain of the greater excommunication which we intend to launch against each one of you, if you do not effectually obey our mandates.

In the first place, we ordain, define and command, that thou, brother Hugh, abbot aforesaid, within the space of three days after notification of these presents made unto thee, dismiss and send away from thy precincts, cohabitation and care, never again to take her back, that Catherine

O'Dogherty, whom thou art said lately to have taken into thee in concubinage.

*Item*, we ordain, define and at the same time command that thou, the abbot aforesaid, altogether desist from all manner of promise whatsoever made for the superinduction [bringing in] of the aforesaid Catherine – and that thou make no promise, nor give any donation for any other woman whatsoever, to be as concubine taken unto thee (which God forbid) but that do rather violate (all such promises) in future.

*Item*, we ordain, define and at the same time command that within the space of ten days, thou revoke and fully and effectually restore to the said house whatsoever goods, moveable or immoveable, belonging to the said house, have been by thee, whilst thou wast guardian of the said house, alienated; so that neither thou nor any other canon whatsoever of the said house, mayest or may give out, expend, or promise, any of the goods of the said house for the keeping of any woman.

*Item*, we ordain, as aforesaid, that no suspected woman be, by thee or any canon of the aforesaid house, introduced within the precincts of the said house or sleep or rest within the precincts aforesaid.

*Item*, we ordain, that thou and each and every one of the canons of the said house eat together in the common refectory, keeping up holy and devout reading during the time of refection, and that ye sleep together in one dormitory, within the house aforesaid.

*Item*, we ordain, define and at the same time command, that on every Lord's Day, and on every solemn feast, all the *Horae Canonicae*,[4] and one solemn Mass with singing, and another without singing, be devoutly recited in the choir of the church aforesaid, and that on every other day one Mass at least be devoutly celebrated in the said church, and the *Horae Canonicae* be recited in the choir, at least without music. Provided always that each brother, who is to celebrate, approach the Lord's altar, contrite for his sins, and after confession in true penitence.

Given under our seal at Banagher in the diocese of Derry, on the fifteenth day of this month of October, in the year of our Lord, one thousand three hundred and ninety seven, and of our consecration the fourteenth.

Moreover, we give and grant to the dean of the cathedral church of Derry, by the tenor of these presents, the power of compelling you and each of you, if necessary, to the observance of the ordinances aforesaid, by all ecclesiastical censures; and – if it happen (which God forbid) – that any contravene them – the power of punishing you, and each of you, canonically.

---

4 The set prayers for the canonical divisions of the day. Counting from the notional time of sunrise: *Prime* – 6am; *Terce* – 9am; *Sexte* – 12 midday; and *None* – 3pm.

References to the abbot (and some of the other monks) keeping a 'concubine' should not unduly surprise us. Although it was undoubtedly contrary to canon law, this sort of practice was not uncommon in the medieval church throughout Christendom. John Colton's predecessor as archbishop of Armagh, Milo Sweetman, had to deal with a similar situation in Derry in 1367 (Leslie 1937, 2). During the election of a dean in that year, complaints were made that the then bishop of Derry, Simon, a Dominican, had been excommunicated for a variety of offences, the most serious of which were concubinage and adultery. Simon was later rehabilitated, but never seems to have returned to the straight and narrow path. Until his death in 1380, he continued to be the subject of similar accusations.[5]

On his third day in Derry, Friday 12 October, John Colton again took his ceremonial position on the tribunal in the choir of the Augustinian abbey so that he could deal with some more of its problems.

> [T]here appeared before him a certain religious man, Brother Reginald O'Hegarty, canon of the said house, and lately abbot of the same, and humbly supplicated the aforesaid Venerable Father, that he the said Venerable Father would be graciously pleased to ratify and confirm the resignation of the said abbey aforetime made by him Reginald, as has been above set forth: yea, that he would be pleased to accept anew, and *ex-abundanti*, the resignation of the said monastery from him the said Reginald. Which the said Venerable Father showed himself extremely reluctant to do, and urgently prayed the said Reginald to exercise the office of abbot continuously, or at least to undertake it anew; to which the said Reginald utterly refusing to consent, resigned the said monastery, the charge and dignity of the same, into the hands of the aforesaid Father; many religious persons, clerks and laymen, standing present. And the said Venerable Father overcome by importunity of the prayers, as well of the said Reginald, as of the others standing by, accepted as judge ordinary and guardian of the spirituality of the aforesaid bishoprick of Derry, the resignation of the said monastery thus made by him the said Reginald. But afterwards, a long and lengthened interval having elapsed, the canons of the house aforesaid, appearing together in presence of the aforesaid lord primate, unanimously besought him that he might be pleased to confirm the election of a certain brother, Hugh M'Gillivray one of their canons, by them harmoniously agreed upon, to the said monastery so vacant as aforesaid, by the resignation of the said Reginald. And the aforesaid Venerable Father inquired of each of them, the said canons individually, whether he consented to the said Brother

---

5 For a fairly detailed study of Simon's episcopacy, see now Devlin 2013, 252–6.

Hugh as his future abbot. And all and every one unanimously replying that they consented to him as their future abbot, the aforesaid Venerable Father caused a public proclamation or cry to be made and set forth in the same place: that if any person wished to object against the aforesaid Brother Hugh thus elected, or against the form of the election made concerning him, he should, on the next day following, viz. on the thirteenth day of this month of October, legally appear in the cathedral church of Derry, at the usual hour of the sitting of the court, and should legally object and oppose at his own pleasure.

That concluded the formal business of the day. The following day was Saturday 13 October. Dr Colton took his place in the choir of the cathedral of the diocese of Derry, the *Tempull Mór*, a short distance away from the abbey.

[A]fter high mass solemnly sung, and sitting on his tribunal, in a place honourably prepared by the officers of the said church; – and certification having been made on the part of Doctor William McCamayll, dean of Derry, by testimony *viva voce*, concerning a certain mandate of the said Venerable Father, the archbishop and primate, guardian as aforesaid, directed to him the said dean, in which mandate it was contained that he the said dean of Derry should summon, or cause to be summoned, peremptorily, on imminent peril of their souls, the archdeacon, and all and every one, the members of the chapter of Derry, as likewise all of whatsoever of the clergy of Derry, promoted to dignities or ecclesiastical benefices, or to holy orders, as also the herenachs, and all officers whatsoever, of the bishoprick of Derry, to appear on the aforesaid thirteenth day of October, before the said lord primate, guardian as aforesaid, in the cathedral church of Derry aforesaid: and then and there to exhibit their letters of dignities, benefices, orders and dispensations; as likewise their charters or letters of herenachships, lands, possessions and offices of whatsoever kind; and to do and to receive what might be just and agreeable to reason ... And certification having been given ... the said Venerable Father caused the archdeacon, and the others of the chapter of Derry, to be called by the crier. And when they did not appear, he graciously awaited them in the same place, until the hour immediately after the none of day [*c*.3pm]. But very many others, beneficed and non-beneficed, presbyters and also herenachs, being summoned by the crier, appeared personally, exhibited their letters of orders and benefices, and their charters of herenachship and lands and offices ...

The missing members of the chapter were listed as follows. It is important to note the number of Cenél nEógain family names among them.[6]

6 The original Latin word *Magister* is here translated as 'Dr'; *Dominus* as 'Sir'.

Dr William O'Cahan, archdeacon of Derry
Dr John McKaig
Dr Donald Mc Loughlin
Dr David O'Moryson
Sir Laurence McCullimore
Dr Maurice O'Kinlay
Dr Roger O'Doyle
Dr Simon O'Feenaghty
Dr Hugh McKaig
Dr Maurice O'Cahan
Dr John O'Cushely

This 'ritual' stand-off between the cathedral chapter and the archbishop – acting in his role as temporary bishop of Derry – would be resolved a few days later. In the meantime, John Colton was obliged to return to the matter of the abbacy of the Augustinian monastery.

> [T]he Canons Regular of the Black Abbey of Derry, with great urgency, begged of the aforesaid Venerable Father a confirmation of the election by them made, of Brother Hugh M'Gillivray, one of their canons, to be their abbot. And the said Venerable Father having held some discourse with the dean of Armagh [Dr Maurice O'Corry] and others of the clergy present, again *ex abundanti* caused and made a public cry to be made, that if any one wished to propound or object anything against the aforesaid election, or against the form of his election, he should do the same forthwith or never after be heard. And no one appearing or objecting, the same Venerable Father, as guardian of the spirituality and spiritual jurisdiction of the bishoprick of Derry, whereof he then and there made public protestation, judicially confirmed before a large assemblage of clergymen and people, the election of the aforesaid Brother Hugh to the aforesaid monastery, called the Black Abbey of Derry; and authoritatively instituted the said Brother Hugh as abbot of the aforesaid monastery; and by the delivery unto him of his ring, invested him with the same, committing to him the care and government of the aforesaid monastery: and caused the said Brother Hugh to take an oath of obedience and fidelity to be yielded and kept unto him the said Venerable Father, as ordinary of the bishoprick of Derry, by virtue of the guardianship aforesaid, and to his successors the archbishops of Armagh, primates of Ireland, the see of Derry being vacant; and also to the future bishops of Derry, canonically entering.

It was then around 4 or 5 o'clock in the evening. The archbishop went back to the Augustinian abbey for refreshment and then returned to take his position

24 The ruins of St Brecan's sixteenth-century church, St Columb's Park, Clooney, in the Waterside district on the east bank of the Foyle. The building is almost certainly on the same site as the church mentioned in earlier medieval sources, but apparently demolished by Bishop Nicholas Weston (1466–84).

once more in the cathedral. The archdeacon and members of the chapter were summoned individually by the crier, but, once again, they failed to appear. The archbishop now resorted to one of the most terrible of his powers.

> [T]he aforesaid Venerable Father pronounced them all and every one contumacious; and for punishment of their contumacy (proof having been given of the malicious and fraudulent latitation ['remaining hidden'] of them and each of them, by Dr Thomas O'Loughran, canon of Armagh, and instructor or promoter of the office of the aforesaid Venerable Father) the said Venerable Father decreed that they and each of them should be cited by public edict of citation in the church of Derry aforesaid, in presence of the clergy and the multitude of people there being, so that knowledge of the aforesaid citation might and ought probably to come to them and each one of them, that they and each of them should appear before the aforesaid Venerable Father or his commissary, one or more, in the village of Dermot O'Cahan [probably at Enagh Lough, Co. Derry] in the diocese of Derry, on the Monday then next ensuing …

At that point, the crier once more, before the assembled congregation and 'with loud and intelligible voice', summoned the recalcitrant members of the cathedral chapter without success. As well as the visiting dignitaries from Armagh and members of the local clergy, the congregation included the dean and bishop of Raphoe,[7] and the 'prior of the house of Preachers [Dominicans] at Derry', Brother Nicholas Lochlinnach (Mac Lochlainn). The archbishop withdrew and the formal business of the day was concluded.

The following day, 14 October, was a Sunday. The archbishop's party crossed the River Foyle by ferry to what was called the 'parish church of St Brecan, situate in the lands of Clooney ... which lands are known to belong to the Church of Armagh'.[8] The dean of Derry was also rector of the parish of Clooney and he requested Dr Colton to 'reconsecrate that church and its cemetery, polluted as he said by the shedding of blood, afterwards ... to celebrate a solemn mass before the thousands of people there assembled out of respect for the said Father'. The archbishop did as requested and reconsecrated the church and its cemetery. An altar had been prepared outside the west door of the church, but apparently before the mass had begun the missing archdeacon and the other members of the chapter of Derry turned up, having been persuaded to do so through the mediation of the bishop of Raphoe. The recalcitrant clergy 'humbly' requested the archbishop to lift the sentences he had laid on them the previous day 'that so, without scruple of conscience, they might be present at the solemn mass'. Colton assented and:

> commissioned *viva voce* the said lord bishop of Raphoe that he, by authority of the said primate and guardian, should absolve them and each of them according to the church's rite – under pain and condition nevertheless of falling a second time under the same sentences, if they did not afterwards obey the mandates and ordinance of the aforesaid lord archbishop. And the said lord bishop of Raphoe accepting this commission, absolved, in due form or law, them, the archdeacon, and other members of the chapter, there present, having first administered to them, and each of them, an oath to abide by the mandates of the church.

When this process was completed, the main liturgy of the day commenced. During the mass, the archbishop solemnly blessed the newly elected Brother Hugh, as abbot of 'the monastery called the Black Abbey of Derry' according to the rite and custom of the church.

---

7 Seoán Mac Meanmain, a Cistercian monk of the monastery at Assaroe, Co. Donegal.
8 The church was almost certainly on the same site as the present ruined St Brecan's Church in St Columb's Park. Apparently, the older church was demolished by Bishop Nicholas Weston, but was rebuilt by Bishop Réamann Ó Gallachair (see below, p. 126).

> And the mass and benediction being finished, the same Venerable Father, with consent of the whole convent [the Black Abbey], and by advice of the dean, archdeacon and chapter of Derry, delivered and yielded up the common seal of the aforesaid convent, which the aforesaid Father had in his custody, to a certain Brother Donald O'Hegarty, a canon of the said house, on behalf of the whole convent – commanded the said Brother Donald, the canon aforesaid, and the whole convent, under penalty of the greater excommunication, to replace, as soon as they conveniently could, and to keep the said common seal in the common chest, under three keys and locks; – and to deliver the said keys unto certain regular persons of the said convent, to be chosen by the whole convent, that is to say, one key to each person, to be by him kept; – and enjoined the said abbot, that he, at no future time, should usurp to himself singly, the custody, the carrying or handling of the said seal; which abbot promised, under debt of oath, to do as enjoined.

When these matters had all been dealt with, the archbishop 'proceeded with his retinue to the village of Dermot O'Cahan', probably at Enagh Lough. No further public business seems to have been transacted for the rest of that day. On the morning of Monday 15 October, the dean and chapter of Derry presented themselves before the archbishop again and asked that they be allowed on the following day, Tuesday, to 'exhibit' the various letters and documents asked of them at the ceremony in the cathedral on the previous Saturday. Colton agreed to their request. Still at Dermot O'Cahan's 'village', the archbishop was obliged to deal with a number of marital disputes. The lady Una O'Connor, 'saying that she was the lawful wife of Magnus O'Cahan, the chieftain of her sept', claimed that her husband had put her away 'without the judgment of the church, and taken another in her stead'. She asked that the archbishop arrange 'that fitting redress should be granted to her upon the case'. Magnus, 'being there close at hand', was summoned to appear to answer 'on account of the imminent peril of souls'. The charge put to him was

> that he had formerly contracted marriage with the aforesaid Una by words of the present tense, and had confirmed the same by cohabitation, and had begotten offspring of her, and that he had afterwards, of his own temerity, without the judgment of the church, put her away and adulterously joined himself to another; wherefore the said father inquired of him if he could show any cause why he ought not to be compelled to take her back, and to do canonical penance for so great an enormity.

Magnus asked for time to consider the charge and to consult his 'council', but, on returning, denied that he had ever 'contracted matrimony with the aforesaid Una'. Una was requested to produce witnesses in support of her case and she promptly produced a certain Donald O'Cahan and Simon O'Feenaghty – the latter a member of the chapter of Derry. Further consideration of the matter was postponed to the following day but, as there is no other mention of it in Kenmore's account, we must assume that harmony was somehow achieved for all the parties involved.

A second marriage dispute was then brought before the archbishop. Catherine O'Dogherty claimed that she was lawfully married to Magnus McGilligan, but that he 'had divorced her without any reasonable cause, and taken other women in her stead'. The hearing of the case continued along the same lines as the previous dispute and further consideration of it was also postponed to the following day.

> These things being thus transacted, the aforesaid Venerable Father having taken with him horses provided by, and at the expense of the dean of Derry, for the carriage of his victuals and baggage, proceeded together with his retinue, and with the dean, archdeacon and others of the chapter of Derry, to Banagher [about twenty miles to the south-east], in the diocese of Derry; at whose arrival, the herenachs and inhabitants of that place, made arrangements, at their own expense, for provisions to the men and horses of the said Venerable Father, and of his officers, as also for the night-watch.

On the following morning, 16 October 1397, the archbishop and his party travelled the short distance – two miles or so – from Banagher to the 'house of the Blessed Virgin, for Canons Regular of the order of St Augustine' at Dungiven. Various pieces of business were transacted and the party then returned to Banagher. A tribunal had been set up in the church there and as soon as all were present a ceremony began in which the archbishop set out the legal reasons why he had come to the diocese of Derry. The members of the chapter who had absented themselves from what was to have been a similar ceremony at the cathedral in Derry on the previous Saturday now all 'gave their corporal oath, touching the Holy Gospels', of obedience to the archbishop in his role as temporary guardian of the diocese of Derry. Various other commitments were given on both sides.

> [A]nd a horse having been given to the aforesaid lord archbishop, by the aforesaid dean of Derry, and another horse by the archdeacon of Derry, on account and in part payment of the rents and other episcopal emoluments, by them or any of them received during the vacancy of the see, the same not being to them due and payable.

Certain other administrative arrangements were put in place by the archbishop, who 'commanded and caused his letters thereupon to be made patent'. The marital case of Catherine and Magnus McGilligan was raised, but, as there was no time to deal with it, the archbishop deputed its resolution to the archdeacon of Derry and John McKaig, a member of the chapter. He then retired for the night. 'The herenachs and inhabitants of the village provided, at their own expense, the needful requisites and night-watch'. On the following morning, 17 October, after an early mass, various outstanding pieces of business were transacted by the archbishop including the delivery to the dean of Derry of

> letters addressed to divers persons, of monitions, suspensions, excommunications and interdict, against O'Donnell, O'Dogherty, O'Cahan, O'Gormley, Donald and Brian Mór, sons of Henry O'Neill, on account of their usurpation of the episcopal rights of the church of Derry.

There were few, if any, of the local Gaelic lords not included in this 'gang of thieves' and, yet, as one historian of medieval Ireland has pointed out, perhaps surprisingly, Archbishop Colton had been able to move about the diocese 'in peace and harmony, unharassed by any hostile lay power' (Watt 1973, 211). A few other local matters were dealt with by the archbishop in his role as guardian of the bishopric.

> These affairs being settled, having taken with him certain horses from the village of Banagher to the number of five or thereabouts, for his own baggage and that of his retinue, at the common expense of the herenachs and inhabitants of the village of Banagher aforesaid, the said Venerable Father returned towards the diocese of Armagh; the dean, archdeacon and other members of the chapter of Derry accompanying him for the space of two miles or thereabouts; to whom having bidden farewell, and having dismissed them in peace, the said Venerable Father, proceeding with his retinue through the trackless mountains of Glenelly, came in peace to the church of Desertcreat in the [rural] deanery of Tullyhog, within the diocese of Armagh.

Derry returned to its normal pace, but, although the documentation is sparse, there is a general indication of decline and stagnation. The rare reports we get suggest that the main buildings of the settlement were anything but in good condition.[9] In 1423, Pope Martin V granted an indulgence to anyone who assisted with the repair of the Dubreclés. In 1469, the bishop of Derry, Nicholas Weston – the only Englishman to hold that office during the Middle Ages, and who was probably in Rome at the time – presented a petition to Pope

---

[9] Admittedly, the same could be said of major public buildings in many parts of medieval Ireland. It is also likely that some of the reports were exaggerated in order to gain the

Paul II describing the abysmal state of his cathedral church, the famed *Tempull Mór*. It may be that he had exaggerated somewhat. At any rate, on 14 December 1469, an indulgence was granted.

> The pope has learned that the church of Derry, which is notable among the cathedral churches of the realm of Ireland, is, on account of the various misfortunes with which those parts have been afflicted, almost entirely unroofed and that Bishop Nicholas the bishop for the time being has no house which he can inhabit and that the said church in which there used to be a tin chalice only, is without chalices, books, parchments and other ecclesiastical ornaments and that it is feared that, without the help of the faithful, the said church will fall utterly to ruin. The pope, therefore, desiring that the said church may be roofed, that the said bishop may be able to build himself a becoming house and buy the said ornaments, hereby grants a relaxation in perpetuity of seven years and seven quarantines of enjoined penance to all who, being truly penitent and having confessed, visit the said church on the feasts of St Martin in winter [11 November] and St Columba [9 June] and give alms for such rebuilding, restoration and maintenance.[10]

Manus Ó Domhnaill has a curious miracle story about Bishop Weston.

> Once Colum Cille was in the place called Clooney in the port of Derry on the east bank of Lough Foyle, and he blessed the place and built a church there. Speaking through the spirit of prophecy, he said: 'A foreign bishop will come to this place long after me and he will demolish this church that I've made, and he will build something else with its stones at a place called Bun Sentuinne ['mouth of the old wave'?] in the same townland'. Then he made this verse:
>
> > My fear is that foreign strangers,
> > Here to Clooney, yet will come,
> > And bear my church away with them,
> > To Bun Sentuinne, cold and numb.
>
> All this was fulfilled as is clear to everyone today [1532]; that is a foreign bishop called Nicholas Weston came to Derry [bishop of Derry, 1466–84], and destroyed the church in order to make a palace [*cúirt*] from it. But that palace was never finished, and I'm certain that it was because of a miracle of Colum Cille that they weren't able to complete it with the stones of his very own church.
>
> (Lacey 1998, 54)

requested support.    10 CPR, xii (1458–71), quoted in Bonner 1982, 132.

The remains of the church that were 'clear to everyone' in Manus' day were almost certainly on the same site as the ruins now known as St Brecan's Church in St Columb's Park, in the Clooney district of Derry's Waterside.[11] The church was rebuilt in the late sixteenth century by Bishop Réamann Ó Gallachair (Jefferies 1999, 176), but the present ruins may incorporate some of the fabric of those extant in 1532. Sir Nicholas Weston's death is recorded at the years 1474 and 1484 in various sets of annals, but it appears from other sources that the second of these is the correct date (AU).

[11] There is confusion about the dedication of this church in both the medieval and the modern sources. Richard Kenmore, in 1397, called it the 'parish church of St Brecan' (see p. 121, above). Manus Ó Domhnaill, in 1532, associated it with St Colum Cille (see p. 125, above). An annal entry for 1197 (see p. 100, above) adds further to the confusion. See detailed discussion in Mac Giolla Easpaig 1996–7.

CHAPTER 9

# The Uí Domhnaill and the end of medieval Derry

From the mid-thirteenth century onwards, the Uí Domhnaill as senior lords of Tír Chonaill (more or less modern Donegal) were the most powerful dynasty in the north-west of Ireland, rivalled in the rest of Ulster only by the O'Neills of Tír Eóghain. In their heyday, the Uí Domhnaill were among the most accomplished rulers in Ireland. They were the first Irish chieftains to make use of galloglass Scottish mercenaries; later, they were among the first in Ireland to use fire-arms and artillery. They were great patrons of the learned classes and had extensive contacts with foreign aristocrats and royalty. They were also renowned as patrons of the church, particularly – from the end of the fifteenth century – of the innovative Franciscans.

Although their family propaganda claimed otherwise, the Uí Domhnaill (and their distant relatives the Uí Dochartaigh) were descended from an originally fairly insignificant people, the Síl Lugdach (Lacey 2012). They had originated in the sixth and seventh centuries in what must have been a relatively impoverished kingdom. By the end of the thirteenth century, they had taken control of almost the whole of what is now Co. Donegal, with the exception of the Inishowen Peninsula, which had come under Anglo-Norman influence. Elsewhere, they had been successful in excluding Anglo-Norman intrusion into their territories. When Norman power collapsed in Inishowen about 1333, the Uí Dochartaigh – chief supporters of the Uí Domhnaill – moved into that peninsula from their existing territories in Ard Midhair (Glenswilly and Kilteevogue) and Cenél nÉnnai (the Laggan, east Donegal).

Likewise, with the collapse of Mac Lochlainn power in the mid-thirteenth century, the Uí Domhnaill began to exert influence on the settlement at Derry, which also, effectively, became part of their lordship. Although originally their ancestors had no connection with Columba, from at least the early ninth century, as their territories expanded, they cultivated, for propaganda purposes, Columban lore as part of their own patrimony. They claimed, almost certainly falsely, that they shared the same genealogy with the ancient Cenél Conaill to whom Columba had belonged. In fact, they claimed direct descent from close relatives of the saint. As the site, according to legend, of the first and most loved of Columba's churches, Derry was clearly one of the Uí Domhnaill's most prized possessions. The legends of Colum Cille were harnessed – researched and perhaps even 'embroidered' – as part of Uí Domhnaill family propaganda.

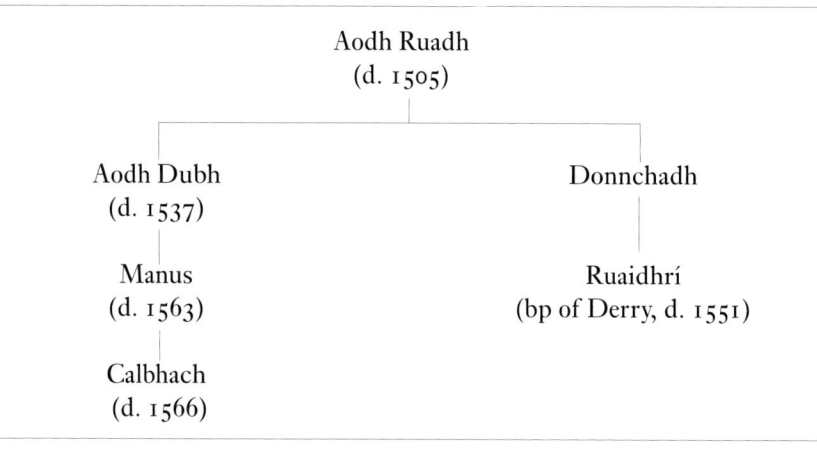

TABLE 7. Genealogy of sixteenth-century Uí Domhnaill lords involved with Derry.

```
                    Aodh Ruadh
                    (d. 1505)
         ┌──────────────┴──────────────┐
    Aodh Dubh                      Donnchadh
    (d. 1537)                          │
        │                          Ruaidhrí
     Manus                    (bp of Derry, d. 1551)
    (d. 1563)
        │
    Calbhach
    (d. 1566)
```

In 1474, Aodh Ruadh Ó Domhnaill introduced the Franciscans to his lordship and established a monastery for them at what is now Donegal town. Among the Observantine Franciscans, the friar minor Domhnall Ó Fallamhain had established a significant reputation as a preacher. He was vicar provincial or leader of the order in Ireland between 1472 and 1475. The Annals of Ulster said of him that he was 'the preacher that did most service to Irishmen since [St] Patrick was in Ireland'. In 1485, Ó Fallamhain was appointed bishop of Derry. No doubt the Uí Domhnaill were involved in his appointment and saw him as a close ally in their own plans for Derry; Uí Domhnaill influence in Derry was clearly strengthened by the bishop's appointment. He died in 1501.

Almost certainly around the same time, a tower house castle was built in Derry by the Uí Dochartaigh for their overlords the Uí Domhnaill. Although there is no documentation as to when it was built, we know something about its origins from a reference in the 1609 inquisition:

> And further, the said jurors doe uppon their oathes finde and point out that the grounde and land whereon the old castle called O'Donell's castle was built, within the lower forte of the citie of Derry, was formerly bought by O'Donell of the erenagh [Mac Lochlainn] beinge parcell of his herenagh land for twentie cows, and the said castle was built thereupon by O'Dogherty for O'Donell's use, in consideracion whereof O'Donell forgave O'Dogherty certen dueties.

We do not know when it was built, but most of those castles were erected in Ireland between 1450 and 1550. Aodh Ruadh himself had built his new castle

*The Uí Domhnaill and the end of medieval Derry* 129

**25** The Uí Domhnaill tower house on the west bank of the River Foyle in Derry, as shown on a map of *c*.1611 (original in Trinity College Dublin). The castle had been built by the Uí Dochartaigh – probably around 1500 – for their overlords in lieu of 'certen dueties', on land bought from the Mac Lochlainn erenagh for 'twentie cows'.

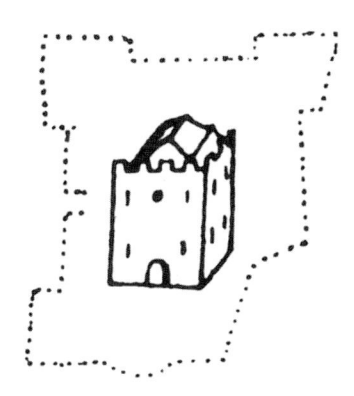

at Donegal in 1505, and in 1512 he set off from Derry with an army on a campaign against Mac William Burke (AConn.). As Derry was certainly not a convenient launching pad for a campaign in Connacht, there must have been some special reason that Aodh Ruadh used it as his departure point. The completion of a new castle there may have been that special reason.

The castle, as shown on several early seventeenth-century maps, was located near what is now the bottom of Magazine Street, close to the old shoreline of the Foyle, which then came right up to what are now the city walls in Shipquay Place. The building survived into the plantation city and gave us names like Castle Street and Castle Gate. The castle was very close to the start of a pilgrimage route (*oilithre*) that Manus Ó Domhnaill described in 1532, and one of the functions of that fortification may have been to monitor the arrival of the pilgrims by boat. Certainly, the story about the pilgrimage in Manus' *Betha Colaim Chille* – the only account of it that survives – shows that the Uí Domhnaill had a renewed interest in Derry in the early sixteenth century. Manus was the eldest son of Aodh Dubh, who was a son of Aodh Ruadh.

The description of the pilgrimage is set out in the context of a legend about a fictional visit by Colum Cille to Pope Gregory the Great in Rome.

> Colum Cille's messengers went back to Iona and explained to him that the pope wanted him to visit. Colum Cille set out then and, when he had come to within fifteen miles of Rome, all the bells of the city rang by

themselves and they could not be stopped. All the people of Rome were startled and filled with wonder. 'Don't be amazed at this', said the pope. 'The holy patron, Colum Cille, is coming to see me and the bells rang in his honour, and they will not be silenced until he comes to the city'.

Then the pope went out with great honour and reverence to meet Colum Cille, together with many of the nobility of Rome. They embraced when they met each other and were truly joyful and glad towards each other. Then they returned to the city and, when Colum Cille had bowed down in the great church of Rome,[1] the bells stopped by themselves. After Colum Cille had been with the pope in great honour for a while, he got permission to return home. The pope sent his blessing with him and Colum Cille left his blessing with the pope. And then the pope gave important gifts to Colum Cille, that is that, whichever of his own foundations Colum Cille would appoint as a pilgrimage destination for everyone, there should be the same indulgence there as for a pilgrimage to Rome. And, although he himself was in Scotland, the place that Colum Cille gave that honour to was Derry;[2] and the place where he ordained that the pilgrimage should be made was from the altar at the ship quay at the east end of the settlement to the 'Righthand-wise Turn' at the west end.

(Lacey 1998, 114)

The story, of course, is not historical, either with regard to Pope Gregory or to Colum Cille, but it does give us two interesting pieces of information about early sixteenth-century Derry: (i) that either based on that legend, or authenticated by it, there was a pilgrimage route (*oilithre*) there between the two named places; and (ii) that the name of one of those, *port na long*, seems to

---

[1] Instead of St Peter's Basilica (or some equivalent), the name actually given by Ó Domhnaill to this church is *Tempull Mór na Romha* – 'the great church of Rome', the same name (*Tempull Mór*) as was used for the cathedral church in Derry. Manus' references to Rome were probably influenced by accounts he had heard from his father, Aodh Dubh, who had gone on pilgrimage there in 1510–11, leaving the young Manus as his deputy at home. The massive redesign and rebuilding for Pope Julian II of St Peter's, familiar to us now, was just commencing about that time.   [2] There is an error at this point in the 1918 printed edition of the *Betha*: the omission of a short section of the English translation that is of crucial importance to the story about Derry (Lacey 1997b, 39–41). The Irish language text as printed by O'Kelleher and Schoepperle contains the sentence: *Acus as é baile dá tucc C.C. an onóir sin .i. do Doire 7 ssé fen a nAlbain; acus asse inadh inar ordaigh se an oilithre sin do denamh .i. ó an ulaidh ata ag port na long 'sa cend toir don baili, conuige an t-impódh dessiul ata 'sa cend tíar de*. The editors translated this as: 'And it is to this place that Columcille gave this honor, to wit, from the calvary that is in the harbor of the ships east of the town, to the turn sunwise that is west thereof' (O'Kelleher and Schoepperle 1918, 212–13). The references to Scotland and Derry are omitted in the 1918 printed translation, although in the index there is a reference to this section of the text that reads '*Port na Long*, on the east side of Derry, 218' (ibid., 482). This would seem to indicate that the omission was a typographical error.

have been the direct predecessor of the equivalent English language place-name 'Ship Quay', which is found in the city in roughly the same place from the seventeenth century onwards. That place-name is usually thought of as dating only from the time of the plantation city of Londonderry and not from the medieval settlement that preceded it (Lacey 1997b, 40). Such pilgrimage routes were a popular feature of the cult of Colum Cille. Two survive to the present day in Co. Donegal: at Gleann Cholm Cille (Herity 1989; 1995) and at Churchtown near Gartan, the saint's alleged birthplace (Ó Gallachair 1963, 263). *Port na long* was evidently at what is now Shipquay Place. Elsewhere in the *Betha*, Ó Domhnaill narrates another legend that tells us that *an t-impódh deissiul* was in the general area close to the *Tempull Mór*, now the precincts of the Long Tower church.

> Having received, moreover, the very noble and very honourable order of priesthood, and having been chosen against his will as the abbot of the black monks in that settlement of Derry, and having blessed it and made his dwelling there, he took it in hand to feed a hundred poor people every day for the sake of God. And he had a particular person to give that food to the poor. One day, after the poor had been fed, another poor man came begging. But Colum Cille's servant said that he had already fed the customary number, so he told the poor man to return on the following day when he would get alms like the rest of the poor. But he did not come on the following day until after all the poor had been fed, and again he begged alms. He got nothing from the servant but the same answer. And he came begging a third day after the poor had been fed but only got the same answer from Colum Cille's servant.
>
> At that point the poor man said: 'Go to Colum Cille and tell him that ... he should not decide just to provide only for a hundred each day'.
>
> The servant went to Colum Cille and told him what the poor man had said to him. When Colum Cille heard this, he rose suddenly, not staying for his cloak or shoes, but he pursued the poor man and overtook him eventually at the place that is called *An t-Impodh Deisiul* on the southwest side of the *Tempull Mór*. He recognized that it was the Lord that was there and he fell on his knees before Him and he spoke with Him, face to face and was filled with the grace of the Holy Spirit. Among all the gifts that he got from God that time, he received knowledge of all mysteries in the scripture ... And from then on he provided not only for a hundred, but the great gifts that he got without measure from God he gave them without stint for the sake of God.
>
> (Lacey 1998, 46–7)

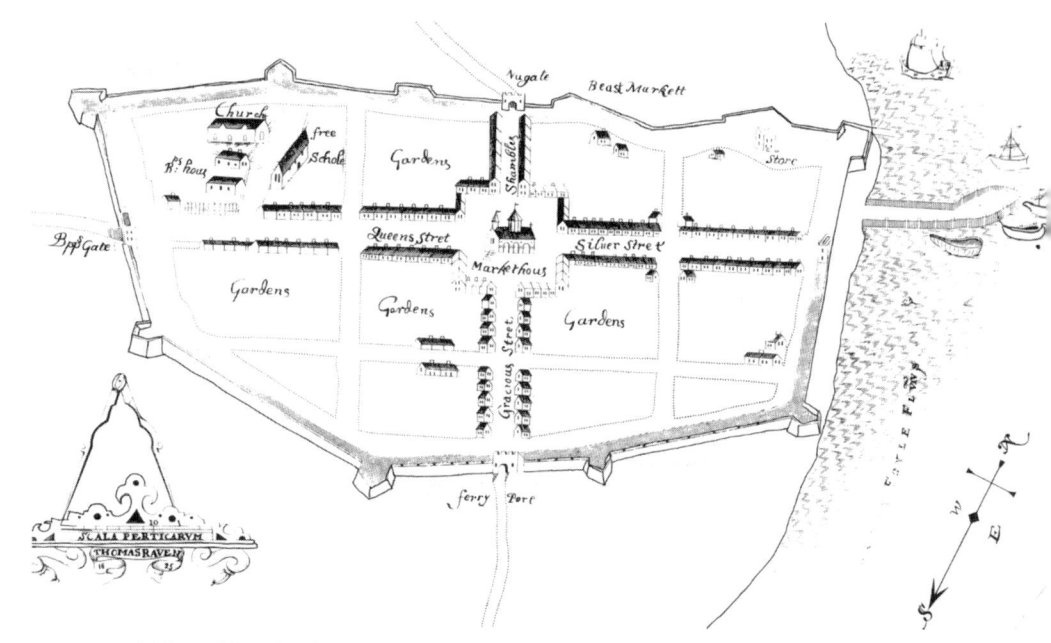

26 Map of Londonderry, c.1625. The former Uí Domhnaill castle is marked 'store' (also known as the 'magazine'). The slightly zig-zag line of Magazine Street and the adjacent city walls (top), defying the otherwise geometric layout of the city, probably reflects a pre-Plantation pathway that may have been the route of the medieval pilgrimage (*oilithre*) described by Manus Ó Domhnaill in 1532.

The legend of an apparition of the Lord to Colum Cille in Derry will have served to strengthen the value of any pilgrimages made there.

Contrary to the geometric layout of the plantation city, the unexpected somewhat zig-zag line of Magazine Street and the adjacent city walls may be a survival of an older medieval street, which was probably the route of the pilgrimage dating back at least to the early sixteenth century (Lacey 1997b). It looks very much as if the Uí Domhnaill could have been trying to develop the pilgrimage as a kind of medieval tourism and that Manus' book, which he may have intended to be printed, was in part designed to have a central role in such a 'promotional campaign'. As an Ó Domhnaill, Manus believed, almost certainly incorrectly, that his ancestors had been related to Colum Cille, 'his high saint and kinsman in blood' as also 'his own dear patron'. Manus' cousin, the very effective Ruaidhrí Ó Domhnaill, had been appointed bishop of Derry in 1520 – the one thousandth anniversary of Colum Cille's birth, as the family well knew.[3]

[3] The only *Anno Domini* dates used by Manus in the *Betha Colaim Chille* are 520 – the date of its subject's birth – and 1532, the year the text was completed. Bishop Ruaidhrí, who died in 1551, had to negotiate the difficult situations arising from Henry VIII's reforms, both

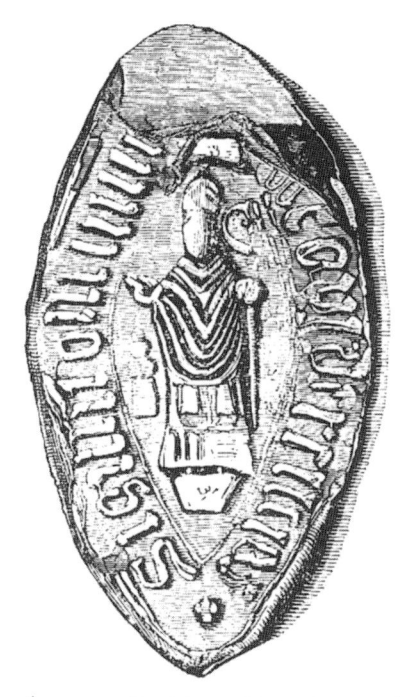

*The Uí Domhnaill and the end of medieval Derry*　　　　　　　　　　　　　133

27 The seal of Ruaidhrí Ó Domhnaill, bishop of Derry (1520–50) (after Colby 1837, 34).

Although the *Betha* was composed by Manus at his castle of *Port na Trí namat* – the junction of the rivers Finn, Foyle and Mourne – we would be justified in claiming the work as part of Derry's historiography. As well as much else of course, it contains the most comprehensive account of the alleged foundation of Derry as well as several other stories about Colum Cille that are set there. If it was not written consciously to boost the pilgrimage there as a form of economic development, the account certainly underpinned such a project. The *Betha* also gives us incidental information about Derry that we cannot find elsewhere. Some of those stories have what we might call a distinctively Irish twist to them. For instance, it is the earliest source for the existence of an institution that was to become a lot more common in the later city:

> Another time when Colum Cille was in Derry, a gambler and a poor man came to him. And he gave a *bonn* ['groat'?] to the gambler and a penny to the poor man. And it seemed strange to all that he should give more to the gambler than to the poor man. God revealed to Colum Cille that everyone was amazed at this, but he said to some of them that were present that they should follow the gambler and the poor man to see what

secular and ecclesiastical. For his political and diplomatic career, see Devlin 2000b, 115–18 and now Devlin 2013, 264–8.

each would do with the money he had given them. And they found the gambler in a tavern (*taibeirne*) drinking the value of the *bonn* and sharing it with every needy person who came to him. And this was the way that they found the poor man: dead on the road, and the penny that Colum Cille had given him sewn into his clothes along with five marks. They returned to Colum Cille with the news.

Then Colum Cille said: 'God let me know that the poor man had only a short time to live but, even if it had been longer, he wouldn't have used for himself or anyone else what he'd been given, but hoard it as he did with the five marks. And although the gambler was a bad man, he didn't hoard what he got but, to the value of the *bonn*, he satisfied himself and the others that were in need. That's why I gave him more than the poor man'.

(Lacey 1998, 50–1)

Whatever its intention, the story certainly indicated Colum Cille's support for the 'hospitality industry' in medieval Derry; this would have been very useful for those promoting the pilgrimage there. Audrey Horning has suggested that taverns and inns were an essential part of the urban package associated with the plantation (2009, 118). But this story – even though it is fictional – shows that taverns, and commercial transactions in them, were not entirely unknown in north-west Ulster almost a hundred years before the plantation.

Whatever the Uí Domhnaill planned for Derry, it was not to be. For much of the later part of the Middle Ages, the English crown had paid little attention to Ireland as a whole, confining their policies to ensuring that the island did not become a base for foreign enemies or a drain on royal resources. All that changed with the arrival on the throne of Henry VIII. His policies required active intervention, as did those of his successors. Initially, these events left most of Gaelic Ulster, including the tiny settlement at Derry, largely unaffected. With the death in 1559 of Conn O'Neill, who had been created earl of Tyrone in 1542 under the policy of 'surrrender and regrant', supremacy in Ulster had passed to Shane 'the proud' O'Neill. But Shane's authority rested on Gaelic Irish (rather than English) custom and rights. By then, Queen Elizabeth I and her lord lieutenant for Ireland, the earl of Sussex, had been extending English-style local government throughout Munster and Connacht – it was already reasonably well established in Leinster. They now turned their attention to Ulster. They sought to break up the vast Gaelic bloc under Shane's control and achieve, instead, a series of separate treaties with the individual local leaders. Sussex's advice to his queen was: 'if Shane be overthrown, all is settled. If Shane settle, all is overthrown'.

In 1565, Sir Henry Sidney was appointed lord deputy with a commission to bring Shane to obedience. In September 1566, Sidney marched into Ulster from the south in search of O'Neill. The latter eluded the English who had to be content with confirming the allegiance to the crown of the Uí Domhnaill chieftain, Calbhach. Ancient rivalries between the O'Neills and the Uí Domhnaill – who believed themselves to be the latter-day representatives of the Cenél nEógain and Cenél Conaill respectively – prevented a united front against the advancing English forces.

Sidney's progress into the north was part of a pincer movement, the other arm of which was an English force transported by sea, which entered Ulster via the 'back-door' of Lough Foyle. The sea-borne expedition consisted of one thousand foot soldiers and fifty horse under the command of Col. Edward Randolph. They set sail from Bristol on 6 September 1566 and subsequently arrived in the vicinity of Derry. According to Ciarán Devlin, Randolph and Sidney were both encamped on the Waterside by 12 October. On that day, a party led by the Ó Dochartaigh chieftain and the bishop of Derry, Eoghan Ó Dochartaigh, came to offer them 'the platte of ground where the ancient city of Derry stood, now totally ruined and yet some monuments remaining, in the hope that [Her] Majesty [Elizabeth I] would build, or cause to be built, a city there' (2000b, 119). It appears that, prior to the arrival of the English, Shane O'Neill had burned Derry, then part of the territory of his enemy (and ally of the English), the Uí Domhnaill (ibid.).

Randolph made camp in Derry amid whatever had survived of the various medieval structures. The soldiers threw up earthen defence works and, according to tradition, used the stone-built *Tempull Mór* cathedral as their ammunition magazine. The seventeenth-century writer, Philip O'Sullivan Beare, in his *History of Catholic Ireland*, ignoring any damage done by O'Neill, described the situation in his characteristic manner:

> The English heretics having landed in this town against the wish and command of O'Donnell expel the priests and monks, invade the holy churches and in one church place for safe-keeping gunpowder, leaden bullets, tow-match, guns, pikes and other munitions of war. In other churches, they performed the heretical rites of Luther, Calvin and others of the class of impious men. They left nothing undefiled by their wickedness. St Columba did not long delay the punishment of this sin.

The English, who began to succumb quickly to the damp conditions of the north-west of Ireland and the harassment by their Irish enemies, held on in Derry. They complained that they got no support from their supposed ally, Calbhach Ó Domhnaill, who himself died on 26 October. On 15 November, supported by the Uí Dochartaigh of Inishowen, the English marched out of Derry to an encounter with O'Neill's men. The English won the battle, but their commander Randolph was killed. Various local Gaelic lords submitted to the crown, but the English garrison itself continued to decline. On 21 April

1567, a fire broke out in the camp and spread rapidly. The flames caught the ammunition store and there was a huge explosion. At least thirty people were killed. The cause of the fire was variously attributed: on the English side, an accident in the blacksmith's forge was blamed; O'Sullivan Beare had another explanation:

> The natives confidently assert that a wolf of huge size and with bristling hair, coming boldly out of the nearest wood to the settlement, and entering the iron barriers, emitting from his mouth a great number of sparks, such as fly from a red-hot iron when it is struck, proceeded to the place in which the powder was stored, and spitting out sparks, set fire to the powder and church. I will not take upon myself to vouch for the truth of this story; upon fame and long-standing tradition let it rest.

O'Sullivan Beare claimed that the survivors were well aware of the real author of the tragedy. The English, he says, cried out: 'The Irish *god* Columba killed us all'. The new Ó Domhnaill chieftain wrote to the lord deputy from his castle at Bundrowes expressing his 'grief for the ruin of the Derry'. According to a 9 May letter from Cecil, chief advisor to Queen Elizabeth, 'Her Majesty perceiving it to come by God's ordinance, beareth it well'. The remains of the garrison were withdrawn from Derry and, although there were various plans up to 1600 to replace it, these came to nothing.

Whatever remained of Derry after Shane O'Neill's onslaught seems to have been more or less finished off by the fire and explosion of 1567. But there was one swan song. A document preserved by the seventeenth-century antiquarian Sir James Ware demonstrates that some form of ecclesiastical life continued there after the English left, at least intermittently (Martin 1968). The document is a certificate of ordination to the priesthood of Patrick Mac Entagart (peculiarly of the diocese of Clogher), with the consent of his own bishop, Cornelius Mac Ardle, by Réamann Ó Gallachair, bishop of Derry (1569–1601) (fig. 28).[4]

According to the certificate, the ordination took place on 10 June 1590, Pentecost Sunday, in *ecclesia cathedrali Derensis* – the cathedal church of Derry. It is not clear what building is implied by that designation. Tradition claims that the *Tempull Mór* had been used as the ammunition store and was destroyed in the 1567 explosion. There were, however, at least two other churches on the 'island' of Derry at the time – the Cistercian convent chapel at the top of the hill and the church of the Augustinian abbey. Either of these could have functioned as a pro-cathedral; from other evidence the Cistercian church seems more likely. It is not clear why this Clogher ordination should

---

[4] For excellent biographical essays on Bishop Ó Gallachair, see Devlin 2000b, 120–33 and now 2013, 270–87.

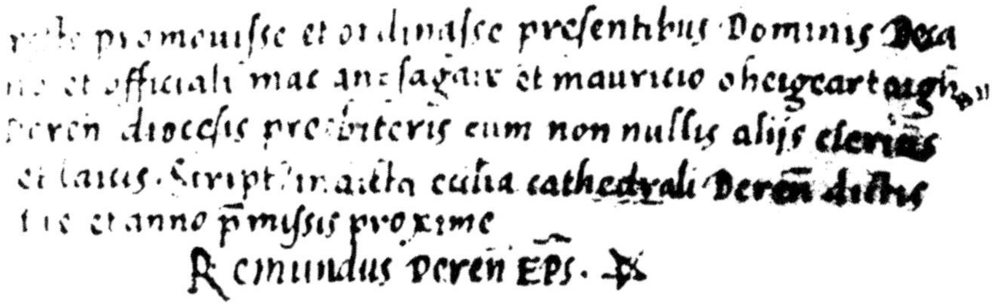

*The Uí Domhnaill and the end of medieval Derry* 137

*[handwritten Latin manuscript image]*

28 Certificate of ordination to the priesthood of Patrick Mac Entagart, 10 June 1590, '*in eclesia cathedrali Deren[sis]*, the cathedral church of Derry'. It bears the signature *Remundus Deren[sis] eps [episcopus]*, that is, Réamann Ó Gallachair, bishop of Derry (1569–1601) (British Library, Add. MS 4783, fo. 29r; see Martin 1968).

have taken place in Derry. The dean of Derry at the time, who was said to be present, was William Mac Entagart, who may have been a relative of the new priest. William, unlike his bishop, who was slain by crown forces in 1601, later conformed to the established church and continued as Protestant dean. He spoke Latin as well as Irish and served on the jury at the Limavady Inquisition in 1609.

Within a few years of the Derry ordination, the Nine Years War – the last ditch effort of Gaelic Ulster – began. It would see the arrival of Docwra in 1600, bringing about the absolute end of medieval Derry and the commencement of a totally new phase in the history of that settlement. The Dubreclés Augustinian community had disappeared in the tumults of the sixteenth century, although the ruins of its church may have survived for use in the plantation city.[5] The titular position of abbot and *comarba* of Colum Cille was taken over by bishops Eoghan Ó Dochartaigh (1554–68) and his successor Réamann Ó Gallachair, and later for a while by the bishops of Raphoe (Devlin 2000a, 110). The Cistercian convent also disappeared, but its church survived to be used for secular purposes by Docwra in 1600. The Dominican house went the same way, although Docwra was said to be kind – providing a parcel of land – to the elderly prior Seán Ó Luinín, who was still living there in 1600 (Fenning 1978, 53; 2009, 96). The new English bishop, George Montgomery, was not so indulgent. He tried to persuade Ó Luinín to 'embrace Protestantism', warning him that he would have him hanged for celebrating mass (Jefferies 2000, 162). The friar was later executed along with his brother William, another Dominican, by English troops during Sir Cathair Ó Dochartaigh's rebellion in 1608 (ibid.).

[5] Various lists of clerics for late medieval Derry are available; for example, anon. (Ciarán Devlin?) 1978, 18–52, esp. 25–6 for the Dubreclés; Daly and Devlin 1997; Leslie 1937, esp. 28–31, 47, 68–72; and other references cited in those publications. See also now Devlin 2013.

CHAPTER 10

# Memorializing and reinterpreting Columban Derry

From 1600 onwards, Derry was absorbed into the English system in Ireland, first as a garrison camp and from 1604 as the new city of Derrie. Some of the medieval buildings survived and were put to various uses by the settlers. However, in April 1608 the 'infant city' was attacked and burned by Sir Cahir O'Doherty. Thomas Ridgeway, writing in July, pointed out that, amid the destruction, the Augustinian church, which seems to have been used as the colony's place of worship,[1] and:

> whose timber work, either in respect of the height or in devotion to their solemn Collam Kill, the patron of that place, and whose name they use as their word of privity and distinction in all their wicked and treacherous attempts, was not fired.

Within a few years, the city of Londonderry was being built; allegedly parts of its walls were made from the debris of the medieval buildings. The new Protestant cathedral was constructed between 1628 and 1633. The 'apostolic' succession from its medieval predecessor seemingly confirmed with a stone brought especially from the ruined *Tempull Mór* (fig. 30); as also the fact that it was built, more or less, on the site of the nuns' church, which may itself have functioned lately as a pro-cathedral. Perhaps unexpectedly, the dedication of the new cathedral was to the ancient patron, St Columba. Although elsewhere the reformed Church of Ireland had simply held on to the ancient cathedrals along with some of the traditions of their patron saints, the situation in Londonderry was different. The medieval cathedral had been destroyed and, allegedly, on that occasion, according to O'Sullivan Beare, the English garrison that was occupying the building were heard to cry out: 'The Irish *god*, Columba, killed us all'. That idea that Columba was a sort of pagan deity was sarcastically echoed in other sources.[2] Given all those circumstances, it is surely surprising that the Londoners dedicated their new cathedral to Columba rather than, as might have been expected, to a saint with whom they

---

1 But see p. 87, above.   2 In 1584, the lord deputy, Sir John Perrot, having acquired a relic as booty from Sorleyboy MacDonald's castle at Dunluce, Co. Antrim, sent it to Cecil with the message: 'And for a token I have sent you Colum Cille's Cross, a god of great veneration with Sorleyboy and all Ulster, for so great was his grace that happy the man thought himself who could get a kiss of the said cross'.

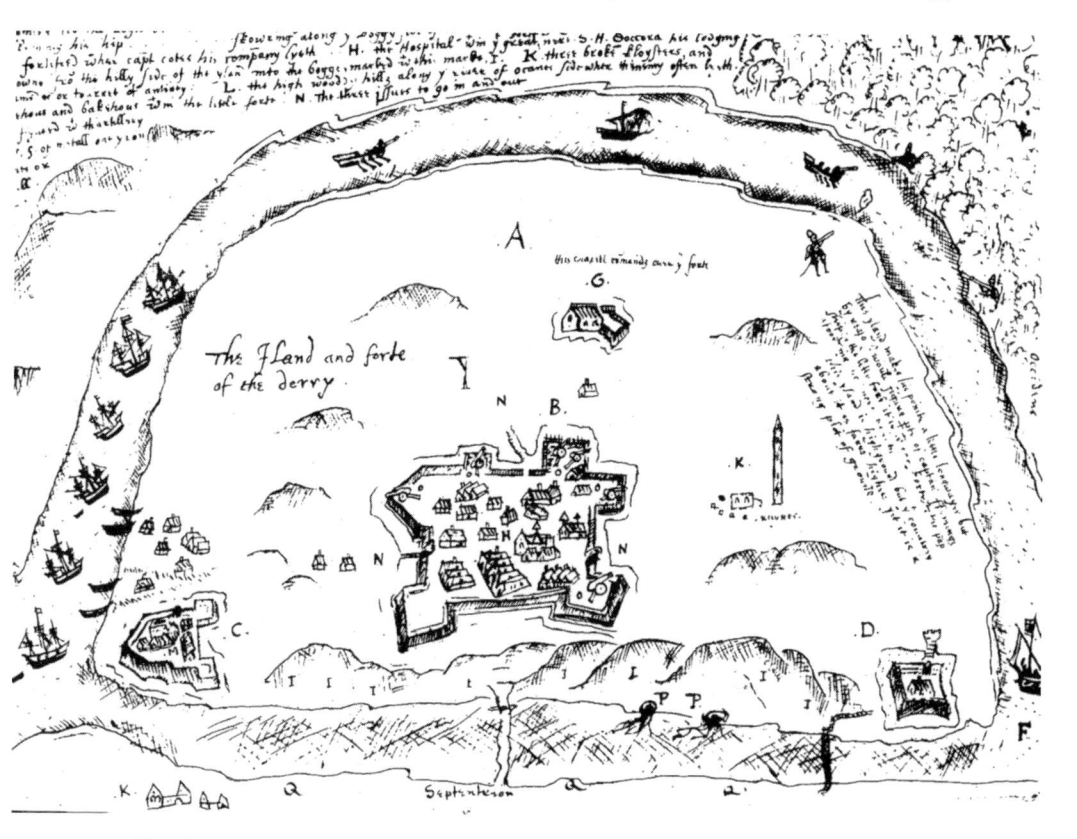

*Memorializing and reinterpreting Columban Derry* 139

29 Sketch map of Derry: National Archives, London: PRO SP 63/207, pt vi, no. 84 (I). It dates to slightly earlier than 19 December 1600 and is the oldest known map of Derry. It depicts the 'island' some months after it had been captured and garrisoned by Sir Henry Docwra, and includes depictions of a number of the medieval buildings and structures discussed in the main text (pp 86–92).

were better acquainted: St George or St Paul, for example. Otherwise, we must assume that public devotion to Columba in Derry had come to an end.

Outside the city walls, some of the traditional monuments and practices associated with the saint's cult probably continued among the local *ab original* population. Some relevant sites are marked on Francis Neville's map of the Siege of Derry of *c*.1690. John Bryson has shown that some of the pre-1600 property lots also survived the upheaval of the plantation, particularly those associated with the dean and bishopric of Derry (2001, 194–6). As conditions following the penal period improved towards the end of the eighteenth century, a new Catholic church was built in 1784 on or close to the site of the *Tempull Mór*. The medieval holy wells seem to have been preserved and resorted to by the increasing Catholic population that began to settle in their vicinity, the area that would become known later as the Bogside. Most of those Catholics came

30 Inscribed stone plaque in the west entrance porch of St Columb's Cathedral (1628–33). Set into the top of the plaque, which mainly commemorates the Londoners who built 'this church and cittie', is a smaller inscribed stone said to have been brought from the ruins of the medieval cathedral, the *Tempull Mór* (see p. 88) (after Colby 1837, 103).

into Derry seeking work from neighbouring Donegal, where, outside the areas that had been heavily 'planted' by English and Scottish colonists, traditional beliefs and practices associated with Colum Cille continued to be part of everyday life, as to some extent they still do.

Columba's story figured in many of the partisan Catholic and Protestant ecclesiastical histories of the seventeenth and eighteenth centuries. The controversial Catholic cleric John Lanigan (1758–1822) critically reviewed some of those in his *An ecclesiastical history of Ireland: from the first introduction of Christianity among the Irish to the beginning of the thirteenth century* published in Dublin in 1822. That book was arguably the first study to apply modern critical approaches to the story of the foundation of Derry (Lanigan 1822, 118–25).

A significant advance came with the publication in 1837 of Colby's *Ordnance Survey of the County of Londonderry … memoir … parish of Templemore*. The section on the medieval history of the city and its structures was written by the great Gaelic scholars George Petrie and John O'Donovan. The eminent Columban scholar William Reeves said:

> This admirable work … will always, and deservedly, be cited as the highest authority on the history of Derry, and will couple with the name of that ancient city, and the Ordnance Survey, as the quickening cause, the revival in Ireland of genuine antiquarian research.
>
> (1857, 277–8)

Information about the medieval precursor to the plantation city began to make its appearance in more general studies such as Robert Simpson's *The Annals of Derry*, published in 1847. The publication of the *Annals of the Four Masters* in the 1840s and 1850s, magisterially edited with translation by John O'Donovan, also influenced thinking about medieval Derry. William Reeves' stunning annotated editions of *Acts of Archbishop Colton in his metropolitan visitation of the diocese of Derry* in 1850 and *The Life of St Columba, founder of Hy, written by Adamnan, ninth abbot of that monastery*, published in 1857, both with

31 Fr William ('Willie') Doherty (1861–1931), re-builder of the Long Tower church and the greatest promoter of devotion to St Colum Cille in Derry in the late nineteenth and early twentieth centuries.

numerous references to Derry, placed the medieval and particularly the Columban history of Derry in its widest context. Other histories – both at a local and at a 'national' level – followed in that vein.

The major medieval study of Colum Cille had been Manus Ó Domhnaill's *Betha* of 1532, which included the most comprehensive (alleged) account of the foundation of the Derry monastery by that saint. Those stories, apparently having all but disappeared locally, were put back into circulation in Derry by Fr William Doherty (1861–1931) around the end of the nineteenth century (fig. 31). In that form, they were to have an enormous impact on the modern understanding of the foundation of Derry and its medieval layout.

Doherty was curate at St Columba's 'Long Tower' church from 1890 until 1903; in 1903 he was made 'administrator' (effectively parish priest) there and continued in that position until 1917. He was responsible for three major achievements in terms of the evolution of the modern understanding of the legend of Colum Cille and Derry. In 1897, he masterminded the great Catholic celebrations in Derry marking the 1300th anniversary of the death of the saint. Subsequently, he wrote a highly influential account of those events: *Derry Columbkille: souvenir of the centenary celebrations, in honour of St Columba, in the Long Tower church, Derry, 1897–99*.[3] More importantly, he was also responsible for the reconstruction of the Long Tower church, a building that he turned, effectively, into a shrine – even an interpretive centre – to the Derry Columban story. The new Long Tower was – what we saw Tomás Ó Carragáin describe above in a medieval context – a church as an associative relic (2010, 149–56).

The Long Tower church had been built originally in 1784. It was the first Catholic church erected in Derry since the Reformation and the building of Londonderry (Lacy 1990, 152–4). The church was constructed outside the city walls, allegedly close to a well-known Hawthorn Tree under which mass had been said during Penal times (Anon. 1946, 30–1). Apart from those late eighteenth-century associations, the church was almost certainly on or close to the site of the *Tempull Mór*. Whether or not that connection was recognized at the time of its construction, it was made explicit in the encyclopaedic *Ordnance Survey memoir* published in 1837. The memoir also contended that the original monastic church of Derry was 'adjacent'.

The Long Tower was the only Catholic church in Derry (that is, in the 'old city' area on the west bank of the River Foyle) until work began on St Eugene's Cathedral in 1850. Doherty was convinced that it was located on the site of the original Columban monastery. With great dedication, he set out to revive the traditions and cult of St Columba.

> Up to this time, if the name of Colmcille was familiar, the life and personality of the saint of the Long Tower were as unfamiliar to the great mass of those whose privilege it was to worship on the spot where he was

---

3 The 'souvenir' is actually a 181-page, relatively large-format, hardback book. Fr Doherty wrote other relevant material, for example articles in the *Derry Journal* – pers. comm., John Bryson.

wont to pray. Father Doherty set himself to change that. With the enthusiasm and singleness of purpose of the pioneers of great Irish devotions of the past, he began in a way all his own to tell the people of the glorious memories and holy traditions of the Long Tower, and to preach devotion to the patriot saint who over thirteen centuries before had laid its foundation and consecrated it to God.

(Anon. 1946, 35)

Doherty was curate at the Long Tower in the years around the celebration of the 1300th anniversary of St Columba's death, in 1897. He recorded the magnificent and inspiring Catholic ceremonies held in Derry, as well as the general background to them, in the book *Derry Columbkille*, mentioned above. The book retells the story of Colum Cille with particular reference to Derry, quoting from a range of sources such as: Bede's *Historia Ecclesiastica*; Skene's version of Reeve's edition of *The Life of St Columba* and Reeve's edition of 'Colton's Visitation'; the 'Book of Lismore' (the version of the Middle Irish Life of Colum Cille published by Whitley Stokes in *Lives of the saints from the Book of Lismore* (Oxford, 1890)); the works of John Colgan and, of course, Manus Ó Domhnaill's *Betha Colaim Chille*. It is clear from a number of references to the *Vita Quinta* when mentioning Ó Domhnaill's work (Doherty 1899, 16, 17, 32, 48 and esp. 68, 134), that Doherty (who was writing twenty years or so before the appearance of the O'Kelleher and Schoepperle edition and English translation of the *Betha*) was using John Colgan's translation into Latin in the *Trias Thaumaturga* of 1647 of the original Irish language text.

Doherty was convinced from his reading of those works that the Long Tower church had been built on the site of the monastery founded in Derry in the sixth century by (as he understood) Colum Cille. Referring to this foundation, he says:

> Though often burned in times of war, it was as often rebuilt, on the very same site, and in the very same style, stones, however, being substituted after a time for timber. Its ruins were still extant in 1520 when O'Donnell examined them, and described their position, relative to the Templemore, whose exact situation we learn from Neville's map, made in 1689, ere yet its traces had been obliterated.
>
> From his detailed description and the nature of the ground, apart altogether from unmistakable traditions, one may fairly conclude without much risk of error that the altar on which Columba offered the Holy Sacrifice of the Mass – the altar before which he loved most of all spots in the world to kneel in prayer – the altar whose lovely angel-guards he used so often to see peering from behind its veil of mystery – that altar lay within the lines of the present church.

(Doherty 1899, 16–17)

32 The title page of *Derry Columbkille* (1899), mainly written – anonymously – by Fr William Doherty.

A later writer on the history of the church added to this sense of certainty:

> When it [the Dubreclés] finally fell into disuse we do not know, but we have it that its ruins were still to be seen when Manus O'Donnell visited the spot in 1520. Its exact position has been fixed beyond yea or nay by the discovery of the foundations during the excavations preparatory to the erection of the present church [finished 1909]. Father William Doherty made a careful examination of the remains and, after comparing them with the seventeenth-century manuscript maps, and [Manus] O'Donnell's description, was able to define the original outline.
> 
> (Anon. 1946, 11)

Doherty's 'discoveries' were memorialized in a series of plaques inserted in the floor of the church and the surrounding churchyard. The belief about its situation was given what might be called its 'canonical' form at the dedication of the new Long Tower church on Pentecost Sunday, 30 May 1909. The sermon on that occasion was preached by the Bishop of Raphoe, Dr (later Cardinal) O'Donnell, who spoke of the matter in the following way:

> I know no better way to characterize this beautiful building, with all its memorials of the hallowed past, its eloquent religious symbolism and its rich, artistic finish, than to say it is worthy of its place, worthy of its name and worthy of its purpose ... It is no small distinction for this church that it has kept its ground ... Comprising the exact site of St Columba's first church, the Dubh Regles, and adjoining the position of [Flaithbertach] Ó Brolchán's Teampull Mór, it is the renovated Long Tower church of later years, altogether renewed, on the ground which an Irish Ard Rí gave his saintly relative for the foundation of his famous monastery in days when beautiful surroundings were wont to raise men's minds to thoughts of the Creator ... The stronghold of Aileach is long desolate for our sins ... But the Derry foundation remains and, defying the evanescence of secular power, St Columba's sway continues on his old domain ...
> 
> (Anon. 1946, 40–1)

With hindsight, it is easy to be critical of Fr Doherty. He was, however, almost certainly mistaken about his findings and their meaning. No doubt his enthusiasm led him to some hasty conclusions. Yet given the divisive atmosphere between the city's Catholic and Protestant populations at the time, we cannot overlook the possibility that a form of sectarian thinking may have influenced the priest's ideas. It is clear that around that time Derry Catholics had begun to use the associations and legends of Colum Cille in much the same mythic way that Protestants exploited the legacy of the Siege of Derry. Protestant expression through – for example, the building of the Apprentice Boys Memorial Hall (1873), and the establishment of marching bands named after Siege heroes – was mirrored by the Catholic St Columb's Hall (1888) and St Columb's band, as well as by the 'balancing' of other similar memorial institutions. Indeed, Trevor Semple has drawn attention to the contemporary suggestions that the idea for the Catholic events commemorating Colum Cille's anniversary in 1897 may actually have been stimulated by a desire to match the 'Protestant' celebrations marking the Diamond Jubilee of Queen Victoria, which also occurred that year (2002, 94–5).

At the beginning of the twentieth century, Derry Catholics would have found it very difficult to accept that the original monastic church, irrespective of who actually founded it, was probably on the site occupied by St Augustine's Church of Ireland, chapel-of-ease (see ch. 6). There would have been little in the way of objective history or archaeology to help anyone come to a 'scientific' conclusion on the matter.

CHAPTER 11

# Summary and conclusions

It is likely that Derry, with its excellent strategic location on the River Foyle and the varied environment in its vicinity, was considered as a desirable location for human settlement throughout much if not all of the prehistoric period from the Mesolithic (*c*.8000BC) onwards. Archaeological finds made in and around the city confirm this (Ó Baoill, forthcoming). At times during the prehistoric past, Derry had been a true island in the Foyle. By the beginning of the historic period, however, the channel on the western side had receded, although the isolated 'island' nature of the hill remained.

In the early to mid sixth century AD, Derry was probably the location of a fortified settlement belonging to the tiny Cenél nÉnnai kingdom, marking their northern border. The first part of the name by which it was known then – Daire Calgaich – seems to have reflected a notable stand of oak trees that may have had some ritual significance. A memory of protective taboos associated with those trees lasted throughout the whole of the Middle Ages. The second part of the oldest name we have for Derry, Calgach, was a personal name; probably of one of the Cenél nÉnnai kings. It may be that the record of the death of Tipraite mac Calgaich (almost certainly also a king) in 595 records the names of that king and his son.

Probably around 578, the powerful and expansive Cenél Conaill dynasty that ruled a small but wealthy kingdom to the south of the Cenél nÉnnai defeated and conquered the latter. One of the most important consequences in the aftermath of that conquest was that the Cenél Conaill king, Áed mac Ainmerech, seems to have established a monastic church at Derry, which marked the new northern border of his territory and the frontier with his recent neighbours and enemies to the north, the Cenél nEógain of Inishowen. The first abbot and true 'founder' of the church at Derry was probably Fiachra mac Ciaráin, a nephew of king Áed, but one of the most senior churchmen of the time, Columba – a relative of both Áed and Fiachra – may have had some sort of secondary involvement in that foundation. Although Columba had left for Scotland about sixteen years before, he was present in Ireland around the years 578 or 579 to attend the so-called Convention of Drum Cett, held about fifteen miles north-east of Derry. It was possibly then that the first Christian church in Derry was established. Derry seems to have remained a relatively quiet Columban church for the next couple of centuries, although one of the first named persons connected with it – the *scriba* Caech Scuili, who died in 724 – may have been an important scholar with a reputation well outside the locality.

147

Derry was burned in 788 and probably largely destroyed, as we hear little more about it for around a century. Although there is no contemporary information as to why it was burned, almost certainly it was part of the ongoing campaign by the Cenél nEógain against the Cenél Conaill, which had been carried on for most of the eighth century. The decisive battle of that campaign occurred the following year, 789, at Clóitech (Clady, Co. Tyrone), an important fording point on the River Finn. The result was the expulsion of the Cenél Conaill from their rich territories north of the Barnesmore Gap, their confinement to south Donegal and their exclusion from overlordship in Donegal as well as on the wider 'national' sphere of Irish politics. The fortunes of Derry also changed considerably: from then until the middle of the thirteenth century it would form part of Cenél nEógain territory. Although it had been destroyed in 788 – perhaps completely – at least the site itself remained. In 833, we learn of a battle there between the Vikings and leading figures of the Cenél nEógain, the first time we know of members of that dynasty associated with Derry.

The patchy record for Derry begins to improve towards the end of the ninth century. This may reflect a real advance in its fortunes, but it is also clear that some events attributed to Derry should have been assigned to other churches – most notably to Kilmacrenan (Daire Eithne). The apparently improved documentation begins with the record of the death of a Muirchertach son of Niall in 882, who is described in the annals as the abbot of Derry and other monasteries. Muirchertach was not otherwise identified, but there is a strong probability that he was the son of the Cenél nEógain king of Tara, Niall Caille, and, if so, a brother of another king of Tara, Áed Findliath. Although no relevant documentation has survived from this period, if Muirchertach did belong to such an important family, then the consequences for the patronage of, and physical improvements to, Derry at the time should not be underestimated.

From the beginning of the tenth century, we appear to see an energetic propaganda response against Cenél nEógain control of Derry by the defeated Cenél Conaill. This appears for the first time in the annal death notice for Cináed mac Domnaill in 921, where it was claimed that his role of *princeps* extended from Drumhome to Derry, an assertion that could not have been sustained in contemporary *realpolitik*. The oldest written Cenél Conaill propaganda claim to Derry – in the legend of Colum Cille's foundation of that church – occurs in the late tenth-century 'preface' to the poem *Noli Pater Indulgere* in the *Liber Hymnorum*. Some of the poetry, as it were, put into the mouth of Colum Cille around this time or a little later may have also derived from this Cenél Conaill propaganda campaign. The emergence of Cenél Conaill propaganda about Derry may have been in part facilitated by a decline in Cenél nEógain fortunes, particularly in the middle of the eleventh century.

*Summary and conclusions*

All that changed with the arrival of the latter's leading dynast, Domnall Ua Lochlainn, in 1083. Domnall was a ruthless and highly ambitious ruler who appears to have made Derry his capital. His tenure in Derry coincided with the beginnings of a major reform movement in the Irish church. This would lead to many changes, not least in the role of the ancient monastic foundations such as Derry and the division of the country into territorial dioceses based on the contemporary secular political arrangements. The fortunes of Derry continued to be affected by the fact that it was ostensibly founded by the most famous Cenél Conaill saint and yet ruled in the twelfth century by the Cenél nEógain. That ambiguity prevented Derry from becoming the seat of any diocese until the middle of the thirteenth century, a century and a half after most of the other episcopal centres had been so designated.

After Domnall Ua Lochlainn's death, Derry continued as the Mac Lochlainn capital and also continued to develop physically. The twelfth century was clearly a boom time for the settlement, which by then must have been as close to being a town as anything was in Gaelic Ireland. By the middle of the century, Derry had succeeded Kells (Co. Meath) as the headquarters of the Columban churches in Ireland, under the leadership of the influential Flaithbertach Ó Brolcháin. The Derry solution to a Derry problem led to the equivalent of a personal episcopal chair being agreed for Flaithbertach. He subsequently commenced a reorganization of the Columban churches, apparently along the lines of the new religious orders being introduced from the Continent, taking as his model the Augustinian canons. Just at the time that Derry achieved its leading role, however, the *familia* or confederation of Columban churches itself collapsed under the combined challenges of church reforms – including the new diocesan arrangements – and the ecclesiastical consequences of the arrival of the Anglo-Normans in Ireland.

Nevertheless, Derry continued to thrive under Flaithbertach and, perhaps more especially, under the patronage of the Mac Lochlainn kings – some of whom were even recognized as high-kings of Ireland. The domination of Derry by the Cenél nEógain continued to be challenged by the Cenél Conaill, but some sort of compromise seems to have been worked out by 1180 – the sharing of the two most senior offices of the monastery. In the first few decades of the thirteenth century, the power of the Mac Lochlainns transferred gradually to the O'Neills; it finally collapsed in the 1240s. Nevertheless, they managed to cling on to some sort of control in Derry itself and at the end of the Middle Ages they were one of the two erenagh families still in charge there. The seat of the Cenél nEógain diocese, which would eventually evolve into the diocese of Derry – including their old ancestral homeland in Inishowen – was moved to Derry by the middle of the thirteenth century. West of the Foyle, power was taken by the Uí Domhnaill, who began to play a greater role in the affairs of Derry. The Cenél nEógain versus Cenél Conaill conflict continued over Derry, but eventually by the fourteenth century the solution applied to that age-old problem was the actual partition of the island of Derry itself. One part – apparently the northern end – remained in the diocese of Derry, while the southern part was transferred to the diocese of Raphoe. Around 1300, there was also a plan by the de Burghs to develop Derry as an Anglo-Norman town, but nothing came of it.

Derry's fortunes declined over the later Middle Ages, but there was a minor renaissance at the beginning of the sixteenth century – under the auspices of the Uí Domhnaill. An Uí Domhnaill tower house was built in Derry – probably about 1500 – by their kinsmen the Uí Dochartaigh, their subordinate lords, who had been ruling the adjacent Inishowen Peninsula since the late fourteenth century. At the same time, we also hear about a Columban pilgrimage in Derry in what looks like a contemporary attempt to boost the economic fortunes of the settlement through the medieval equivalent of tourism.

With the arrival of Henry VIII and his immediate successors on the English (and, from 1541, on the Irish) throne, and the Protestant reformation, everything began to change in Ireland, particularly in Ulster. Derry remained largely unaffected until the 1560s, when it was captured for the first time by the English in their war with Shane O'Neill. Among the consequences were the final dissolution of its various religious houses and the destruction of its medieval cathedral, the *Tempull Mór*. Although the garrison remained for less than two years, the effects seem to have been permanent. The place recovered somewhat and there is even a record of an ordination of a priest there in 1590. But with the capture of the settlement by the English for the second time in 1600 under Sir Henry Docwra during the Nine Years War, medieval and monastic Derry, which had existed in various forms for the previous thousand years or so, came to an end. All that would survive were fragments of its buildings – eventually to disappear in turn – and memories of its history and its legends, which themselves would become distorted in the coming four centuries.

# Bibliography

Anderson, A.O. and M.O. Anderson (eds), 1961, *Adomnan's Life of Columba* (Edinburgh).
Anon., 1946, *The story of the Long Tower, 546–1946* (Derry).
Anon. (Ciarán Devlin?), 1978, 'Clerics of Derry', *Derriana: the Journal of the Derry Diocesan Historical Society*, 18–52.
Anon. (DOENI), 1983, *Historic monuments of Northern Ireland* (Belfast).
Bannerman, John, 1993, 'Comarba Coluim Chille and the Relics of Columba', *Innes Review*, 44:1 (spring), 14–47.
Bernard, J.H. and R. Atkinson (eds), 1898, *The Irish Liber Hymnorum* (London).
Bhreathnach, Edel (ed.), 2005, *The kingship and landscape of Tara* (Dublin).
Bhreathnach, Edel and Bernadette Cunningham, 2007, *Writing Irish history: the Four Masters and their world* (Dublin).
Bonner, Brian, 1982, *Derry: an outline history of the diocese* (Dublin).
Bryson, John, 2001, *The streets of Derry (1625–2001)* (Derry).
Bryson, John, forthcoming, 'Map of Daire, $c.1512$'.
Byrne, F.J., 1973, *Irish kings and high-kings* (Dublin; 2nd ed. Dublin, 2001).
Byrne, F.J., 1989, 'Bishops, 1111–1534' in T.W. Moody, F.X. Martin and F.J. Byrne (eds), *A new history of Ireland*, 9: *maps, genealogies, lists – a companion to Irish history, part II* (Dublin; pbk ed. 2011), 264–332.
Byrne, F.J., 2005, 'Ireland and her neighbours, $c.1014$–$c.1072$' in Ó Cróinín (ed.), *A new history of Ireland*, 1 (Oxford), 862–98.
Byrne, Paul and Ailbhe MacShamhráin, 2005, 'Prosopography I' in Edel Bhreathnach (ed.), *Tara: kingship and landscape* (Dublin), 159–224.
Charles-Edwards, Thomas, 2001, *Early Christian Ireland* (Cambridge).
Clancy, T.O., 2003–4, 'Diarmait *sapientissumus*: the career of Diarmait, *dalta* Daigre, abbot of Iona', *Peritia*, 17–18, 215–32.
Clancy, T.O. and Gilbert Márkus (eds), 1995, *Iona: the earliest poetry of a Celtic monastery* (Edinburgh).
Colby, T. (ed.), 1837, *Ordnance Survey of the County of Londonderry*, 1: *memoir of the city and north western liberties of Londonderry – parish of Templemore* (Dublin; repr. Limavady, 1990).
Cusack, M.F., n.d., *The* Trias Thaumaturga *or three wonder-working saints of Ireland: St Patrick, St Bridget and St Columba* (London).
Daly, Edward and Kieran [Ciarán] Devlin, 1997, *The clergy of the diocese of Derry: an index* (Dublin).
Devlin, Ciarán, 1983, 'Review – *Derry: an outline history of the diocese* by Brian Bonner', *Derriana: The Journal of the Derry Diocesan Historical Society*, 32–5.
Devlin, Ciarán, 2000a, 'The formation of the diocese' in H.A. Jefferies and Ciarán Devlin (eds), *History of the diocese of Derry from earliest times* (Dublin), 85–113.
Devlin, Ciarán, 2000b, 'Some episcopal lives' in H.A. Jefferies and Ciarán Devlin (eds), *History of the diocese of Derry from earliest times* (Dublin), 114–39.

Devlin, Ciarán, 2013, *The making of medieval Derry* (Dublin).
Dobbs, Margaret, 1921, 'The history of the descendants of Ir', *Zeitschrifte für celtische Philologie*, 13, 308–59.
Dobbs, Margaret, 1955, 'A poem ascribed to Flann mac Lonáin', *Ériu*, 17, 16–34.
Doherty, Charles, 1982, 'Some aspects of hagiography as a source for Irish economic history', *Peritia*, 1, 300–28.
Doherty, William, 1899, *Derry Columbkille: souvenir of the centenary celebrations in honour of St Columba, in the Long Tower church, Derry, 1897–99* (Derry).
Dumville, David, 1999, 'Derry, Iona, England and the governance of the Columban church' in Gerard O'Brien (ed.), *Derry & Londonderry: history and society* (Dublin), 91–114.
Duncan, A.A.M., 1975, *Scotland: the making of the kingdom, the Edinburgh history of Scotland, 1* (Edinburgh; repr. 1978, 1989, 1996, 2000).
Etchingham, Colmán, 1999, *Church organisation in Ireland, AD650 to 1000* (Maynooth).
Fenning, Hugh, 1978, 'The Dominicans of Derry', *Derriana: the Journal of the Derry Diocesan Historical Society*, 53–6.
Fenning, Hugh (ed.), 2009, *Medieval Irish Dominican studies: Benedict O'Sullivan OP* (Dublin).
Ferguson, W.S., 2005, *Maps & views of Derry, 1600–1914: a catalogue* (Dublin).
Fisher, Ian, 2005, 'The heirs of Somerled' in R. Oram and G. Stell (eds), *Lordship and architecture in medieval and Renaissance Scotland* (Edinburgh), 85–97.
Flanagan, M.T., 2005, 'High-kings with opposition, 1072–1166' in Ó Cróinin (ed.), *A new history of Ireland*, 1 (Oxford), 899–933.
Flanagan, M.T., 2010, *The transformation of the Irish Church in the twelfth century* (Woodbridge).
Gilbert, J.T. (ed.), 1870, *Historic and municipal documents of Ireland, AD1172–1320* (London).
Gwynn, Aubrey, 1959, 'Raphoe and Derrry in the twelfth and thirteenth centuries', *Donegal Annual*, 4, 84–100.
Gwynn, Aubrey and R.N. Hadcock, 1970, *Medieval religious houses: Ireland* (Dublin; 2nd ed. 1988).
Gwynn, Edward, 1924, 'The metrical dindshenchas, part iv' in *RIA Todd Lecture Series*, 11 (Dublin).
Heist, W.W., 1965, *Vitae sanctorum Hiberniae e codice olim Salimanticensi* (Brussels).
Hennessy, W.M. and D.H. Kelly (eds), 1875, *The Book of Fenagh* (Dublin).
Herbert, Máire, 1985, 'Beatha Mheán-Ghaeilge Cholm Cille' in Pádraig Ó Fiannachta (eag.), *Léachtaí Cholm Cille*, 15 (Maigh Nuad), 127–36.
Herbert, Máire, 1989, 'The preface to Amra Coluim Cille' in Donnchadh Ó Corráin, Liam Breatnach and Kim McCone (eds), *Sages, saints and storytellers: Celtic studies in honour of Professor James Carney* (Maynooth), 67–75.
Herbert, Maire, 1988, *Iona, Kells and Derry: the history and hagiography of the monastic familia of Columba* (Oxford; repr. Dublin, 1996).
Herity, Michael [Mícheál Ó hOireachtaigh], 1989, 'Seandacht an *Turais* in Éirinn' in Seosamh Watson (eag.), *Oidhreacht Gleann Cholm Cille* (Gleanncolmbkille), 9–30.

Herity, Michael, 1995, 'Early Christian decorated slabs in Donegal: An Turas and the tomb of the founder saint' in William Nolan, Liam Ronayne and Mairéad Dunlevy (eds), *Donegal, history and society* (Dublin), 25–50.
Herity, Michael and Aidan Breen, 2002, *The* Cathach *of Colum Cille: an introduction* (Dublin).
Hogan, Flannan, 1998, 'Derry: the Cistercian connection', *Hallel*, 23:2, 127–35.
Hogan, James, 1940, 'The Ua Briain kingship in Telach Óc' in John Ryan (ed.), *Féilsgríbhinn Eóin Mhic Néill .i. Essays and studies presented to Professor Eoin MacNeill* (Dublin), 406–44.
Holland, Martin, 2005, 'Kells, Synod of' in Seán Duffy (ed.), *Medieval Ireland: an encyclopedia* (New York), 247–9.
Horning, Audrey, 2009, '"The root of all vice and bestiality": exploring the cultural role of the alehouse in the Ulster Plantation' in James Lyttleton and Colin Rynne (eds), *Plantation Ireland: settlement and material culture, c.1550–c.1700* (Dublin), 113–31.
Hughes, Kathleen, 1966, *The church in early Irish society* (London).
Hughes, Kathleen, 1972, *Early Christian Ireland: introduction to the sources* (London).
Jefferies, H.A., 1999, 'Derry diocese on the eve of the plantation' in Gerard O'Brien (ed.), *Derry & Londonderry: history and society* (Dublin), 175–203.
Jefferies, H.A., 2000, 'George Montgomery, first Protestant bishop of Derry' in H.A. Jefferies and Ciarán Devlin (eds), *History of the diocese of Derry from earliest times* (Dublin), 140–66.
Kelly, William, 2003, *Docwra's Derry: a narration of events in north-west Ulster, 1600–1604, edited in 1849 by John O'Donovan* (Belfast).
Kenney, J.F., 1929, *Sources for the early history of Ireland: ecclesiastical* (New York; repr. Dublin, 1979).
Lac[e]y, Brian, 1988, 'The development of Derry, *c.*600 to *c.*1600' in Gearóid Mac Niocaill and Patrick Wallace (eds), *Keimelia: studies in medieval archaeology and history in memory of Tom Delaney* (Galway), 378–96.
Lac[e]y, Brian, 1990, *Siege city: the story of Derry and Londonderry* (Belfast; repr. 1995, 1998).
Lacey, Brian, 1997a, *Colum Cille and the Columban tradition* (Dublin).
Lacey, Brian, 1997b, 'A lost Columban turas in Derry', *Donegal Annual*, 49, 39–41.
Lacey, Brian, 1998a, *The Life of Colum Cille by Manus O'Donnell* (Dublin).
Lacey, Brian, 1998b, 'Columba, founder of the monastery of Derry? – "Mihi manet Incertus"', *Journal of the Royal Society of Antiquaries of Ireland*, 128, 35–47.
Lacey, Brian, 1999, 'County Derry in the early historic period' in Gerard O'Brien (ed.), *Derry & Londonderry: history and society* (Dublin), 115–48.
Lacey, Brian, 2004, 'Revival or re-invention: Columban traditions in nineteenth-century Derry', *Ulster Folklife*, 50, 27–50.
Lacey, Brian, 2006, *Cenél Conaill and the Donegal kingdoms, AD500–800* (Dublin).
Lacey, Brian, 2012, *Lug's forgotten Donegal kingdom: the archaeology, history and folklore of the Síl Lugdach of Cloghaneely* (Dublin).
Lacey, Brian, 2013, *St Columba: his life and legacy* (Dublin).
Lanigan, John, 1822, *An ecclesiastical history of Ireland: from the first introduction of Christianity among the Irish to the beginning of the thirteenth century* (Dublin).

Leask, H.G., n.d., *Glendalough, Co. Wicklow: official historical and descriptive guide* (Dublin).
Leslie, James, 1937, *Derry clergy and parishes* (Enniskillen).
Mac Donald, Aidan, 1984, 'Aspects of the monastery and monastic life in Adomnán's Life of Columba', *Peritia*, 3, 271–302.
Mac Donald, Aidan, 1999, 'Reiclés in the Irish annals to AD1200', *Peritia*, 13, 259–75.
Mac Giolla Easpaig, Dónall, 1996–7, 'Breccán Cathe: a forgotten Derry saint', *Ainm: Bulletin of the Ulster Placename Society*, 7, 75–88.
Mac Niocaill, Gearóid, 1972, *Ireland before the Vikings* (Dublin).
Mac Niocaill, Gearóid, 1975, *The medieval Irish annals* (Dublin).
MacShamhráin, Ailbhe, 2000, 'The making of Tír nÉogain: Cenél nÉogain and the Airgialla from the sixth to eleventh centuries' in C. Dillon and H.A. Jefferies (eds), *Tyrone: history and society* (Dublin), 55–84.
Manning, Aidan, 2002, *Glencolumbkille, a history: 3000BC–1901AD* (Letterkenny).
Márkus, Gilbert, 2010, '*Adiutor laborantium*: a poem by Adomnán?' in J.M. Wooding, Rodney Aist, T.O. Clancy and Thomas O'Loughlin (eds), *Adomnán of Iona: theologian, lawmaker, peacemaker* (Dublin), 145–61.
Martin, F.X., 1968, 'Derry in 1590: a catholic demonstration', *Clogher Record*, 6:3, 597–605.
Mc Carthy, D.P., 2008, *The Irish annals: their genesis, evolution and history* (Dublin).
McCracken, Eileen, 1971, *The Irish woods since Tudor times: their distribution and exploitation* (Belfast/Newton Abbot).
McErlean, J., 1914, 'Synod of Ráith Breasail: boundaries of the dioceses of Ireland', *Archivium Hibernicum*, 3, 1–33.
McNeill, T.E., 1980, *Anglo-Norman Ulster: the history and archaeology of an Irish barony, 1177–1400* (Edinburgh).
Meckler, Michael, 1997, 'The Annals of Ulster and the date of the meeting at Druim Cett', *Peritia*, 11, 42–52.
Meyer, Kuno, 1893, 'Anecdota from Irish Mss X', *Gaelic Journal*, 4:46 (July), 229.
Ní Bhrolcháin, Muireann, 1986, *Maoil Íosa Ó Brolcháin* (Maigh Nuad).
Ó Baoill, Ruairí, forthcoming, *The archaeological story of Derry-Londonderry* (Belfast).
O'Brien, M.A. (ed.), 1962, *Corpus Genealogiarum Hiberniae*, 1 (Dublin; repr. 1976).
O'Byrne, Emmet, 2005, 'Mac Lochlainn, Muirchertach (*c*.1110–1166)' in Seán Duffy (ed.), *Medieval Ireland: an encyclopedia* (New York), 295–8.
Ó Canann, Tomás, 2009, 'Surveying County Donegal', *Aimn: A Journal of Name Studies*, 10, 27–100.
Ó Carragáin, Tomás, 2010, *Churches in early medieval Ireland* (New Haven, CT).
Ó Ceallaigh S., 1951, *Gleanings from Ulster history* (Cork; repr. Draperstown, 1994).
Ó Clabaigh, Colmán, 2012, *The friars in Ireland, 1224–1540* (Dublin).
Ó Corráin, Donnchadh, 1972, *Ireland before the Normans* (Dublin).
Ó Corráin, Donnchadh, 2001, 'Muirchertach Mac Lochlainn and the "Circuit of Ireland"' in A.P. Smyth (ed.), *Seanchas: studies in early and medieval Irish archaeology, history and literature in honour of Francis J. Byrne* (Dublin), 238–50.
Ó Corráin, Donnchadh and Fidelma Maguire, 1981, *Gaelic personal names* (Dublin).

Ó Cróinin, Dáibhi (ed.), 2005, *A new history of Ireland*, 1: *prehistoric and early Ireland* (Oxford).

O'Doherty, J.K., 1902, *Derriana: essays and occasional verses, chiefly relating to the diocese of Derry* (Dublin).

Ó Floinn, Raghnall, 1995, 'Sandhills, silver and shrines: fine metalwork of the medieval period from Donegal' in William Nolan, Liam Ronayne and Mairéad Dunlevy (eds), *Donegal, history and society* (Dublin), 85–148.

Ó Floinn, Raghnall, 1997, 'Insignia Columbae I' in Cormac Bourke (ed.), *Studies in the cult of Saint Columba* (Dublin), 136–61.

Ó Gallachair, Pádraig, 1960, 'Coarbs and erenaghs of County Donegal', *Donegal Annual*, 272–81.

Ó Gallachair, Pádraig, 1963, 'Columban Donegal', *Donegal Annual*, 262–76.

O'Kelleher, Andrew and Gertrude Schoepperle (eds), 1918, *Betha Colaim Chille: Life of Columcille* (Chicago; repr. Dublin, 1994).

Ó Lochlainn, Colm, 1940, 'Roadways in ancient Ireland' in John Ryan (ed.), *Féilsgríbhinn Eóin Mhic Néill* (Dublin), 465–74.

O'Loughlin, Thomas, 2005, 'Canon Law' in Seán Duffy (ed.), *Medieval Ireland: an encyclopedia* (New York), 63–4.

Ó Riain, Pádraig, 1983, 'Cainnech *alias* Colum Cille, patron of Ossory' in R.A. Breatnach (ed.), *Folia Gadelica* (Cork), 20–35.

Ó Riain, Pádraig, 1985a, 'Trí eachtraí as beatha bhéil Cholaim Chille' in Pádraig Ó Fiannachta (eag.), *Léachtaí Cholm Cille XV: Ár Naomhsheanchas* (Maigh Nuad), 115–26.

Ó Riain, Pádraig, 1985b, *Corpus Genealogiarum Sanctorum Hiberniae* (Dublin).

Ó Riain, Pádraig, 1997, *Trias Thaumaturga: John Colgan – with an introduction by Pádraig Ó Riain* (Dublin; facs. repr. of 1647 Louvain ed.).

Ó Riain, Pádraig, 2011, *A dictionary of Irish saints* (Dublin).

Ó Riain, Pádraig, 2013, 'The O'Donohue Lives of the Salamancan Codex: the earliest collections of Irish saints' Lives' in Sarah Sheehan, Joanne Findon and Westley Follett (eds), *Gablánach in scélaigecht: Celtic studies in honour of Ann Dooley* (Dublin), 38–52.

O'Sullivan, Jerry, 1999, 'Iona: archaeological investigations, 1875–1996' in D. Broun and T. Clancy (eds), *Spes Scotorum, hope of Scots: Saint Columba, Iona and Scotland* (Edinburgh), 215–44.

O'Sullivan, Jerry and Tomás Ó Carragáin, 2008, *Innishmurray: monks and pilgrims in an Atlantic landscape* (Dublin).

Porter, J. Scott, 1853, 'Metropolitan visitation of the diocese of Derry, AD1397, 2', *Ulster Journal of Archaeology*, 1, 184–97.

RCAHMS, 1982, *Argyle: an inventory of the monuments*, 4: *Iona* (Edinburgh).

Reeves, William (ed.), 1850, *Acts of Archbishop Colton in his metropolitan visitation of the diocese of Derry* (Dublin).

Reeves, William (ed.), 1857, *The Life of St Columba, founder of Hy; written by Adomnan, ninth abbot of that monastery* (Dublin).

Rowan, Alistair, 1979, *The buildings of Ireland: north-west Ulster – the counties of Londonderry, Donegal, Fermanagh and Tyrone* (London).

Ryan, Michael, 1983, *The Derrynaflan Hoard*, 1: *a preliminary account* (Dublin).

Semple, Trevor, 2002, *Saint Columba: a Protestant dilemma revisited* (Derry).
Sharpe, Richard, 1991, *Medieval Irish saints' Lives: an introduction to* Vitae Sanctorum Hiberniae (Oxford).
Sharpe, Richard (ed.), 1995, *Adomnán of Iona: Life of St Columba* (London; repr. 2005).
Simms, Katharine, 1995, 'Late medieval Donegal' in William Nolan, Liam Ronayne and Mairéad Dunlevy (eds), *Donegal, history and society* (Dublin), 183–201.
Simms, Katharine, 1999, 'Tír Eoghain "north of the mountain"' in Gerard O'Brien (ed.), *Derry & Londonderry, history and society* (Dublin), 149–74.
Simms, Katharine, 2008, 'The Donegal poems in the Book of Fenagh', *Ériu*, 58, 37–53.
Smyth, A.P., 2003, *Warlords and holy men: Scotland, AD80–1000* (Edinburgh).
Thomas, Avril, 2005, *Irish Historic Towns Atlas, 15: Derry – Londonderry* (Dublin).
Walsh, Paul (ed.), 1918, Genealogiae Regum et Sanctorum Hiberniae *by the Four Masters* (Dublin).
Watt, J.A., 1973, 'John Colton, justiciar of Ireland (1382) and archbishop of Armagh (1383–1404)' in J.F. Lydon (ed.), *Ireland in the later Middle Ages* (Dublin), 196–213.

# Index

A few issues should be noted when using this index. The name used for Derry for almost the first five and a half centuries of its history is Daire Calgaich and variations, including the shortened form Daire/Doire. Daire/Doire Coluim Chille appears for the first time in the contemporary annals in the obituary for Domnall Ua Lochlainn, under the year 1121. In the index below, all instances of Daire/Doire Calgaich occurring in the text have been entered, but only those for Daire/Doire Coluim Chille that arise, apparently, prior to 1121 have been listed. From then on, Daire/Doire Coluim Chille and variations seem to become the norm and so have not been indexed. The various sets of annals have been noted in the index only when they themselves are the subject of discussion, as distinct from when they are the sources of other historical references.

Rather than as subheadings of 'Derry', named individuals connected with the settlement have been entered in the correct place in the general alphabetical arrangement. In some Gaelic surnames, such as Ua/Mac Lochlainn, the terms Ua (Ó) and Mac are interchangeable. There is little or no standardization in the original sources, although an attempt has been made to impose one in the main text above. The matter is further complicated by the use of common anglicized forms. Readers should note that a particular surname can be listed below under the headings: Ó, O', Mac, Mc, Ua or Uí (plural of Ua or Ó).

Adhlann mac Éichnecháin, 47–8
*Adiutor Laborantium* (poem), 17
Adomnán, 4, 6, 8 n. 7, 17 n. 5, 28–30, 34, 48, 67, 80, 90–1; Law of, 46; *Vita Columbae*, 4, 6, 28–30, 39, 46, 48, 68, 80, 114 n. 3, 140
Áed Allán, 42, 61 n. 18
Áed Findliath, 42, 148
Áed mac Ainmerech, vii, 13–14, 18–22, 24–7, 31–2, 34–6, 44–5, 64, 99, 147
Áed Oirdnide, 38, 42
Áedán mac Gabráin, 35
Agricola, 9
Aileach (Elagh), 50–1, 58
Ainmere mac Sétnai, 27, 34, 36, 44
Aitheman, 11
*Altus Prosator* (poem), 17
*Amra Coluimb Chille*, 63–4
Andersons, A.O. and M.O., 28
Anglo-Normans (*see also* Scottish Normans), 19–20, 67, 69, 73, 76, 83, 85, 97, 100, 102, 104, 109–11, 127, 149–50
Annals of the Four Masters, 28, 31–4, 36, 48–9, 51, 140; 'foundation' of Derry, vii–viii, 27
Annals of Roscrea, 31–3
Annals of Tigernach, 27, 31, 33
Annals of Ulster, 31, 36, 48, 51, 95; 'foundation' of Derry, vii, 27–8, 36
Antrim, Co., 39
Ardgar (d. 1124) 57
Ard Midhair, 102, 110 n. 35, 127
*Ard na scéla* (poem), 49
Argyll, 66
Armagh, Ard Mhacha, 19, 52, 56, 57 n. 9, 72, 87, 93, 121; abbey of SS Peter and Paul, 56, 66–7, 74–5; archbishop (*comarba*), 51, 56, 62, 70, 72, 75, 86, 94, 111–24; diocese of, 60, 111, 124; ecclesiastical province, 60

Árd nGobhaill, 104
Ardstraw, 60–1, 71, 100, 113
Arrouaise/Arroasian, 66–7
Assaroe, 53, 60, 100, 121 n. 7
Assylin, 68
Áth na Dairbrighe (Dervor) 63–4
Áth Meadhon, 104
Attacots, 107–8
Augustin (Iona high-priest), 66
Augustinians (*see also* Derry/*Cella Nigra*), 66–7, 71, 73–5, 86, 89, 94, 123, 149

Báetán mac Cairill, 35
Báetán mac Ninnida, 26
Baítán nepos niath Taloirc, 29
Baithéne (Mobhaoi), 14, 23–4, 28; Tech Baithéne (Taughboyne/St Johnstown), 24
Ballinascreen, 65 n. 65
Ballougry, 98 n. 11
Ballymagroarty (*see also* Derry/Ballymagrorty), 45, 49, 70
Ballyshannon, 100
Banagher, 65 n. 29, 82, 115–16, 123–4
Bann, River, 35, 56, 65 n. 27, 100, 104
Barnesmore Gap, 38, 40–1, 45, 53
battles, *see* Caméirge, Clóitech, Desertcreat, Druim Meic Ercae, Dunbo
*Béarla Féine*, 46
Bé Bhinn (wife of Domnall Ua Lochlainn), 57
Bede, 143
Beltany Stone Circle, 60
Bethóc, daughter of Somerled, 74
Birdstown (*Lathreg Inden?*), 29 n. 6
Blessed John of Vercelli, 107
Blackwater, River, 65
Bluestacks, 102
Bole, John (archbishop), 67
Book of Fenagh, 11, 26, 58; *Estid re Conall Calma*, 26
Book of Lecan, 95
Book of Lismore, 143
Bovevagh, 65 n. 29, 82

Bradley, John, 85
Bran, nephew of Columba, 6, 14, 30–1
Brian Boru, 57 n. 10
Bridge End, 50
Brí Mic Thaidhg, synod, 63
British Library, 4
Brugach mac Dega, 11–12, 17
Bryson, John, x, 90, 139, 142
Bundrowes, 136
Burnfoot (*Lathreg Inden?*), 29 n. 6
Byrne, F.J., 52, 72

Caech Scuili (*scriba*), 38–9, 147
Caencomhrac mac Maeluidhur, 46, 48
Calgach mac Aitheman, 3, 9–12
Calann, River, 42
Calvin, John, 135
Cambridge University, 113
Caméirge, battle of, 105
Campbell/Caulfield (Uí Cathmail), 49
Cappagh, 113
Carn Glas/Beltany, 60
Carrickmore, 111
Cashel ecclesiastical province, 60
*Cathach*, 45, 49, 69–70, 95
Cecil, William (Lord Burghley) 136, 138
Celestinus/Cellach (of Iona), 74
Cell Dara (Kildare), 46
Celts, 4
Cenél Conaill (*see also* diocese), 11, 24, 37–8, 40, 75, 97–8, 101, 103, 107, 127, 135; *cenn adchomairc*, 43; Conall of, 14–16, 26; Derry involvement, 9, 13, 21, 23, 25–7, 31, 34, 36, 39, 60, 85, 105–6, 108, 147–9; king, 18, 31–2, 45, 47, 64, 99–100; territory, 41, 46–7, 51, 53–4
Cenél Duach, 26
Cenél Feradaigh, 57, 93 n. 2
Cenél mBinnig, 56, 103–4
Cenél mBogaine, 46
Cenél nÉnnai, 7–8, 10–13, 23, 25–6, 49, 54, 81, 127, 147
Cenél nEógain (*see also* diocese), 9, 13, 34, 37–8, 40, 55, 71, 101, 135; members of, 55–7, 62–3, 70, 76,

93–4, 97–8, 118–19; monuments, 43, 54; ruling Derry, 21, 41, 51, 59, 103, 105, 108; territory, 41, 50–2, 58 n. 11, 60, 64, 104, 147–9
Cenél Tigernaich, 62
*Chronicum Scotorum*, 31, 33
Churchtown, 131
Cináed mac Domnaill, 43–5, 48, 148
Cistercians (*see also* Derry, Dunbrody, Jerpoint), 73; Mellifont, 87–9; Newry, 71
Clancy, T.O., 98 n. 12
Clann Chearnaigh, 104
Clann Cholmáin, 52
Clann Diarmata, 81, 93
Clann Sínaich, 57 n. 9
Cleirchéne mac Conalláin, 46–7
Cloghaneely, 47
Clogher, 49, 60
Clóitech, battle of, 38, 40–1, 47, 148
Clonard, 23
Cloncarney, 104
Clonfert, 18
Clonmacnoise, 2, 31–3, 82
Clonmore, 68
Cnoc Nascain, 100
Colby, Thomas, vii, 140, 142
Colcu mac Domnaill, 44
Coleraine/Mountsandel, 100–1
Colgan, John, vii–viii, 24, 27, 30–1, 33, 35, 43–5, 47; *Trias Thaumaturga*, vii, 27, 33, 143
*Collectio Canonum Hibernenses*, 38
Colmán Ela, Life of, 39
Colton, John, 75, 86, 88, 111–24, 140
Columba/Colum Cille, 15–21, 29, 39, 44, 48, 69, 73, 96, 99, 103–4; churches (*see also familia Columbae*), 68, 73, 75, 102, 126 n. 11, 149; cult/celebration of, 47, 49, 58–9, 80, 95, 127, 131, 138, 140, 142–3, 146; feastday (9 June), 19, 67, 125; 'founder'/patron of Derry, vii–viii, 14, 18–22, 27, 34, 36–7, 45, 52, 66, 68, 77–8, 94, 130, 132–6, 139, 141, 145; Middle Irish Life of, 12, 19–21, 24, 34, 47–8, 64, 66 n. 32, 67–9, 83, 86, 90, 95, 103

Conall Cú, 31
Conall Gulban, 14–16, 26, 36
Conchobor son of Colcu, 44
Corpraige of Fanad, 16
Croaghan Hill/Cruachan, 11, 16
Cuanu, 33
Cú Chuimne (of Iona), 38
Cuimne, 14, 16
Cuirenrige/Culenrige, 29
Culmore, 1, 3
Cummery, 105 n. 26
Cusack, Sr Mary Frances, 22

Da (Do) Cualén, x, 21, 103–4
Daire/Doire Calgaich (*Roboretum Calgachi*), 3–4, 6, 9–10, 18, 26, 28–31, 33, 39–40, 43, 46, 48–9, 51, 81, 147
Daire/Doire Coluim Chille, 27–8, 47–9, 51, 57–8, *et seq.*
Daire Eithne (*see also* Kilmacrenan), 16, 46, 48–9, 51
Dálach (*dux*), 47
Dál Coirpre, 65
Dál Riata (Scottish), 35
Danes (*see* Vikings)
de Burgh, family, 150
de Burgh, Richard, 109
de Burgh, Walter, 110
de Burgh, William the Brown, 110
de Courcy, John, 100–1
de Galloway family, 101
Derc bruach (Gransha), 100
Derry, Abbey St., 108 n. 33; *airchinnech*/erenagh, 43, 46–7, 49, 51, 56, 61–2, 82, 94, 97–9, 102–3, 105, 108, 149; *ancoire*, 49; *an t-iompódh desiul*, 92, 130–1; apparition of the Lord, 131–2; Apprentice Boys hall, 146; as border/frontier, 7; Ballymagrorty, 49, 70; *banairchinnech*, 56, 89; bishop of, 61 n. 16, 71–2, 74, 82, 106–7, 109, 117, 120, 121 n. 7, 128,

Derry, Abbey St. (*continued*)
132, 139; Bogside, 8, 139; Book of, 95; Brandywell Rd, 91; Bridge St., 92; bullaun/St Columb's Stone, 91; Bun Sentuinne, 125; burial/graveyard, 6, 14, 29–31, 35, 58, 80, 83, 86; burning, 38–40, 61; castle/tower house, 1, 89, 92, 128–9, 132, 150; *Cella Nigra*/Dubreclés/Black Church, 17, 23, 56, 66–7, 72–5, 78, 81–7, 91–2, 108, 114–19, 121–2, 136–7, 145; *Cellóir Mór* (cellarer), 86; chapter of, 119, 121–4; Cistercian *Conventus Sanctae Mariae*, 56, 83, 88–9, 108, 136–8; Clondermot, 81; Clooney (Cluain Í), 8, 100, 120–1, 125–6; coat of arms, 109–10; *comarba* (abbot), 47–8, 51, 62, 66, 71, 73–5, 82, 84, 93–5, 98, 102–4, 108, 114, 137; commerce in, 85; concubinage, 116–17; *corn*/chalices/goblets, 81, 85, 99; dean of, 114–16, 118, 121–2, 139; *disiurt* ('hermitage'), 56, 57 n. 8, 81; Dominicans, 89, 106–8, 117, 121, 137; dormitory, 116; English in, 88, 134 *et seq.*; executions, cross of, 99; exorcism/ritual cleansing, 79; Fahan St., 91; ferry, 92, 113, 121; *fir léighinn/ardfir léighinn*, 93–4; Franciscans, 89, 108; Galliagh/Rosnagalliagh, 56; guest-house, 86; harbour/port/ship quay, 1, 30, 71, 80, 84, 92, 100, 125, 130–1; hawthorn tree, 142; holy wells, 2, 65, 83, 90–1, 139; houses, 81–3; *Journal* (newspaper), 142; literature of (*see also* Columba/Middle Irish Life of), 67, 95; Londonderry/plantation/walled city, 60, 77, 85, 89, 129, 131–2, 134, 138, 142; Long Tower church, viii, 86, 88, 91, 106 n. 27, 131, 141–5; Long Tower St., 91–2; Magazine St., 129, 132; malediction, 82; maps, 3, 65, 87–8, 90, 132, 139, 143; marching bands (Protestant), 146; meteor, 72; *muinnter* ('Community of'), 55, 57, 74, 81, 83, 85, 93–4, 101; oaks/trees, 3–4, 6, 17, 19–20, 22, 58, 77–80, 84, 86–7, 142; orchard, 82, 92; Orchard St., 92; partition of, 101 n. 17, 108, 150; Pennyburn Depression, 8–10, 13, 25, 50; pilgrimage, 56, 129–33, 150; place-name, 5–6; *princeps/abb/abbas*, 43, 46, 148; prior (*secnabuigecht*) of, 21, 103, 108; *proinntig* ('refectory'), 82, 86, 116; quarry, 1, 92; relics, 18–21, 24, 69, 86, 95–6; Rossville St., 108 n. 33; round tower, 2, 88; 'saints' of, 24, 30, 33, 43–5, 47; St Augustine's chapel, viii, 87 n. 11, 146; St Columb's Cathedral, 87, 89, 106 n. 27, 138, 140; St Columb's Hall, 146; St Columb's Stone/bullaun (Long Tower), 91; St Columb's Stone (Pennyburn), 43; St Columb's Wells, 90–2; St Eugene's Cathedral, 142; *sámad Coluim Chille*, 70, 79, 83, 87, 94; *scriba*, 38–9, 147; seals, 14, 115, 122, 133; Shipquay Place, 129, 131; Siege of, 65, 92, 139, 146; taboos, 77–9; *taiberne*, 134; *Tempull Becc*, 65 n. 28, 72, 81–3; *Tempull Mór*/cathedral, 1, 65–6, 83, 85, 87–9, 91–2, 99, 101?, 106 n. 27, 108, 118, 125, 135–6, 139–40, 142, 145, 150; *toisech* ('leader' of students), 70, 93; township, 61, 83; treasures, 85, 101; *ulaidh* ('altar'), 92; Waterside, 8; William St., 108 n. 33; yew tree, 79

Derryloran, 38
Derrynaflan, 6
Dervor, 63–4
Desertcreat, 112, 124; battle of, 107
Devenish, 2, 82
Devlin, Ciarán, 38, 53, 59, 61 n. 18, 135

# Index

Diarmait *alumnus* Daigre, 98 n. 12
Diarmait (*princeps* of Derry), 43
diocesan restructuring, 60
diocese of Cenél Conaill/Raphoe, 59, 61, 74, 98, 105–9, 113, 150
diocese of Connor, 60–1, 72, 104
diocese of Cenél nEógain/Derry, 59–61, 71, 74, 88, 105–6, 111–24, 149–50
dissolution, of monasteries, 75
Dobbs, Margaret, 49
Docwra, Henry, 1–3, 6, 88, 137, 139, 150
Doherty, Charles, 63
Doherty, Fr William, viii, 141–5
Domnach Mór Maige nItha (Donaghmore), 16, 81, 85
Domnall Daball, 55
Domnall mac Áedo, 18 n. 6, 31–2, 44
Domnall mac Éichnecháin, 47
Dorbéne, 4
Druim Meic Ercae, battle of, 13, 34–5
*Druim Monach*, 68
Druim Tuama (Drumhome), 43, 45, 100, 148
Drum Cett, Convention of, 34–5, 63, 147
Drumcliff, 75
Dumville, David, 31, 33, 39
Dubsidhe (Iona lector), 66
Dunbo, battle of, 69
Dunbrody, 74 n. 41
Duncrun, 72, 93 n. 2
Dungiven, 65 n. 29, 82, 123
Dunluce, 138
Durrow, 17, 68, 73, 95

Éichnechán mac Dálaig, 47
Edinburgh (*see also* Scotland, National Library), 66
Edward II, 109
Eithne, 14, 16
Elizabeth I, 134–6
Enagh Lough, 53, 100, 120, 122
Énán, 14, 16, 48
Énna (of Cenél nÉnnai), 11
Eoin (Derry lector), 93–4
Erchelaidh (*abbas*), 62 n. 21
Erganagh townland, 105 n. 26

Erne, River, 37, 53, 60
Eshkaheen Mountain, 13
Ess craibhe (The Cutts), 100

*familia Columbae* (*see also* Columba/churches), 10, 19, 62–3, 66, 68–9, 73, 75, 84, 149
Fanad, 16, 37, 108
Faughan river, 100 n. 15
Fedelmid, 14, 16, 36, 44
Fergal mac Máele Dúin, 42
Fiachra mac Ciaráin, 31–3, 35–7, 39, 147
Fidh Ó nEchtach (The Fews), 70
Finn, Lough, 102; River, 77, 113–14
Fir Bolg, 107
Fir na Craibhe, 82
Fisher, Ian, 65
Fitton, Roitsel, 100
Fogartach (*abbas*), 49
Foyle, Lough, 1, 6–8, 77, 93, 110, 114; River, 1–3, 7–8, 37, 50, 60, 77, 113–14, 121, 147
Francis, Dermot, 2, 9
French Revolution, 6

Galgachus/Calgachus, 9
galloglass, 127
Gartan, 16, 48, 84, 104, 131
Gelasius/Gilla Meic Liac, 61, 63, 72, 75
*Genealogiae Regum et Sanctorum Hiberniae*, 32
Glencolumbkille, 84, 131
Glendalough, 73, 82, 88 n. 14
Glenswilly, 127
Gransha, 100 n. 14
Greenan Mountain (*see also* Grianán), 7, 11, 13, 106 n. 27
Greencastle, 109–10
Grianán of Aileach, 7, 9, 51, 54
Gweedore, River, 47
Gwynn, Edward, 51

Hebrides, 66, 74
Hegarty, Walter, 38
Henry VIII, 132, 134, 150
Herbert, Máire, 19, 31, 45, 67

Holywell Hill/Knockenny/Cnoc
    Énnai, 7, 9, 11, 106 n. 27
*Horae Canonicae*, 116
Horning, Audrey, 134
Hughes, Kathleen, 68
Hyde, Douglas, 58
Hymn of St Cummain, 18

Inch Island, 8, 29
Inchcolm, 66 n. 33
Inishmurray, 82
Inishowen, 13, 42–3, 50, 52, 54, 93,
    102, 110 n. 35, 127, 147
Inishtrahull, 29 n. 7
Inis Saimer, 100
Inquisitions, 82, 84, 98, 105, 107, 137
*In te Christe* (poem), 17
Iona, 17, 30, 58, 65, 74–5, 98 n. 12, 129;
    abbots of, 14, 24, 28, 37, 62 n. 24,
    74, 98; anchorites, 66;
    Benedictines, 74; *Céile Dé*, 66;
    Chronicle, 4, 31, 33 n. 9, 39;
    excavations, 75; leadership of
    *familia Columbae*, 10, 62, 64; St
    Oran's chapel, 65
Isles, the (of Scotland; *see also*
    Hebrides), 74

Jefferies, Henry, 87
Jerpoint, 74 n. 74
Jesus, staff of (*see also*
    Derry/apparition), 70

Kells, 19, 60–2, 64, 68, 71, 149
Kenmare, 'Nun of ' 22
Kenmore, Richard, 111–24, 126 n. 11
Kilcummin, 18
Kilmacrenan (*see also* Daire Eithne), 14,
    16, 47–9, 68, 75, 97, 148
Kilteevoge, 127
Kings/Queens of England, 71, 100–1,
    104, 109, 111, 113, 132, 134–6, 146,
    150
Kings of Tara/'Ireland', 16, 24, 32, 38,
    40–2, 52, 56, 149

Laggan, the, 127
Lambay, 68, 73
Lanigan, John, 140
Lappan, Lough (Portlough), 49, 109
Larne, 101
*Lathreg Inden* (Birdstown?), 29
*Leabhar Breac*, 17
*Leabhar Clainne Suibhne*, 20, 103 n. 21
Leckpatrick, 113
*Liber Hymnorum*, x, 64; *Noli Pater
    Indulgere*, 17–18, 20, 22–4, 45, 59,
    79, 81, 148
Librán, 30
Limavady, 34–5
Lochlann, 55
Louvain, 33
Luther, Martin, 135
Lynally (Co. Offaly), 39
Lyon, Council of, 107

Mac Ardle, Cornelius, 136
Macarius (of Tours), 96
Mac Cathmail, 94, 111, 118
Mac Colmáin, Maelfinnen, 98 n. 11
Mac Comhaltáin, Cathasach, 93
Mac Conchaille family, 56, 103
Mac Conchaille, Bé Bhinn, 56, 89
Mac Conchaille, Conchobor, 56
Mac Conchaille, Congalach son of, 56
MacDonald, Aidan, 29, 86
MacDonald, Sorleyboy, 138
Mac Entagart, Patrick, 136–7
Mac Entagart, William, 137
Mac Forcellaigh (Iona *Céile Dé*), 66
MacGeoghegan, Fr Ross, 106
Mac Gilladuff (Iona anchorite), 66
Mac Lochlainn, Áed, 84
Mac Lochlainn, Argal, 100 n. 15
Mac Lochlainn, Domnall (d. 1241), 55,
    104–5
Mac Lochlainn, Geoffrey, 109
Mac Lochlainn, Niall, 55, 59, 63
Mac Lochlainn (Lochlinnach),
    Nicholas, 121
Mac Lochlainn, Muirchertach (d.
    1166), 55, 63, 65–6, 70–1, 75, 82,
    84, 87, 97

# Index

Mac Lochlainn, Muirchertach (d. 1196), 55, 93, 99
Mac Lochlainn family (*see also* Ua Lochlainn, Domnall), 21, 52–3, 55, 57, 60–1, 75, 82, 84, 92, 97–101, 103–5, 127–9, 149
Mac Meanmain, Seoán, 121
Mac Uchtrach, Thomas (earl of Athol), 101
Mac William Burke, 129
Máel Coba, 31
Máel Brigte mac Tornáin, 51
Maelfinnen, 46–7
Máel Fothartaig mac Suibne, 37
Mailodranus (Máelodran) mocu-Curin, 29–30
Maghera (Machaire Ráith Luraigh), 61, 71, 88, 106
Magheraroarty, 49
Magilligan Point, 93
Malin Peninsula, 29 n. 7
*maor cána Adhamnáin*, 46
Márkus, Gilbert, 66 n. 33
M'Camayll (Mac Cathmail), William, 114, 118
Mc Carthy, Daniel, 4 n. 2, 33, 35, 95 n. 9, 103 n. 19
McCullimore, Sir Laurence, 119
McCarthy, Dermot (of Desmond), 71
McErlean? (*mac in fhir léighinn*), 94
McGilligan, Magnus, 123–4
McKaig, Dr John, 119, 124
McLoughlin, Dr Donald, 119
McNeill, Tom, 109
Mincoleth, 14, 16, 48
Milesians, 107
Mo Bíí, 18, 20–1, 23–4, 28; belt of (relic), 18, 20–1, 24, 86
Mo Chuaróc the wise, 57
Monasterboice, 69
Moyola, River, 65 n. 27
Montgomery, George, 87 n. 11, 137
Moone, 68, 73
Mourne, River, 77, 114
Muirchertach Mac Ercae, 13

Muirchertach mac Niall (abbot), 41–2, 148
Mullagh Hill (Limavady), 34–5
Mulroy Bay, 50
Munster, 18
Murchad son of Máel Dúin, 40–2

Neagh, Lough, 65 n. 27
Neville, Francis, 65, 88, 90, 139
Niall Caille, 40–2, 148
Niall Frossach, 42
Niall Glúndub, 55
Niall Noígiallach, 14–16
Niall son of Aedh (Armagh abbot), 61
Ní Bhrolcháin, Muireann, 57 n. 9
Nine Years War, 1, 137, 150
Ninnid mac Fergus mac Conall Gulban, 26
Norse (*see* Vikings)

(*see also* surnames starting with Ua and Uí)
Ó Breslein, Donn, 108
O'Brien, Muirchertach king of Dál Cais), 71
Ó Brolcháin, Domnall (prior), 74
Ó Brolcháin, Donald, 65 n. 29, 75
Ó Brolcháin, Flaithbertach, 62–6, 70, 73, 75, 82–4, 97, 102, 145, 149
Ó Brolcháin, Flann, 94
Ó Brolcháin, Máel Bhríde, 62 n. 22
Ó Brolcháin, Máel Coluim, 56, 81
Ó Brolcháin, Máel Íosa, 57 n. 9, 62
O'Cahan family, 124
O'Cahan, Dermot, 120, 122
O'Cahan, Magnus, 122
O'Cahan, Dr Maurice, 119
O'Cahan, Dr William, 119
Ó Caireallan, Donnchadh, 81, 85
Ó Caráin, Giolla an Choimhde, 56
Ó Carragáin, Tomás, 56, 86, 142
O'Carroll (king of Airgialla), 71
Ó Ceallaigh, Seamus, 104
Ó Clabaigh, Colmán, 106–7
Ó Conchobhair, Ruaidhrí, 70–1
O'Connor, Brendan (Bonaventure), 33

O'Connor, Una, 122
Ó Corráin, Donnchadh, 55
O'Corry, Dr Maurice, 119
O'Cushely, John Dr, 119
O'Deery, *see* O'Derry/Ua Daighre
O'Derry (O'Deery/Ua Daighre?), Donogh, 98
Ó Dochartaigh, Eoghan, 135, 137
O'Dogherty, 124
O'Dogherty, Hugh M'Gillivray (Mac Giolla Bhríde), 114–15, 117–19, 121
O'Dogherty, Catherine, 123–4
O'Doherty, Cahir, 85, 87 n. 11, 137–8
O'Doherty castle (Elagh), 3, 50
O'Doherty, Catherine, 56, 115–16
Ó Domhnaill, Aodh Dubh, 128–30
Ó Domhnaill, Aodh Ruadh, 128–9
Ó Domhnaill, Calbhach, 128, 135
Ó Domhnaill, Cathbarrr, 45
Ó Domhnaill, Domnall Óg, 107, 109
Ó Domhnaill, Éigneachán, 102
Ó Domhnaill, Manus, 75, 128, 145; *Betha Colaim Chille*, viii, 21, 23, 24 n. 12, 34, 77 9, 83, 86, 90 1, 95 6, 125–6, 129–33, 142–3
Ó Domhnaill, Ruaidhrí, 128, 132–3
O'Donnell, 124
O'Donnell, Cardinal Patrick, 145
O'Donohue group, 39
O'Donovan, John, vii, 49, 57 n. 11, 62 n. 21, 69, 75, 140
O'Doyle, Dr Roger, 119
Odrán, 30
Ó Fallamhain, Domhnall, 128
O'Feenaghty, Dr Simon, 119, 123
Ó Firghil (O'Friel), Conchobor (*see also* Ua Fergail), 108
Ó Firghil (O'Friel), Fergal, 109
Ó Floinn, Raghnall, 24
Ó Gallachair, Réamann, 121 n. 7, 126, 136–7
O'Gormley family, 124
O'Gormley, Niall, 81
O'Hegarty, Donald, 122
O'Hegarty, Reginald, 114, 117

O'Kinlay, Dr Maurice, 119
O'Kelleher and Schoepperle, 143
O'Loughran, Dr Thomas, 120
Ó Luinín, Sean & William, 137
O'Maelseachlainn, Dermot (king of Meath), 71
Omagh, 113
O'Moryson, Dr David, 119
O'Neill, Áed, 94, 101, 104
O'Neill, Brian, 106
O'Neill, Brian Mór, 124
O'Neill, Conchobar, 108
O'Neill, Domnall, 104
O'Neill, Henry, 124
O'Neill, Shane, 134, 150.
O'Neill family/Uí Néill, 52 n. 13, 55, 57 n. 10, 76, 89, 97, 105, 107, 127, 149
*Ordnance Survey Memoir ... Templemore*, vii, 140, 142
Ó Riain, Pádraig, x, 39, 104
O'Rourke, Tigernan (Ui Briún and Conmaicni king), 71
Ó Scuapa, Cairpre, 107
Osraige, 63–4, 71
O'Sullivan, Benedict, 106
O'Sullivan Beare, Philip, 135–6, 138

papal legate, 63
Perrot, Sir John, 138
Petrie, George, vii, 62 n. 21, 140
Pisa, Dominican chapter in, 107
Popes, Alexander IV, 106; Gregory I ('the Great'), 129–30; Gregory VII/Hildebrand, 60; Julian II, 130 n. 1; Martin V, 124; Paul II, 125
Portlough (Lough Lappan), 49, 109

Raghnall (Reginald) mac Somhairle, 74, 101
Ráith Maige Oenaig/Enaig, 11–12
Randolph, Edward, 135
Raphoe, 12, 59, 68, 73; bishop (*see also* diocese of Cenél Conaill), 49, 56, 121, 145
Rath Breasail, synod, 59–61

# Index

Raven, Thomas, 89
Reeves, William, vii, 9 n. 10, 31, 46, 56, 62 n. 21, 111, 113, 140, 143
Reformation, 142
Reginald (Raghnall) son of Somerled, 74, 101
Reichenau (Lake Constance), 6
Ridgeway, Thomas, 138
*Robertus de deri*, 85
Rory mac Raghnall mac Somhairle, 101
Rossguill, 37
Romans, 60
Rome, 60, 67, 108, 124
RTÉ, tv mast, 7
Ruben (of Dairinis), 38

St Brecan, 100, 120–21, 126
St Buite, 69
St Cainnech, 100
St Cummain, hymn of, 18
St Dominic, 106–7
St Finnian, 23
St George, 139
St John's feastday, 19
St Johnstown (Tech Baithéne/Taughboyne), 24
St Malachy, 67
St Martin (*see also Soiscél Martain*), 69, 90–1, 95 n. 10, 96, 125
St Patrick, 12, 16–17
St Paul, 139
St Peter's Basilica, 130
Scalp Mountain, 13
Scandlán mac Colmáin/Cinn Fáelad, 64
Schaffhausen Stadtbibliotek, 4, 30
Scotland (*see also* Argyll, Edinburgh, Hebrides, Iona, the Isles), 17, 108 n. 32; National Library of, 20, 103 n. 21
Scottish Normans (*see also* Anglo-Normans), 83, 97, 101
*scriba* (of Derry), 38
Sharpe, Richard, vii, x, 6, 18 n. 7, 30–1, 35, 39
Shaw, Robert, 10, 15, 25, 37, 41

Síl Cathasaigh, 65 n. 27
Síl Lugdach, 12, 41, 47, 97, 101, 127
Simms, Katharine, 26, 100 n. 15, 109
Simon (Derry bishop), 117
Simpson, Robert, 140
Skene, W.F., 143
Slighe Midhluachra, 77
*Soiscél Martain*/Gospel of (St) Martin, 19, 69, 95–6
Somerled (Somhairle), 66, 74, 101
Spain, 106
Spanish Dominican archive, 106
Sperrins, 113
Srubh Broin (Stroove), 60
Stokes, Whitley, 33 n. 10, 143
Sulpicious Severus, 69
Sussex, earl of, 134
Sweetman, Milo (archbishop), 117
Swillyburn, 10, 11, 61 n. 15
Swilly, Lough (*see also* Glenswilly), 7–8, 13, 29, 50, 100; River, 47, 102
Swords, 68, 73
Sydney, Sir Henry, 134–5

Telach Óc/Tullyhogue, 57 n. 10, 101, 124
Templedouglas, 47
Termonmagurk, 111–12
Tipraite mac Calgaich, 10–12, 147
Tír Luighdeach, 47
Tyrconnell, Prince of, 106
Toome, 100
Tops Hill, 60
Tory, 49, 69–70, 93 n. 4, 96
Tours, 69, 91, 96
Tuathal Teachtmhar, 107–8

(*see also surnames starting with Ó and O*')
Ua Branain, Gilla Mac Liac, 62 n. 23, 73
Ua Branain, Máel Íosa, 62, 97, 102
Ua Briain, Cennétigh, 57
Ua Briain, Muirchertach (*see also* O'Brien), 53–4
Ua Bronáin, Fonachtan, 93
Ua Bronáin, Maolcolum, 93 n. 4

Ua Canannáin, Domhnall, 79, 99
Ua Canannáin, Ruaidhrí, 99
Ua (Mac) Cathmail family, 49, 114
Ua Cathmail, Cinaed, 49
Ua Cellacáin, Maghnus, 97
Ua Cerballáin, Florence, 74
Ua Cerballáin, Gilla an Choimded (Germanus), 106–7, 109
Ua Cernaigh, Eogan, 51
Ua Cernaigh, Gilla Críst, 51, 62 n. 23, 94, 104
Ua Cobthaigh, Ainmire, 74
Ua Cobthaigh, Muiredach, 61, 71–2, 75
Ua Conaingen, Fionn, 61
Ua Daighri, Amhlaim, 98
Ua Daighri, Goffraigh, 94, 98 n. 13, 102
Ua Daighri, Mac Craith, 98, 102
Ua Daighri, Máel Íosa, 95 n. 9, 98 n. 13, 102–3
Ua Daighri, Máel Ruanaid, 98
Ua Dochartaigh, Domnall (d. 1199), 102
Ua Dochartaigh, Domnall (d. 1339), 110 n. 35
Ua Dochurtaigh, Aindiles, 97
Ua Dochurtaigh, Echmarcach, 99–100, 102 (see also O'Doherty et al.)
Ua Domnaill (see Ó Domnaill)
Ua Dorig, Mael Ísu, 74
Ua Duimen (Devine?), Dunchadh, 51
Ua Duinnsléibhe family, 65
Ua Duinnsléibhe, Eochaid, 70
Ua Eochada (king of Ulaid), 71
Ua Fercomais, Maolcainnich, 93
Ua Fergail, Amalgaidh (see also Ó Firghil), 74
Ua Lapáin, Aengus, 49 n. 8
Ua Lapáin, Uisíne, 49
Ua Lochlainn, Domnall (see also Mac Lochlainn), 27, 48, 53–8, 149; Bé Bhinn (wife of) 57
Ua Maelcholuim, 51

Ua Maelcoluim, Muiredach, 51
Ua Máel Doraidh, Flaithbertach, 99–102
Ua Máel Doraidh, Gilla Críst, 98
Ua Millugáin, Muirchertach, 93–4
Ua Muiredaigh, Amhlaim, 72, 93 n. 93
Ua Muiredaigh, Domnall, 93, 94 n. 7
Ua Muiredaigh, Maolíosa, 93
Ua (Mac) Robhartaigh, 49, 70
Ua Robhartaigh, Aenghas, 49
Ua Toráin, Máel Eoin, 48, 51
Uí Brolcháin (see also Ó Brolcháin), 57
Uí Canannáin family, 97, 99
Uí Catháin family (see also O'Cahan), 82
Uí Daighre, 98–9, 102–3, 105
Uí Dochartaigh (see also O'Doherty), 12, 97, 102, 105, 110, 127–9, 135, 150
Uí Domnaill (O'Donnells), 47, 89, 97, 102, 104, 106–7, 127–36, 149–50
Uí Echach Ulad, 65
Uí Fearáin, 104
Uí Fercomais, 93 n. 3
Uí Lapáin, 49
Uí Máel Doraidh, 97, 99
Uí Nialláin, 56
Uí Néill dynasty (see also O'Neills), 14, 52 n. 13
Uí Robhartaigh, 70
Uí Tuirtre, 37–8, 65 n. 27
Ulaid, 35
Ulster, earl of (see also de Burgh), 109
universities, 93 n. 1
Urney, 113

Victoria, Queen, 146
Vikings (Norse), 38, 40, 50–1, 53, 71, 74, 148

Weston, Nicholas, 120, 121 n. 7, 124–6
Ware, Sir James, 136